Transformation from Below

STUDIES OF COMMUNISM IN TRANSITION

General Editor: Ronald J. Hill
*Professor of Comparative Government
and Fellow of Trinity College,
Dublin, Ireland*

Studies of Communism in Transition is an important series which applies academic analysis and clarity of thought to the recent traumatic events in Eastern and Central Europe. As many of the preconceptions of the past half century are cast aside, newly independent and autonomous sovereign states are being forced to address long-term, organic problems which had been suppressed by, or appeased within, the Communist system of rule.

The series is edited under the sponsorship of Lorton House, and independent charitable association which exists to promote the academic study of communism and related concepts.

Transformation from Below

Local Power and the Political Economy of Post-Communist Transitions

Edited by
John Gibson
Senior Lecturer in Local Government
University of Birmingham
and
Philip Hanson
Professor of the Political Economy of Russia and Eastern Europe
University of Birmingham

STUDIES OF COMMUNISM IN TRANSITION

Edward Elgar
Cheltenham, UK. Brookfield, US

Published by
Edward Elgar Publishing Limited
8 Lansdown Place
Cheltenham
Glos GL50 2HU
UK

Edward Elgar Publishing Company
Old Post Road
Brookfield
Vermont 05036
US

British Library Cataloguing in Publication Data
Transformation from Below: Local Power and
the Political Economy of Post-Communist
Transitions. – (Studies of Communism in
Transition)
  I. Gibson, John II. Hanson, Philip
  III. Series
  352.00091717

Library of Congress Cataloguing in Publication Data
Transformation from below : local power and the political economy of
  post-communist transitions / edited by John Gibson and Philip
Hanson.
    (Studies of communism in transition)
    Includes bibliographical references and index.
    1. Local government—Europe, Eastern. 2. Local government—Former
Soviet republics. 3. Decentralization in government—Europe,
Eastern. 4. Decentralization in government—Former Soviet
republics. 5. Europe, Eastern—Politics and government—1989–
6. Former Soviet republics—Politics and government. 7. Post
-communism—Europe, Eastern. 8. Post-communism—Former Soviet
republics. I. Gibson, John, 1944– . II. Hanson, Philip.
III. Series
JS3000.2.T73 1996
352.047—dc20   95–42287
                                     CIP

ISBN 1 85898 122 0

Printed in Great Britain by the Ipswich Book Company, Suffolk

Contents

Figures

Tables

Contributors

Andrzey Bukowski is an assistant in the Institute of Sociology, Jagiellonian University, Crakow.

Adrian Campbell is a Senior Lecturer in the Department of Local Government Studies, University of Birmingham.

Ana Cielecka is an Honorary Research Fellow in the Centre for Russia and East European Studies, University of Birmingham.

Kenneth Davey is a Professor Development Administration, Department of Development Administration, University of Birmingham.

Artashes Gazaryan is Director, Centre of Self-Government Studies, Klaipeda.

John Gibson is a Senior Lecturer in the Department of Local Government Studies, University of Birmingham.

Philip Hanson is a Professor of the Political Economy of Russia and Eastern Europe, Centre for Russian and East European Studies, University of Birmingham.

Daniel Hanšpach is a doctoral student at the Institute of Sociology, Czech Academy of Sciences, Prague.

Max Jeleniewski is a consultant based in Rotterdam at the Institute for Housing and Urban Development Studies.

Peter Kirkow is a research fellow at the Centre for Russian and East European Studies, University of Birmingham.

Elizabeth Teague is Adviser to the High Commissioner on National Minorities, Organization for Security and Cooperation in Europe, the Hague.

Zdenka Vajdová is a doctoral student at the Institute of Sociology of the Czech Academy of Sciences, Prague.

Acknowledgements

The general scheme of this book, and most of the individual contributions to it, stem from research funded by the Economic and Social Research Council (project L.309.25.3001) as part of its East–West Programme. ESRC support is gratefully acknowledged. The editors are also deeply grateful to Marea Arries, without whose unstinting secretarial and editorial help publication would probably have been delayed until the next millennium, and to Elizabeth Teague, who, in addition to contributing as an author, provided valuable guidance on constitutional and other matters relating to the former Soviet Union.

Introduction

Philip Hanson and John Gibson

Devolution is the theme of this book. The chapters that follow all deal with the role of local and regional government in the social and economic changes that are being attempted by the countries of Eastern Europe. The economists and political scientists who have written those chapters have been looking, as social scientists usually do, at the events and experiences of the recent past. Commonly they have tried to derive from the experience of that recent past some generalizations that could help in assessing the future. And the first thing to be said by way of introduction is that they have been observing, analysing and writing during one of those periods – so apt to embarrass social scientists – when history has gone into overdrive.

In the five years since the fall of the Berlin Wall, economic and political analysis of developments in Eastern Europe and the former Soviet Union has looked, at times, a little like bird-watching on a rocket trip to Mars: something that had its uses in the world you had just left, but which was a little beside the point during your present trajectory. History, at a time like this, can make social science look foolish.

Our own original research plans, certainly, have been considerably disrupted by the largely unforeseen course of events. The project on which this book is based was originally formulated in 1990 and the early months of 1991. The idea was to bring specialists on Eastern Europe and specialists on local government together to analyse, with East European colleagues, the development of local government[1] in the region as an element in, and influence on, the attempts at building democratic political institutions and the economic institutions of capitalism.

Much of what has happened in the region since then has been fission rather than devolution. Initially there were six candidates for our attention: the former Warsaw Pact countries less East Germany (already absorbed into a united Germany); in other words, the USSR,

Bulgaria, Czechoslovakia, Hungary, Poland and Romania. Now (January 1995) these six have become twenty-one, following the break-up of the USSR and Czechoslovakia. Peripheries became centres. Debate about the survival of a Soviet federation segued into debate about the survival of a Russian federation. Indeed, at the time of writing, Russian tanks and aircraft are attacking what the Moscow government considers to be a subject of the Russian Federation: Chechnya. In such circumstances, the bloodlessness of a discussion of, say, fiscal federalism may seem its only recommendation.

Despite the turmoil, however, we believe the studies reported in this book provide useful knowledge. There are lessons to be drawn from them about the conditions in which democratic and market institutions begin to take reasonable shape, and the conditions in which they do not. There are also lessons about the feasibility of some neat solutions to the problem of managing radical change, such as so-called 'authoritarian marketization' for Russia, for example.

Conclusions, however, are for the final chapter. Here we will concentrate on introducing the theme of the book, and the problems addressed in it.

The starting-point for this study is that local government is important in the former communist countries. Anna Cielecka and John Gibson have shown (Cielecka and Gibson, 1994) that in East–Central Europe, at any rate, this view was widely held by the population. They quote a survey conducted in Hungary, Poland and Czechoslovakia in January 1991, in which local government emerged at the head of a list of what respondents believed to be the most influential means to strengthen democracy – ahead of parliament, national government, trade unions, the press and other institutions. Perhaps, as Cielecka and Gibson speculate, the remarkably high expectations of local government reflect, as much as anything, its virtual absence under communism: a parliament, a government, a press – of sorts, in each case – they had had. Visible and representative local government they had not had.

To many Westerners it may seem that nothing but an upbringing with this particular deprivation could lead anyone to attach such importance to local government. But received thinking on the subject suggests at least two ways in which healthy institutions of elected local government are important: as schools for democracy and as means to more efficient resource allocation by the state.

First, the political side. Functioning democracies commonly have at least one sub-national layer of elected government. The institutions vary enormously across Western countries, but a linkage of political careers and party organizations between levels of government is standard. Conversely, one indication of the importance of local government in a political system is whether it does or does not perform these functions. As Robert Putnam wrote of the introduction of elected (instead of prefectural) regional government in Italy in 1970: 'The first test for any new political institution is that it must engage the aspirations and harness the ambitions of serious politicos' (Putnam, 1993, p. 28). The Italian regions passed this test. Considered simply as an institution that facilitates the working of representative democracy, elected local government can serve this training and transmission-belt function.

In countries that contain compact settlements of ethnic minorities (minorities, that is, in comparison with the main ethnic group, if there is one, in the national population), another set of political issues arises. It might be argued that the establishment of elected regional government for such enclaves risks providing platforms and power-bases for separatists. But it can equally be argued that, if ethnic cleavages are deep and the relevant enclaves have little autonomy, discontent, denied a representative outlet, will mount. This was one of the arguments put forward for a federal constitution in the new South Africa. The Inkatha Freedom Party might fail to get the 5 per cent national representation needed to qualify for a cabinet seat at national level, but might well get 35–40 per cent in a Natal-KwaZulu region; if that region were a component of a federation, representation there could bring real power.

Whatever the real force of these arguments in any particular set of circumstances may be (a Scottish Assembly, for example?), several developed western nations have arrangements that entail special powers for such enclaves. These arrangements are not necessarily federal. (In general, the dividing line between federations and other state structures with devolved regional powers is arbitrary, though Elizabeth Teague, in the first chapter, describes the clear division that is made in constitutional theory.) The Swedish cultural autonomy arrangements in Finland and the five special regions out of twenty in Italy are examples. Whatever the exact set-up is, the existence of ethnic-minority enclaves with a special constitutional status reflects a belief that the powers of local government matter.

The economic case for devolved local government is well-established (see Oates, 1992, on which much of the discussion in this and the next paragraph is based). Briefly, it is that, with total state economic functions of a given scope and scale, the efficiency of resource allocation and use will be greater with locally-devolved spending and taxation decisions, if the local governments responsible for the decisions are elected. The grounds for believing this are of a classical liberal kind. The populations of particular localities are likely to have different wishes so far as the level and character of public spending and taxation are concerned. They also will have important information advantages and greater incentives to secure greater efficiency and effectiveness. Information about local tastes and preferences will be more cheaply gathered and acted upon by local than by national governments. And – as opposed to decentralized agencies appointed by the centre – elected local governments will have strong incentives to get the tax and spending mix right in order to get elected again.

This stimulus to public-sector efficiency is reinforced if residents can vote, not only at the ballot-box, but with their feet – moving to a different jurisdiction if it offers a combination of taxes and spending that is more to their liking (Tiebout, 1956). This is a mechanism more easily observed in North America than in Europe (as when Quebec residents moved to other Canadian provinces as the separatist Lévesque government increased the provincial tax burden). But it exists even in smaller countries with less mobile populations.[2] Business, after all, is relatively footloose everywhere in the capitalist world. Thus, in Hirschman's terminology, both exit (going elsewhere) and voice (voting) can exert pressure towards a matching of state resource allocation to voters' preferences.

This line of argument does not, of course, lead to the conclusion that all government, to be efficient, should be local. National public goods like defence and a sound currency require national governments. There are strict limits to the ability and desirability of local governments pursuing redistributional objectives financed by local taxes and independent macro-economic policies (King, 1984, Ch. 1). Some of what the state does may entail economies of scale that require that it be done nationally. Even where these considerations do not apply, a national shortage of capable and honest people in public service may make a centralized order more desirable than it would be without that shortage. In general, however, the economic case for some substantial degree of devolution of the state is a strong one.

Perhaps we should also think of local representative government as performing a role in the former communist countries that is rather grander than assisting the effective functioning of competing political parties and the efficient allocation of resources within the state sector. All the former communist countries, whether they are nominally new nations or not, are engaged in constructing national institutions almost from scratch. In doing so, they start with a weak and damaged civic culture. The rebuilding of local government can thus be seen as a crucial part of the restoration, or development, of civic culture.

Free association, even for the formation of choirs or fan clubs, ranged from the difficult to the almost impossible in the various countries under communist rule. Most of what looked like grass-roots groupings of people even for 'unpolitical' activities were directly or indirectly supervised by the Communist Party. Between the party-state and the individual citizen, in communist societies, there was a large and almost empty space. Nobody in their right mind would want that space to be filled solely by the institutions of local government. But the creation of local government is part of the process of filling what George Kolankiewicz has called 'the missing middle' in former communist societies (Kolankiewiz, 1992). In other words, it should perhaps be seen as part of the re-invention of a civil society, in ways that do not apply so strongly to the building of political institutions on the national level.

Differences between the old order and the new should not be exaggerated. Studies of local politics in the communist order showed that what happened in particular communities was not determined entirely by decisions taken in some omnipotent centre. The role of local participation and local interests and pressures was documented (e.g., Bahry, 1987; Hahn, 1988). In Soviet economic management, Western social scientists variously described the centre's control through regional 'prefects' (regional Communist Party first secretaries) as effective in the 1950s and 1960s (Hough, 1969), and ineffective in the 1970s and 1980s (Rutland 1993). The divisions of interests and procedures within the 'centre', when it came to regional economic development, were also brought out, particularly by Jonathan Schiffer (1989). In the case of Russia, Gavin Helf (1994) has shown that the centre's control of regional leadership appointments was lost in late 1988, not with the collapse of communist rule three years later.

None of these studies, however, undermined the conventional wisdom about local politics in the European communist countries. Local self-government was lacking. The processes by which social and economic developments came about in particular communities and regions were dominated by top-down management and control in what Rutland labels a 'post-totalitarian' political order. In addition, the effective powers of local governments were heavily constrained by either a lack of fiscal resources or a lack of ability directly to command physical resources in the more heavily centrally planned economies (Regulski *et al.*, 1993; Illner, 1992a).

It is therefore not unreasonable to see the development of post-communist local politics and local economic change as starting with a *tabula rasa*. The fact that competitive elections began to be introduced before the fall of communism does not alter this.

The potential of local self-government amply justifies, we believe, the attention given to it in this book. But how can the actual developments so far best be assessed?

We have assumed throughout our work that it is worth focusing on the question of whether changes at the local level assist or impede the overall process of liberalization – both economic and political – in the country in question. A secondary concern has been the compatibility of changes at the local level with maintenance of the territorial integrity of the state.

The existing scholarly literature has little to say about territorial devolution as part of the process of economic and political liberalization.

There is a well-established body of Western literature on local administration and finance. Similarly, much has been written on the role of local elected government in democratic countries (Putnam, 1993, being a notable recent addition). There is, as has already been noted, a public finance literature that provides the grounds for expecting that some degree of local fiscal autonomy, with local elected government, is likely to be more efficient economically than highly centralized fiscal decision-making (see Oates, 1992). But this literature is about functioning liberal societies, not about nations trying to move from a post-totalitarian to a liberal order. The writings on transition to democracy from authoritarian rule in Latin America and Spain, Portugal and Greece are not much concerned with issues of regional devolution, though the work by Linz and Stepan (1992) on electoral sequences (see below) has been of some interest in our study.

Initially, we intended to test hypotheses about factors facilitating the development of local democracy and well-functioning local government, as well as the relationship between political devolution and economic liberalization. In the course of our studies, these aims were modified.

The main reason for the modification of our plans has already been mentioned: the project began before the break-up of the USSR and of Czechoslovakia. Our initial research agenda was altered by those rearrangements of our subject-matter. The work has in the event been focused on changes since 1990 in Russia, Estonia, Lithuania, Poland, the Czech Republic and Hungary, with some comparisons with Ukraine, Moldova and Romania.

One consequence is that comprehensive coverage of former communist countries became impossible. The chapters that follow deal with only nine of the twenty-one possible cases (more, if Albania, Mongolia and the former Yugoslavia are brought into the frame). Nor are our nine in any obvious way representative. In particular, the poorest half-dozen former communist countries are not within our coverage at all. Our general conclusions apply to the nine countries – or perhaps to the 'middle-income' and 'high-income' former communist states (these designations are relative) and not to the 'low-income' category.

The main ideas that we sought, after some reconsideration, to test were the following:

that strong central government, with minimal devolution to regions, is necessary in former communist countries if economic stabilization and liberalization are to be pushed through quickly – an element of the 'authoritarian modernization' advocated by, among others, Migranyan (1989);

that in a liberalising former communist country with compactly settled ethnic minorities and a risk of fragmentation, the sequence of the first competitive elections (regional before national or vice versa) is critical to the maintenance of the integrity of the country (cf. Linz and Stepan 1992, who argue, chiefly from experience in Spain, that parties and their political agendas begin to be formed by the holding of elections, and that the holding of regional before national elections would strengthen centrifugal tendencies);

that the democratization of local government and the establishment of an agreed distribution of powers and responsibilities between levels of government will be more difficult, the greater is the diversity amongst a country's regions in ethnic composition and development level.

Dealing with a small number of countries, we were not able to make statistical tests of hypotheses from comparative data across those countries. We did however expect that there would be some scope for statistical analysis across Russia's regions (77 or 89 administrative territories, varying by the data source used). The idea was to identify factors that assisted the maintenance of local governmental power by the communist-era (*nomenklatura*) local elites in some regions, rather than others, and to assess the influence of local leadership on the rate of economic change across regions.

The eleven chapters that form the core of the book are, with one exception, studies dealing with individual countries or case-studies of particular regions or municipalities. The exception is Adrian Campbell's comparative review of the resistance to local autonomy in Moldova and Romania. The studies are either of the design and building of institutions for devolved government or of the interaction of local power and local government with processes of economic change. In the concluding chapter we draw conclusions from a comparison of the various national studies.

One difference amongst the countries considered in this book, however, is so obvious and so important that it would be odd to make no reference to it here. In Russia the stresses between centre and periphery are enormous; the continued development of Russia as a single state with democratic institutions is in some doubt; and there are large regional differences in the rules of the economic game, and no single market. In the Czech Republic, Hungary, Poland, Estonia and Lithuania centre–periphery relations are simply not so problematic, or so critical to future development. Moreover, Russia, unlike those other five countries, has seen the communist-era elites retaining power at the local level.

Elsewhere among the countries we have studied, the development of local institutions is apparently closer to being a return to business as usual – in a Western sense. Already in 1991, in a case-study of a small Czech town, Michal Illner found 'new people' coming into local office (Illner, 1992b). And centre–periphery relations have not been at the centre of the national political agenda for long in the other five countries, in the way they have in Russia.

The difference is real. Yet again, Russia is special. Or rather, it is special by the standards of countries to the west of it. Some likely reasons for this are obvious: size, ethnic diversity, the wide spread of regional development levels and resource endowments. But arriving at agreed rules of the game in any sphere in Russia seems to be harder than in East–Central Europe, and the origins of that difficulty may lie outside the obvious geographical and demographic circumstances.

At the same time, even the more successful transformers in East–Central Europe have not found the re-invention of local democracy and effective regional devolution plain sailing. The formation of effective new institutions is in some degree problematic there, too. The tensions in Polish politics over regional powers are discussed by Cielecka and Gibson below. Even in the habitually exemplary Czech Republic, the formation of party structures linking the regions with national politics, for instance, is a slow process. In the November 1994 local council elections in the Czech Republic, very nearly 50 per cent of the seats were won by independents, and the largest share of the vote gained by any national party was less than 30 per cent (*RFE/RL Daily Report*, 23 November 1994). As we shall see, the transformation attempt in all these societies encounters many of the same difficulties over centre–periphery relations, despite the wide differences in national circumstances.

Notes

1. The term 'local government' will be used here, unless notice to the contrary is given, to cover all levels of government below the national level.
2. Teske *et al.* (1993) have demonstrated how the mechanism of competition between local governments can be driven by a small subset of informed, sensitive, 'consumers'.

References

Bahry, Donna (1987), *Outside Moscow*, New York: Columbia University Press, 1987.

Cielecka, A. and J. Gibson (1994), 'Great Expectations: Local Government and Democracy in East Central Europe', paper presented at the ESRC Workshop on Local Democracy and Local Initiatives, London, September.

Hahn, Jeffrey W. (1988), *Soviet Grassroots: Citizen Participation in Local Soviet Government*, London: I.B. Tauris, 1988.

Helf, Gavin (1994), *All the Russias: Centre, Core and Periphery in Soviet and Post-Soviet Russia*, University of California at Berkeley, PhD.

Hough, Jerry F. (1969), *The Soviet Prefects: The Local Party Organs in Industrial Decision Making*, Cambridge, MA: Harvard University Press.

Illner, Michael (1992a), 'Municipalities and Industrial Paternalism in a real socialist society', in Petr Dostál, Michael Illner, Jan Kára and Max Barlow (eds.), *Changing Territorial Adminstration in Czechoslovakia*, Amsterdam: Instituut voor Sociale Geografie, University of Amsterdam.

Illner, Michael (1992b), 'Continuity and Discontinuity. Political Change in a Czech Village after 1989', *Czechoslovak Sociological Review*, 28 (August): 79–92.

King, David (1984), *Fiscal Tiers: The Economics of Multi-Level Government*,

London: George Allen & Unwin.

Kolankiewicz, George (1992), 'The Missing Middle', University of Essex, Department of Sociology, mimeo.

Linz, Juan J. and Alfred Stepan (1992), 'Political Identities and Electoral Sequences: Spain, the Soviet Union and Yugoslavia', *Daedalus* 121:2 (Spring): pp. 123–41.

Migranyan, A. (1989) 'Dolgii put' k evropeiskomu domu', *Noviy mir*, no. 7: 166 –84.

Oates, Wallace E. (1992), 'Fiscal Decentralization and Economic Development', *National Tax Journal* XLVI:2; pp. 237–44.

Putnam, Robert D. (1993), *Making Democracy Work*, Princeton, NJ: Princeton University Press.

Regulski, Jerzy, Susanne Georg, Henrik Toft Jensen and Barrie Needham (eds.), (1988), *Decentralization and Local Government: A Danish Polish Comparative Study in Political Systems*, Oxford: Transaction Publishers.

Rutland, Peter (1993), *The Politics of Economic Stagnation in the Soviet Union. The Role of Local Party Organs in Economic Management*, Cambridge: Cambridge University Press.

Schiffer, Jonathan R. (1989), *Soviet Regional Economic Policy. The East-West Debate over Pacific Siberian Development*, London: Macmillan.

Teske, Paul, Mark Schneider, Michael Mintrom and Samuel Best (1993), 'Establishing the Micro Foundations of a Macro Theory: Information, Movers and the Competitive Market for Public Goods', *American Political Science Review*, vol. 87, no. 3, pp. 702–13.

Tiebout, Charles M. (1956), 'A Pure Theory of Local Expenditure', *Journal of Political Economy*, vol. 64, no. 5, October, pp. 416–24.

Part I. Studies in Democratic Development: Former USSR

1. Russia and the Regions: The Uses of Ambiguity

Elizabeth Teague*

Its name notwithstanding, the Russian Federation that emerged from the rubble of the Soviet Union was not a federation but a highly centralized, unitary state. This chapter is an account of the attempts since 1991 to modify this inherited structure in ways that might make political sense.

It is necessary to start with a few definitions. The two concepts of state organization – unitary or federal – reflect two approaches to the question of sovereignty. While sovereignty is one of the most disputed concepts in political science, it may be briefly summed up as 'the ultimate authority and power to decide in a state' (Finer, 1974, p. 80). In unitary states such as Britain, Sweden or France, sovereignty is held to reside in the centre. Though local governments jealously protect their prerogatives, it is, in the final analysis, the central government that has the legal power to determine what the powers and duties of the cities and regions are to be.

In federations such as Switzerland, the United States of America, Canada, Germany or Australia, on the other hand, sovereignty is considered to be shared between the centre and the regions (cantons, states, provinces, *Länder* and so on). The regions not only enjoy a large degree of autonomy; autonomy is their inalienable, constitutional right (Dahl, 1963, p. 37). One example will suffice to indicate the difference in the two approaches. In unitary Britain, decisions relating to criminal law are the exclusive prerogative of parliament. In the USA, on the other hand, each state has its own penal code, and even so weighty a matter as whether or not to apply the death penalty is decided at the state level.

There is no ideal type of federation, however, and there are several ways in which sovereignty may be deemed to be shared between the centre and the regions. Under one model, sovereignty is deemed to originate in the centre, which devolves some of its powers to theregions. All powers that are not specifically described in the constitution as belonging to the regions remain the prerogative of the centre. Under another model, sovereignty is deemed to originate in the regions, which transfer some of their powers upward to the federal centre while retaining certain attributes of sovereignty at the regional level. All powers not specifically granted by the constitution to the centre remain the prerogative of the individual regions. The latter model implies a more radical devolution of power than the former.

The federation that began to take shape in Russia in 1994 represented yet another model – where the issue of who is delegating sovereignty to whom is deliberately obscured. Powers are shared between the centre and the provinces without any mention being made of where sovereignty originates. Thus, the agreement signed in February 1994 between the Russian Federation and the Republic of Tatarstan, which served as the model on which Russian leaders hoped to reconstruct the Russian Federation, spoke merely of the 'mutual delegation of powers' between the parties.

Russia's Administrative Structure

The administrative system of the Russian Federation dates from the early days of Soviet power. It consists of a hierarchy of ethnic and territorial subdivisions which, as Paul Henze has observed, 'vary so enormously in area, size of population, ethnic composition and economic status that it is difficult to find any common denominators among them' (Henze, 1991, p. 10).

On the top rung of the ladder are twenty-one republics formed according to the ethnic principle. These were designed to act as 'national homelands' for the largest ethnic groups – Tatars, Chuvash, Bashkirs, Mordvins, Chechens and so on – that had for centuries inhabited the territory over which the Russian Federation now extends (Schwartz, 1990). They account for 28.6 per cent of Russia's land mass and 15.2 per cent of its population (Sheehy, 1993). (During the Soviet period, the republics were known as 'autonomous republics', to distinguish them from the fifteen Union republics that made up the Soviet Union, but the word 'autonomous' has since been dropped.)

The second rung is occupied by six krais (territories) and forty-nine oblasts (provinces). These are purely territorial in character and bear no ethnic connotations. Two 'cities of federal significance', Moscow and St. Petersburg, have the same rights as the krais and oblasts.

The third rung is occupied by Russia's sole autonomous oblast and its ten autonomous okrugs (districts). Like the republics, these are ethno-territorial in nature. In all, more than half the territory of the Russian Federation (54 per cent) consists of ethnically-based divisions (republics, autonomous okrugs and a single autonomous oblast). However, ethnic Russians not only make up more than 80 per cent of the population of Russia, they are also widely dispersed. This means that, although all the 'autonomies' purport to be founded on the ethnic principle, in many of them the indigenous nationality is heavily outnumbered by ethnic Russians. In only five of Russia's twenty-one republics, in fact, did the titular nationality form a majority of the population at the time of the 1989 census. These were Chechen-Ingushetia (which subsequently split into Chechnya and Ingushetia), Chuvashia, Dagestan, North Ossetia, and Tuva. In Kalmykia and Tatarstan, the titular nationality formed the largest group, as did the Kabardins in Kabardino-Balkaria. In all the others, ethnic Russians were either a majority or a plurality (for details, see Table 1.1). This fact reduced the pressure for the Russian Federation to break up along ethnic lines. So too, as Leokadia Drobizheva has argued, did the fact that, except for Chechnya, Dagestan, Tatarstan and Tuva, most of the titular nations of Russia's republics had no historical tradition of independent statehood (Drobizheva, 1994, p. 54). Finally, the majority of Russia's republics have no external borders (the exceptions being Buryatia, Karelia, Sakha, Tuva, and the North Caucasian republics).

Under Soviet rule, the ethnically-based republics enjoyed privileges that the territorially-based krais and oblasts did not, being endowed with the trappings of statehood (flag, national anthem and so on). A number of posts in the republic leadership were reserved for representatives of the titular nationality, no matter how few in number that group might be. But the chief source of inequality was, and still is, taxation.

Russia's krais and oblasts are generally more populous and more industrialized than the republics, and tend on average to pay more in taxes to the federal centre than they receive in state subventions (though net contributions were heavily concentrated in a dozen of them – see Chapter 9). Many of the republics, by contrast, are net recipients of state funding. This might not matter if Russia's tax system were seen to be fair and if it were applied to all the provinces equally, but it is neither. How much each province pays depends on how much clout it has in Moscow and whether or not it can negotiate a special rate for itself with the centre. Former Finance Minister Boris Fedorov has described Russia as the only country where you can get what you want by standing outside the Ministry of Finance and yelling (*Financial Times*, 10 February 1994). For example, the Republic of Sakha/Yakutia, Russia's major producer of diamonds, has negotiated a special deal whereby it keeps for itself all the taxes it collects and passes none at all on to the centre. This causes great resentment among the krais and oblasts, which feel they pay for the privileges of the republics. Not surprisingly, the krais and oblasts also try to get such privileges. Nizhnii Novgorod oblast, one of Russia's most market-oriented regions, has for example put forward a proposal under which it would contract with the centre to pay an agreed amount into the federal budget but be allowed a free hand as to how it raised the money (*Segodnya*, 3 September 1994).

Table 1.1: The population of Russia's autonomous formations at the time of the 1989 Census

		Titular Nationality %	Russians %
Republics			
Adygeya		22	68
Altai Republic		31	60
Bashkortostan		22	39
Buryatia		24	70
Chechnya (1994)	approx.	75	20
Chuvashia		68	27
Dagestan		80	9
Ingushetia (1994)	approx.	90	10
Kabardino-Balkaria:			
Kabardins		48	32
Balkars		9	
Kalmykia		45	38
Karachaevo-Cherkessia:			
Karachai		31	42
Cherkess		10	
Karelia		10	74

Khakassia	11	79
Komi Republic	23	58
Marii-El	43	47
Mordovia	32	61
North Ossetia	53	30
Sakha (Yakutia)	33	50
Tatarstan	49	43
Tuva	64	32
Udmurtia	31	59
Autonomous oblast		
Jewish	4	83
Autonomous okrugs		
Aga Buryat	55	41
Chukchi	7	66
Evenki	14	67
Khanty-Mansi:		
Khants	0.9	66
Mansi	0.4	
Komi-Permyak	60	36
Koryak	16	62
Nenets	12	66
Taimyr:		
Dolgans	9	67
Nents	4	
Ust Orda Buryat	36	56
Yamal Nenets	4	59

Sources: 1989 census as reported in USSR State Committee on Statistics, *Natsionalnyi sostav naseleniya SSSR*, Moscow: Finansy i statistika, 1991.

Constitutional Impasse

Conflict over the division of powers destroyed the Soviet Union. One after another, the Union republics declared themselves sovereign and announced that their laws took precedence over Soviet laws. Encouraged by their example, Russia's ethnically-based republics also began to declare themselves sovereign states. (The reader should be aware that, with a few exceptions, the Russian republics did not use the terms 'sovereignty' or 'state' in the way those words are customarily understood in international law; precisely what was meant was not defined.) In August 1990, as part of his campaign to increase Russia's position *vis-à-vis* the centre, Russian leader Boris Yeltsin enjoined the leaders of Tatarstan – and, by implication, those of Russia's other autonomies – to 'take as much autonomy as you can swallow' (TASS, 7 August 1990).

By the end of that year, almost all of Russia's autonomous republics had followed Yeltsin's advice. Like the Union republics, they declared that all the land, industrial assets and mineral resources on their territory belonged to them. Many claimed the right to enter into treaties and economic agreements with other governments. Some declared that their laws took precedence over those of the Russian Republic; others asserted the right to self-determination and secession. Most of them did this not because they really wanted to secede but because they hoped to reap the benefits of exploiting their rich natural resources (Sheehy, 1990; Osborn, 1993)

When the Soviet Union collapsed in 1991, Russia's republics demanded the autonomy Yeltsin had promised them. That put the boot on the other foot, and Russian leaders began to express alarm that the next phase of the process would see the disintegration of the Russian Federation. At first, Yeltsin hoped the adoption of a new Russian constitution (on which work had begun in 1990) would ward off centrifugal tendencies and establish an equitable division of power both between the republics and the krais and oblasts and between Moscow and the provinces. Drafting a text that was acceptable to all concerned proved an almost impossible task, however.

The first draft, which was presented in November 1990, sought to replace the system of ethno-territorial units with a federation of territories, each of which would have equal rights. The aim was to turn Russia into a federation consisting of some fifty new territorial divisions modelled on the *Länder* that make up the Federal Republic of Germany. Ethnic distinctions would be abolished; all of Russia's provinces would become equal in status, and ethnicity would be disentangled from the state.

At the same time, members of staff at the Institute of Geography in Moscow were asked to make proposals about how Russia's territorial and administrative boundaries might be redrawn so as to do away with ethnic distinctions and make all federal subjects equal in status. Their initial proposal – that Russia should be divided up along the lines of its existing eleven economic zones – was abandoned because the Russian government feared that, instead of preventing the break-up of

Russia, splitting it up into such large territorial groups might facilitate Russia's disintegration. In addition, the republics put up strong opposition to the scheme, which would have deprived them of their privileged place in the pecking order. As a result, the idea of switching Russia to a system modelled on Germany's was shelved (author's conversation with Andrei Treivish, Moscow, 4 May 1994; see also, Glezer, 1992, p. 7). Academics, including some of Yeltsin's advisers such as Leonid Smirnyagin and Mark Urnov, still advocate the 'republicanization' of the krais and oblasts as a desirable long-term objective (*Izvestiya*, 24 August 1994). In the immediate term, however, only Vladimir Zhirinovsky is actively promoting the idea. The nationalist leader has sworn that, if he is elected president, he will abolish the 'ethnic' republics, restore a unitary state, and divide the territory into 'Russian *guberniyas*' modelled on the administrative units of the Czarist era, abolished in 1924.

The Federal Treaty

Russia's first two years of independence were overshadowed by an increasingly bitter struggle between President Yeltsin and the Russian parliament, or Supreme Soviet. The devolution issue, like everything else, became a football in this struggle and, with the centre in gridlock, the provinces seized the opportunity to go their own way. Alarmed by the impossibility of adopting a new constitution even as parts of the country were escaping from central control, Yeltsin's leadership concluded that, if the Russian Federation was to be prevented from falling apart, some other solution would have to be found. In March 1992, it settled for a multilateral Federal Treaty which codified relations between the centre and the provinces. To sweeten the pill, the centre agreed to devolve to the provinces more powers than they had previously enjoyed. Several of the republics were nonetheless unhappy with Yeltsin's proposals and complained that they were not being given enough autonomy. It proved so difficult to reach agreement over the respective rights of the republics, the krais and oblasts, the two cities of federal significance, the single autonomous oblast and the autonomous okrugs, that in the end three separate treaties had to be signed (for the texts, see *Etnopolis*, no. 1, 1992, pp. 17–32.) Even then, the Republics of Tatarstan and Chechen-Ingushetia (as, technically, Chechnya and Ingushetia still were at that time) refused to sign.

The Federal Treaty outlined the division of authority between Moscow and the provinces, specifying which functions were to be exercised by the centre alone, which were to fall into the category of functions exercised jointly by the centre and the provinces, and which residual functions were to be devolved to the provinces' exclusive control. Under Article I the federal centre was granted exclusive jurisdiction over:

- the adoption and amendment of the Russian constitution and other federal laws and the enforcement of federal law;
- the establishment of bodies of executive, legislative and judicial power at the federal level;
- the approval of changes in internal borders and regional subdivisions as well as the protection of Russia's international land borders, territorial waters and airspace;
- deciding citizenship issues and protecting the human and civil rights of citizens of the Russian Federation;
- the federal procuracy, the criminal code, criminal procedure and legislation on amnesties and pardons;
- federal fiscal policy, including drawing up the federal budget, monetary emission, levying federal taxes and customs, running the central bank and allocating federal funds for regional development;
- energy policy, transport and communications, space exploration and weapons production;
- foreign policy, making war and peace, signing international treaties, and defence and security policy;
- foreign trade;
- administration of federal property.

While the centre's powers were clearly delineated, Article II, which stipulated which functions should be shared between the centre and the provinces, was a potential source of confusion. Included in this category were the administration of border areas, the collection of taxes, the maintenance of law and order, the protection of public safety, environmental protection, health care, culture, and education. How these joint functions were to be carried out was not specified; as a consequence, considerable scope remained for subsequent disagreement over who had the right to do what.

Article III, which dealt with the residual rights of the provinces, was the vaguest of all. It stated merely that 'all spheres of state power' not explicitly assigned to the centre or to the joint jurisdiction of the centre and the provinces were to be exercised by the provinces independently.

One distinction that the Federal Treaty made between the republics and all the other parts of the Russian Federation was that it gave the republics control over the land and natural resources on their territory. It did not grant such control to the krais, oblasts, cities of federal significance, autonomous oblast or autonomous okrugs. How significant this really was is questionable, however, since the centre reserved the right to decide the uses to which the republics might put their natural resources, but it certainly created the impression that the republics had gained more than the other territorial formations from the Federal Treaty.

In the months that followed the signing of the Federal Treaty, there were constant complaints from the provinces that the centre was not implementing its provisions. In the absence of a mechanism for the exercise of joint powers, the centre went its way while the provinces went theirs, the result being almost total confusion. As things turned out, however, this did not matter very much. For, while the Federal Treaty was a stop-gap measure that left many issues of competence obscure, nonetheless it served its purpose. As an exercise in what has been termed 'constructive ambiguity', the treaty calmed tempers and provided a breathing space. And, since it perpetuated the pre-existing asymmetry in the Russian administrative structure, the Federal Treaty distracted the leaders of the krais and oblasts from the idea of secession and focused their attention instead on trying to catch up with the republics.

The 1993 Constitution

The Federal Treaty did nothing to resolve the increasingly bitter power struggle between Yeltsin and the Supreme Soviet. Both sides appealed to the provinces, promising them increased autonomy in return for their support in the battle over Russia's new political order. The struggle centred on whether the country should have a parliamentary or a presidential system of government. Yeltsin, who was pressing for a presidential system, favoured the ethnically-based republics over the territorially-defined krais and oblasts. His preference was particularly evident in the draft constitution approved in July 1993 by the Constitutional Assembly – an *ad hoc* body convoked by Yeltsin in an effort to circumvent his parliamentary opponents. That draft granted the republics numerous advantages over the krais and oblasts (for the text, see *Izvestiya*, 16 July 1993). It included the Federal Treaty in its entirety, with its inbuilt asymmetry between the rights of the various provinces, and described the republics as 'sovereign states within the Russian Federation', whereas the krais and oblasts were described merely as 'state-territorial formations'. There was, nonetheless, one concession Yeltsin refused to make: the draft stated that the territory of the Russian Federation was indivisible; that is, the republics did not win the right to secede.

When the struggle between president and parliament came to a head in the autumn of 1993, Yeltsin found that, despite all the promises he had made, the leaders of many of the republics did not support him. Thereafter, the president felt no further need to woo the republics. Yeltsin's bloody dissolution of parliament paved the way for the adoption, in December, of a new constitution. This gave considerable powers to the president without introducing any of the checks and balances that in democratic systems ensure that no branch of government can dominate the others.

The new constitution rescinded most of the privileges the republics had been offered in the July draft (for the text of the constitution, see *Rossiiskaya gazeta*, 10 November 1993; for selected extracts, see the Appendix; pp. 33–7 below). Most significantly, the final draft deleted the text of the Federal Treaty and all but two references to it, stipulating that, where the Federal Treaty contravened the constitution, the constitution should prevail. With the adoption of a new constitution, therefore, the Federal Treaty became a dead letter.

However, the new constitution did nothing to clarify the ambiguities about joint powers enshrined in the Federal Treaty. The powers granted to the federal authorities under Article 71 of the 1993 constitution were, aside from some minor changes, identical to those reserved for the centre under Article 1 of the Federal Treaty. The final text of the constitution did delete the passages in the July draft constitution that had described the republics as 'sovereign states'. It dropped a clause providing for separate republican citizenship, and asserted that all the 'subjects of the federation' (that is, the republics, krais, oblasts, cities of federal significance, autonomous oblast and autonomous okrugs) were 'equal with each other in their relations with the federal organs of state power'. A clause allowing individual provinces to negotiate separate treaties with the centre was also dropped from the final draft. Moreover, the final draft of the constitution specified that the upper house (the Federation Council) of the new Russian parliament (the Federal Assembly) was to consist of two representatives from each subject of the Russian Federation. Therefore, the krais and oblasts, autonomous oblast and autonomous okrugs were guaranteed equal representation with the republics, something they had not been offered in earlier drafts of the constitution.

The constitution's assertion that all subjects of the federation were equal was untrue, however. The republics still clung to higher status than the krais and oblasts. For example, the constitution gave the republics the right to have their own constitutions and to elect their own presidents, whereas the krais and oblasts were given the right to have only 'statutes'. The krais and oblasts were placed at a further disadvantage by being administered by 'governors' or 'heads of administration' who, while they were originally supposed to be elected democratically, have in fact in most cases been directly appointed (and removed) by the president without reference to the population.

Building a Federation From the Ground Up

Because the 1993 constitution did not resolve the issue of the division of powers between the centre and the provinces, pressure for autonomy did not abate after the constitution entered into force. On the contrary, horse-trading between the centre and the periphery has continued. The republics, krais and oblasts have gone on demanding financial concessions and have grabbed increased powers whenever they could get away with it. The centre has responded by negotiating a series of bilateral treaties between the Russian Federation and its most auton-omy-minded provinces. Though the idea of the whole signing a treaty with part of itself is unorthodox, the legal basis of sorts exists in Article 78.2 of the constitution (see Appendix). So far, the method has proved surprisingly effective.

The first such bilateral treaty, between the Russian Federation and the Republic of Tatarstan, was signed in February 1994. Since the late 1980s, Tatarstan had been in the forefront of those republics and regions pushing for the devolution of power within the Russian Federation. It provided an example of an ethnically-labelled territory where the squabble with the centre was not ethnic but economic. Although the republic takes its name from the Tatars, who are, after the Russians themselves, the second largest ethnic group in the Russian Federation, its leaders campaigned not for national self-determination but for economic autonomy and control over Tatarstan's natural resources. This is partly explained by the fact that the Tatars are a plurality but not a majority of the population in the republic that bears their name. It is also explained by the fact that Tatarstan is richly endowed with oil and natural gas. Moreover, the republic is strategically located in the Russian heartland. It lies on one of Russia's main commercial arteries – the River Volga – astride the East–West highways, electric power grids, and energy pipelines that connect European Russia with Siberia.

So determined were Tatarstan's leaders to assert autonomy that they refused outright to sign the Federal Treaty in March 1992. They instead insisted that they wanted 'associate' status with the Russian Federation, and that they would sign only a bilateral treaty recognizing Tatarstan as equal in status with Russia. Their position was expressed in the constitution that the republic adopted in November 1992. In it, Tatarstan was described as 'a sovereign state, a subject of international law, associated with the Russian Federation on the basis of a treaty on the mutual delegation of powers' (*Sovetskaya Tatariya*, 13 December 1992). No such treaty existed at that time, nor was the status of 'association' recognized by either the Russian constitution then in force or that adopted in December 1993. Indeed, Tatarstan's leaders opposed the section of the 1993 constitution that described all the provinces as 'equal subjects' of the Russian Federation; Tatarstan, they said, would agree to 'association' with Russia but would not be 'subject' to it.

In February 1994, after nearly three years' negotiations, Russia and Tatarstan signed a bilateral treaty 'On the Demarcation of Spheres of Authority and the Mutual Delegation of Powers' (for the text, see *Rossiiskaya gazeta*, 17 February 1994). This was the first such bilateral treaty the Russian Federation had signed.

Under Article II of the treaty, Russia recognized Tatarstan's right to have its own constitution and laws, form its own budget and levy republic taxes, conduct its own foreign policy and foreign trade, and set up its own national bank. Like the republics that had signed the Federal Treaty, Tatarstan was assured the right to administer the natural resources on its territory, the republic's substantial oil reserves included. Tatarstan also acquired the right 'to decide questions of republican citizenship'. Even though this is arguably little more than a glorified residence permit, none of Russia's other republics had the right to confer citizenship. Furthermore, Tatarstan won the right to exempt its young men from military service in the Russian army under a programme of alternative civilian service.

These two items (citizenship and alternative service) are what chiefly distinguish Tatarstan's rights under the bilateral treaty from the rights granted the other republics under the Federal Treaty and the 1993 Russian constitution. The exclusive rights of the federal authorities detailed in Article IV of the treaty between Russia and Tatarstan were the same as those in Article 71 of the 1993 constitution (see Appendix). As for the functions to be exercised jointly by the federal government and the Tatarstan authorities, the Russia–Tatarstan treaty was more detailed than the Federal Treaty or the 1993 constitution, and singled out for mention several areas of activity of special relevance to Tatarstan. For example, it assigned to the joint jurisdiction of Russia and Tatarstan the management of military and defence-industry facilities on Tatarstan's territory, as well as the responsibility for ensuring 'unimpeded and duty-free movement of transport and transportation of cargoes and commodities via air, sea, river, railway, road and pipeline'.

On one level, Russia's treaty with Tatarstan has worked just as the parties intended. Only two years before, Moscow had been afraid Kazan would try to leave the Russian Federation. Today, Tatarstan is a model member of the federation, and its treaty is held up as an example to other independence-minded provinces. Until Moscow lost patience with Chechnya and launched its military invasion in December 1994, hopes were expressed that the formula might help resolve Russia's dispute with the breakaway republic. The idea has also been seized on as a model by leaders in Ukraine's Crimea and Georgia's Abkhazia – though it has been rejected by both the countries concerned, neither of which wishes to become a federal state.

Encouraged by these results, the Yeltsin leadership charged a presidential commission, under Deputy Prime Minister Sergei Shakhrai, with preparing treaties with all Russia's republics and regions (*Rossiiskaya gazeta*, 6 September 1994). Since then, Russia has signed similar (though not identical) treaties with the Republics of Kabardino-Balkaria and Bashkortostan (both of which had insisted on amending the Federal Treaty before they signed it in March 1992). A number of other bilateral treaties were in preparation at the time of writing. Next in line were the Republics of North Ossetia, Udmurtia and Buryatia, Krasnodar Krai, and Orenburg and Kaliningrad Oblasts. Legislation laying down the general rules for the conclusion of such treaties was in preparation, as was a law on the general principles of the division of powers between the centre and the provinces.

Shakhrai warned rebellious regions that Moscow would sign treaties only with those whose constitutions or charters were in accordance with the Russian constitution. But this was clearly sabre-rattling since, in places, Tatarstan's constitution flatly contradicted that of the Russian Federation. Shakhrai admitted as much when he said that, 'Sometimes a temporary technical violation of procedure may be less harmful than delay in the resolution of a problem. In that event, you have to choose the lesser of two evils' (*ibid.*).

On another level, Russia's treaty with Tatarstan contains numerous pitfalls. In particular, it cites as its authority two mutually inconsistent documents – the constitutions of Tatarstan and Russia. While the former describes Tatarstan as 'a sovereign state, a subject of international law', the latter does not recognize the sovereignty of Tatarstan or any other Russian republic. Nor is Tatarstan a sovereign state as far as international law is concerned. Squabbles over interpretation are certain, therefore, to erupt at some future date.

One such squabble has already broken out. Citing the bilateral treaty article allowing Kazan 'to conclude with foreign states agreements that do not conflict with the international commitments of the Russian Federation', Tatarstan in August 1994 signed a bilateral friendship treaty with Georgia's secessionist Abkhazia. Its example was immediately followed by Bashkortostan (Radio Russia, 18 August 1994). Moscow leaders reacted with fury, pointing out that Tatarstan's and Bashkortostan's actions conflicted with Russia's commitments under the February 1994 Russo-Georgian Friendship Treaty with Georgia. Under the terms of that treaty, the Russian Federation recognized Georgia's territorial integrity. The Moscow leadership was so angry that, at one point, it threatened to annul its treaty with Tatarstan (Interfax, 6 September 1994), despite the fact that the bilateral treaty itself explicitly rules out unilateral denunciation. Tatarstan's leaders responded by pointing out, in tones of outraged innocence, that Moscow had made no fuss when Tatarstan concluded treaties with many of Russia's provinces and with almost all the members of the Commonwealth of Independent States. In the end, all Moscow could do was shake its fist. Tatarstan and Bashkortostan were not even forced to denounce their treaties with Abkhazia.

Russia's treaties with its republics angered the krais and oblasts, which complained that they did not enjoy the same rights as the republics. The lack of transparency in Russia's taxation system proved a particular source of controversy between centre and periphery. In

August 1994, the authorities in resource-rich Perm Oblast announced that the region would transfer no more federal taxes to Moscow. Their anger was provoked by the conclusion of the bilateral treaty between the Russian federal authorities and Perm's neighbour, Bashkortostan. For, while Perm Oblast paid out more in taxes than it got back in return, the reverse applied to Bashkortostan. To be precise, producers in Perm Oblast were supposed to pay a profits tax of 45 per cent, while in Bashkortostan the rate was only 10 per cent (*Kommersant-Daily*, 23 August 1994; *Izvestiya*, 24 August 1994). Perm's leaders demanded that Moscow should give the regions the same rights as the republics.

The Provinces Write Their Own Laws

Meanwhile, other krais and oblasts were adopting charters (the functional equivalent of the republics' constitutions) and awarding themselves additional powers. Since the charters were drafted by provincial governors they tended to concentrate increased powers in the hands of local executives. Democratically elected legislatures were often the first casualty. Civil rights were another, and there were frequent allegations that leaders in far-flung places were building personal fiefdoms that had little in common with pluralism or democracy. In Maritime Krai and Bryansk Oblast, for example, local newspapers were shut down by order of regional leaders. The threat to press freedom was especially worrying since national newspapers had grown increasingly hard to obtain in the provinces. This meant that the press was not able to perform the watchdog role assigned to it in democratic societies.

As of October 1994, constitutions had been adopted by seventeen of Russia's twenty-one republics (the only ones not yet having done so were Adygeya, Altai, Khakassia, and Karachaevo-Cherkessia), and the krais and oblasts were preparing charters (*Segodnya*, 21 October 1994). Sergei Filatov, Yeltsin's chief of staff, complained that many of these constitutions and charters contained features at odds with the norms codified in the 1993 Russian constitution, and the centre was having great difficulty trying to persuade local leaders to bring their legislation into conformity with federal law (*Rossiiskie vesti*, 31 August 1994). For example, the charters drafted by Sverdlovsk and Tambov Oblasts asserted that laws passed by the regional legislatures took precedence over federal laws. So too did the constitutions of the Republics of

Bashkortostan, Buryatia, Chechnya, Ingushetia, Kalmykia, Karelia, Komi, Sakha, Tatarstan and Tuva. As for property rights, Filatov said, Komi and Karelia were the only republics whose constitutions were in full accordance with the 1993 federal constitution, which placed issues relating to the ownership, use and disposal of land, mineral resources, water and other natural resources within the joint jurisdiction of the centre and the provinces; all the other republic constitutions declared these items to be the exclusive property of the peoples living on the territory of the republic in question.

Tuva's constitution granted the republic the right to self-determination and secession from the Russian Federation; in addition, Tuva wanted its own defence policy and customs service and refused to allow the privatization of land. Bashkortostan and Sakha claimed the right unilaterally to decide how much they would contribute to the federal budget. The constitutions of Bashkortostan, Komi and Udmurtia infringed the federal constitution by reserving certain privileges for the eponymous nationalities. Yet another conflict concerned the procuracy. Although the federal constitution stated that all procurators throughout the country were to be appointed by the Procurator General of the Russian Federation in consultation with the subjects of the federation, and that the provinces had no right to appoint procurators on their own, the constitutions of Bashkortostan, Tatarstan, Tuva and Chechnya nonetheless stated that republic procurators were to be appointed by the republic's own legislature, bypassing Moscow.

Most telling was the fact that the constitutions of Bashkortostan, Buryatia, Sakha, Tatarstan and Tuva all defined the powers of the federal centre as the sum of the powers delegated upward by the provinces whereas, according to Filatov, the powers of the Russian Federation spring 'from its own sovereignty as a single, integral, federative state'.

Optimists and Pessimists

Alarm at the centre's lack of control over the provinces was expressed by numerous commentators. The political analyst Vladimir Gelman issued a strong warning that such attitudes are storing up problems for the future (*Novaya ezhednevnaya gazeta*, 3 August 1994). In evidence, Gelman cited the fate of the soviets (councils) – the hierarchy of elected local legislatures that had its roots in the Russian Revolutions of 1905 and 1917, gave its name to the Soviet state, and was institutionalized by Lenin.

In October 1993, fresh from his victory over the Supreme Soviet, Yeltsin issued a decree dissolving the soviets throughout Russia at the lowest levels of the administrative structure, that is raion (district) soviets within cities, town soviets within raions, and settlement and village soviets (Radio Rossii, 9 October 1994). The president ordered the powers of soviets at these levels to be assumed by the heads of local administrations. The decree stripped soviets in the krais and oblasts of their managerial functions, which passed to the regional governor, and of the power to pass budgets without the governor's approval. Yeltsin also specified that, if a soviet dissolved itself or was unable to function because it was inquorate, its functions would automatically pass to the head of the relevant local administration. Finally, the Russian president ordered the holding of elections to new local government bodies. In a concession to the republics, however, Yeltsin did not order the parliaments (Supreme Soviets) of the republics to disband, but merely exhorted them to follow the same procedure.

In fact, very few of the leaders of the republics paid any attention to Yeltsin's instructions. And, since there was little follow-up from Moscow, many krai and oblast leaders were also able to ignore Yeltsin's orders with impunity. The result, in Gelman's words, was that 'the fate of the soviets in each case depended on the balance of power in a given region'. In almost all the republics, the soviets were retained and very little change took place in the system of government. In krais and oblasts where good working relations existed between executive and legislature, soviets were dissolved only after their members had been found new posts in the local administration. In Leningrad Oblast in 1994, for example, twelve of the twenty-three members of the regional duma (the legislative body that replaced the soviet) were former members of the oblast soviet. The 1994 edition of the Voronezh Oblast telephone directory of top administrators allegedly contained 'exactly the same names as the 1990 edition', while in only five of Voronezh Oblast's thirty-nine raions were the heads of local administrations 'new men' (*Izvestiya*, 14 July 1994).

Gelman concluded his report with the observation that the only places where the soviets were disbanded fully and immediately were those in which the leaders of the executive and of the legislature were at loggerheads; in these places, local governors lost no time in shutting down the rival organization. This proved a mixed blessing, however. Imperfect and undemocratic though they were, the soviets had served a useful function as a lobby able to convey the interests of the region to the ears of Moscow; they also played a mediating role between various local interests. Once they had gone, regional governors found it hard to perform these functions. As a result, conflicts at local level tended to grow sharper.

Responding to complaints such as Gelman's, Yeltsin's adviser Leonid Smirnyagin countered (*Segodnya*, 2 August 1994) that Russia's overriding need was for rapid and radical decentralization. 'One can only rejoice', Smirnyagin argued, 'that people in the regions are coming to understand that the main source of local solutions is to be found in the regions themselves, not in Moscow'. Haphazard though it was, he argued, the devolution of power to the provinces meant that Russia had embarked on 'the high road to genuine federalism'.

Conclusions

The evolution of Tatarstan's relations with Moscow suggests that, in the short term, ambiguity may be a valuable tool enabling politicians and lawmakers to sidestep issues that are too contentious to tackle head on. In the intervening lull, the sides can concentrate on building new relations based on mutual interests rather than on competing claims.

Tatarstan's relations with Moscow presented one model for keeping the Russian Federation intact. Russia's relations with Chechnya presented another. There were predictions that Russia's military intervention in Chechnya in December 1994 would sow such distrust between the centre and the regions that it would provoke the disintegration of the Russian Federation as a whole. How long Russia would be able to hold on to the republics of the North Caucasus became an open question in light of the violent solution chosen by Moscow in Chechnya. Would the other Russian provinces seek the path of compromise exemplified by Tatarstan or the path of rebellion opted for by Chechnya?

Whatever the answer to this question, the contrast between the two models should not obscure the fact that the Tatarstan model hinged on a temporary expedient. The wide disparities that exist between Russia's provinces as regards geographical size, historical legacy and natural resource potential may well favour the evolution of an 'asymmetrical' federation in which the centre's relations with the periphery will not be forced into a single pattern but vary from region to region. But, if the federation that emerges is to be stable and lasting, it will require substantial modifications. Disparities between the civil rights of inhabitants of different regions must be eliminated. A system of taxation that is seen to be fair will have to be devised. Regional charters and republic constitutions must be amended.

Respect for the rule of law is the most important ingredient of any democracy. If Russia is to become a stable democracy, the ambiguities characterizing Moscow's relations with its provinces will have to be ironed out. Sooner or later, a day will surely come when Tatarstan's perceived interests come into conflict with those of Moscow. The current situation is reminiscent of Humpty Dumpty's boast that, 'When *I* use a word, it means just what I choose it to mean – neither more nor less'. As long as ambiguity is present in the legislation on which Russia's political structure is founded, it will be hard for Russia to become a stable democracy or a full-fledged federation.

Appendix: Extracts from the 1993 Constitution of the Russian Federation

Section 1, Article 5.1: The Russian Federation consists of republics, krais, oblasts, cities of federal significance, an autonomous oblast, and autonomous okrugs which are equal subjects of the Russian Federation.

Article 5.2: A republic (state) has its own constitution and legislation. A krai, oblast, city of federal significance, autonomous oblast, or autonomous okrug has its own charter and legislation.

Article 5.3: The federal structure of the Russian Federation is based on its state integrity, the unity of the system of state power, the demarcation of areas of responsibility and powers between organs of state power of the Russian Federation and organs of state power of the subjects of the Russian Federation, and the equality and self-determination of the peoples in the Russian Federation.

Article 5.4: All subjects of the Russian Federation are equal with each other in their relations with the federal organs of state power.

Section 1, Article 11.3: The demarcation of areas of responsibility and powers between the organs of state power of the Russian Federation and the organs of state power of subjects of the Russian Federation is effected by the present constitution, the Federal Treaty, and other treaties concerning the demarcation of areas of responsibility and powers.

Section 1, Article 71: The following fall within the jurisdiction of the Russian Federation:

(a) the adoption and amendment of the constitution of the Russian Federation and federal laws, and the monitoring of compliance with them;

(b) the federative system and territory of the Russian Federation;

(c) the regulation and protection of human and civil rights and freedoms; citizenship of the Russian Federation; the regulation and protection of the rights of national minorities;

(d) the establishment of a system of federal organs of legislative, executive, and judicial power, the procedure for their organization and activity; the formation of federal organs of state power;

(e) federal state property and the management thereof;

(f) the establishment of the fundamentals of federal policy and federal programmes in the sphere of state, economic, ecological, social, cultural and national development of the Russian Federation;

(g) the establishment of the legal foundations of the single market; financial, currency, credit, and customs regulation, monetary emission and the foundations of pricing policy; federal economic services, including federal banks;

(h) the federal budget; federal taxes and duties; federal regional development funds;

(i) federal energy systems, nuclear power generation, fissile materials; federal transport, railways, information, and communications; activity in space;

(j) the Russian Federation's foreign policy and international relations and the Russian Federation's international treaties; issues of war and peace;

(k) the Russian Federation's foreign economic relations;

(l) defence and security; defence production; the determination of the procedure for the sale and purchase of weapons, ammunition, military hardware and other military property; the production of toxic substances, narcotic substances and the procedure for their use;

(m) the determination of the status and protection of the state border, territorial seas, airspace, the exclusive economic zone, and the continental shelf of the Russian Federation;

(n) the judicial system; the procuracy; legislation in the field of criminal, criminal-procedure, and criminal-executive law; amnesty and the granting of pardons; legislation in the field of civil law, the law of civil procedure and the law of arbitration procedure; the legal regulation of intellectual property;

(o) federal law relating to the conflict of laws;

(p) the meteorological service, standards and standard weights and measure-
     ments, the metric system and measurement of time; geodesy and carto-
     graphy; geographic names; official statistical records and accounting;

(q) state awards and honorary titles of the Russian Federation;

(r) the federal civil service.

Section 1, Article 72.1: The following fall within the joint jurisdiction
of the Russian Federation and the subjects of the Russian Federation:

(a) guaranteeing that the constitutions and laws of republics, and the charters,
     laws, and other normative legal acts of krais, oblasts, cities of federal
     significance, the autonomous oblast, and autonomous okrugs accord with the
     constitution of the Russian Federation and federal laws;

(b) the protection of human and civil rights and freedoms; the protection of the
     rights of national minorities; the guaranteeing of legality, law and order and
     public safety; the arrangements relating to border zones;

(c) issues relating to the ownership, use, and disposal of land, mineral
     resources, water, and other natural resources;

(d) the demarcation of state property;

(e) the use of the natural environment; environmental protection and the
     guaranteeing of ecological safety; natural sites under special protection; the
     protection of historical and cultural monuments;

(f) general issues of nurture, education, science, culture, physical fitness and
     sport;

(g) the coordination of questions of public health; the protection of the family,
     mothers, fathers and children; social protection, including social security;

(h) the implementation of measures for combating catastrophes, natural disasters
     and epidemics, and the elimination of their consequences;

(i) the establishment of general principles of taxation and levying of duties in
     the Russian Federation;

(j) administrative, administrative-procedural, labour, family, housing, land,
     water and forestry legislation, and legislation on mineral resources and on
     environmental protection;

(k) cadres of judicial and law-enforcement organs; attorneys and notaries;

(l) the protection of the primordial habitat and traditional way of life of
     numerically-small ethnic communities;

(m) the establishment of the general principles for the organization of a system
     of organs of state power and local self-government;

(n) the coordination of the international and foreign economic relations of
     subjects of the Russian Federation, and the fulfilment of the Russian
     Federation's international treaties.

Section 1, Article 72.2: The provisions of this article extend in equal
measure to the republics, krais, oblasts, cities of federal significance,

the autonomous oblast, and autonomous okrugs.

Section 1, Article 73: Outside the compass of the Russian Federation's jurisdiction and the powers of the Russian Federation as regards the terms of reference of the joint jurisdiction of the Russian Federation and the subjects of the Russian Federation, the subjects of the Russian Federation possess state power in its entirety.

Section 1, Article 78.2: The federal organs of executive power, by agreement with the organs of executive power of the subjects of the Russian Federation, may hand over to them the implementation of part of their powers provided that this does not conflict with the Constitution of the Russian Federation and federal laws.

Section 1, Article 78.3: By agreement with the federal organs of executive power the organs of executive power of the subjects of the Russian Federation may hand over to them the implementation of part of their powers.

Section 2, Article 1: In the event of noncompliance with provisions of the constitution of the Russian Federation of provisions of the Federal Treaty – the Treaty on the Demarcation of Areas of Responsibility and Powers Between Federal Organs of State Power of the Russian Federation and Organs of State Power of Sovereign Republics Within the Russian Federation, the Treaty on the Demarcation of Areas of Responsibility and Powers Between Federal Organs of State Power of the Russian Federation and Organs of State Power of Krais, Oblasts, and the Cities of Moscow and St. Petersburg in the Russian Federation, the Treaty on the Demarcation of Areas of Responsibility and Powers Between Federal Organs of State Power of the Russian Federation and Organs of State Power of the Autonomous Oblast and Autonomous Okrugs of the Russian Federation, and also other treaties between federal organs of state power of the Russian Federation and organs of state power of subjects of the Russian Federation, and treaties between organs of state power of subjects of the Russian Federation – the provisions of the constitution of the Russian Federation shall prevail.

Source: *Rossiiskaya gazeta*, 10 November 1993, pp. 3–6; with minor modifications, the translation is that made by the Foreign Broadcast Information Service.

* Elizabeth Teague is an Adviser to the OSCE High Commissioner on National Minorities. The views expressed here are her own and do not necessarily reflect those of either the High Commissioner or the OSCE.

References

Dahl, Robert A. (1963), *Modern Political Analysis*, Englewood Cliffs, NJ: Prentice-Hall.

Drobizheva, Leokadia (1994), 'Processes of Disintegration in the Russian Federation and the Problem of Russians', in Vladimir Shlapentokh, Munir Sendich and Emil Payin (eds), *The New Russia Russian Minorities in the Former Soviet Republics*, Armonk, NY: M.E. Sharpe, pp. 45–55.

Elazar, Daniel (1972), 'Federalism', in David L. Sills (ed.), *International Encyclopedia of the Social Sciences*, New York, NY: The Macmillan Company and The Free Press, vol. 5, pp. 353–67.

Filatov, Sergei (1994), 'Sub"ekty Federatsii kak osnovnye sostavlyayushchie konstitutsionnogo polya Rossii', *Rossiiskie vesti*, 31 August, p. 1.

Finer, S.E. (1974), *Comparative Government*, Harmondsworth: Penguin Books.

Gaidar, Yegor (1995), 'Russia Can't Enter the Future by Turning to the Past', *International Herald Tribune*, 10 January.

Gelman, Vladimir (1994), 'Reform of the Institutions of State Power', *Novaya ezhednevnaya gazeta*, 3 August, as translated in *Current Digest of the Post-Soviet Press*.

Glezer, Olga (1992), 'Russian Republic: No Longer Soviet Socialist Federative', *Moscow News*, no. 7.

Hannum, Hurst (1990), *Autonomy, Sovereignty, and Self-Determination: The Accommodation of Conflicting Rights*, Philadelphia, PA: University of Pennsylvania Press.

Hanson, Philip (1994), *Regions, Local Power and Economic Change in Russia*, London: Royal Institute of International Affairs.

Henze, Paul B. (1991), 'Ethnic Dynamics and Dilemmas of the Russian Republic', Santa Monica, CA: RAND Corporation.

Izvestiya Analytical Centre (1994), 'Komu prinadlezhit vlast' v Rossii? 6. Kozyrnye tuzy rossiiskikh regionov', *Izvestiya*, 14 July, p. 5.

Kibbick, Andrei (1994), 'Territorial Reform: Projects and Prospects', *Moscow News*, no. 7.

Kux, Stephan (1990), 'Soviet Federalism: A Comparative Perspective', New York, NY: Institute for East-West Security Studies.

Osborn, Robert J. (1993), 'Russia: Federalism, Regionalism and Nationality Claims', paper delivered at a conference held at the University of Pennsylvania in February, mimeo.

Petrov, Nikolai and Andrei Treivish (1994), 'Riski regional'noi dezintegratsii Rossii', mimeo.

Safire, William (1993), *Safire's New Political Dictionary*, New York, NY: Random House.

Schwartz, Lee (1990), 'Regional Population Redistribution and National Homelands in the USSR', in Henry R. Huttenbach, *Soviet Nationality Policies*, London: Mansell, pp. 121–162.

Shakhrai, Sergei (1994), 'Iz dvukh zol vybyraem men'shee', *Rossiiskaya gazeta*, 6 September, p. 1.

Sheehy, Ann (1990), 'Fact Sheet on Sovereignty Declarations', RFE/RL Research Institute, Munich, 31 October.

Sheehy, Ann (1992), 'Tatarstan and Bashkiria: Obstacles to Confederation', *RFE/RL Research Report*, no. 22, 1992, pp. 33–7.

Sheehy, Ann, (1993), 'Russia's Republics: A Threat to Its Territorial Integrity?' *RFE/RL Research Report*, no. 20, pp. 34–40.

Sheehy, Ann 'The Disintegration of the Soviet Union', chapter in a forthcoming volume on the collapse of the USSR, edited by Vera Tolz and Iain Elliot, to be published by Macmillan.

Smirnyagin, Leonid (1994), 'Razdeleniya vlastei na mestakh bol'she ne sushchestvuet', *Segodnya*, 2 August, p. 3.

Sobell, Vladimir (1994), *The New Russia: A Political Risk Analysis*, London: The Economist Intelligence Unit, June.

Teague, Elizabeth (1993), 'Center/Periphery Relations in the Russian Federation', paper delivered at a workshop held on 28 May, in Washington, D.C., under the auspices of the Russian Littoral Project and organized by Johns Hopkins University and the University of Maryland, mimeo.

Teague, Elizabeth (1993), 'North–South Divide: Yeltsin and Russia's Provincial Leaders', *RFE/RL Research Report*, no. 47, pp. 7–23.

Teague, Elizabeth (1994), 'Russia and Tatarstan Sign Power-Sharing Treaty', *RFE/RL Research Report*, no. 14, pp. 19–27.

Tregubova, Elena (1994), 'Minnats provel reviziyu regional'nykh konstitutsii', *Segodnya*, 21 October, p. 2.

USSR State Committee on Statistics, (1991), *Natsionalnyi sostav naseleniya SSSR*, Moscow: Finansy i statistika.

Volkov, Dmitrii (1994), 'Gosudarstvo beseduet samo s soboi', *Segodnya*, 23 August, p. 2.

Yeltsin, Boris (1994), *The Struggle for Russia*, New York, NY: Times Books.

2. City Government in Russia

Adrian Campbell

Therefore one should treat of the gubernatorial authority ... in respect of members, councillors, and secretaries of the various departments, courts and councils. In my opinion all these individuals are harmful for they do nothing but raise obstacles for the town-governor in his unceasing, as it were, administrative course. (Saltykov-Shchedrin, 1870/1980)

Introduction

The collapse of the Soviet regime bequeathed a set of institutional tensions which, in different ways, continue to plague its successors in different states of the former union. Such institutional conflict may be seen to have two main components:

(1) the respective powers and competencies of the legislature and the executive;
(2) the allocation of powers and competencies between central and regional administration and between regional and city administration.

The two are linked through the prevalence in Russia and other successor-states of two contrasting views of how democratic institutions should work, namely:

(a) the 'top–down' view: that there should be a single line of command, whereby a democratically-elected ruler appoints and controls the 'ruler' at the next level down, who in turn does the same for the next level, and so on;
(b) the 'bottom–up' view; whereby a democratic mandate at any level is taken as absolute, and as excluding any interference from the next level up (or below), regardless of any democratic mandates these other levels may themselves have.

These extreme and mutually opposed views on the nature of the democratic mandate are operating in a political culture which lacks a strong tradition of popular participation or public accountability. On both sides of the argument democracy often appears to be seen purely in terms of the power attached to a political office, rather than as a process involving representation of legitimate interest groups.

To an extent the conflicts referred to derive from tensions which occur in any democratic state, between politicians and administrators (professionals), and between centre and periphery. In Russia they are not only taken to extremes, but also compounded by the political culture's inclination towards a monopoly of power, the pursuit of political power being regarded as a 'zero-sum game'.

More significantly, the collapse of the Soviet system gave rise to more fundamental issues of constitutional relationships and styles of government than was the case in former communist Central Europe, where, to varying degrees, traditions of more or less democratic government and administration were there to be rediscovered. In parts of the former Soviet Union the experience of local and regional government since 1992 suggests that, in the absence of other native traditions, many of the characteristics of Tsarist provincial government returned, albeit in a modified form.

The Imperial Tradition of Local Government

At the risk of over-generalization, one may point to a number of historical traditions which would complicate any attempt to establish effective local democracy in Russia.

(1) The tradition whereby local and (more particularly) regional government are outposts of the central state, and consequently define themselves in relation to the higher-standing authorities rather than in terms of the population they serve.

In much of Russia and other former Soviet republics the state (local or national) appears to be estranged from the population to a remarkable degree, almost as if the administrations concerned were the creations of an occupying or colonial power. This tradition arises from the same set of historical influences which distinguish Russia from other colonial empires, as the country which colonized not only other nations, but itself as well.

(2) The tradition of the 'rebel autocracy' at the local level, whereby regional and local administrators would attempt to keep the central state at bay, whilst attempting to reproduce its brand of centralized, autocratic rule within their own domain.

This may coincide with what might be seen as a more positive trait, that of supporting local interests against the centre. Strongly evident at certain times under tsarism, this tendency was held within limits under Soviet rule, only to emerge more strongly after the collapse of the Union. In this respect Dzhokar Dudayev in Chechnya is not simply a separatist in the Western understanding of the term, but also an extreme version of those such as Eduard Rossel, the former governor of Sverdlovsk Oblast, and others keen to raise their status, and that of their region, against the centre (Campbell, 1994a):

> Now that we've rid ourselves of the Soviet dictatorship, every village administration is trying to act as a miniature Soviet Union, dictating downwards whilst recognizing no higher authority. (Interview with G. Shmakov, Moscow City Government, December 1991)

(3) The tradition of an unaccountable command structure, with only a weak link between authority and responsibility.

In Tsarist times, problems and responsibilities were routinely passed to regional level, with little or no support in terms of resources, and little assistance in implementation. Where centrally-led programmes were thoroughly implemented, it was a case of forced military-style crash programmes geared to output targets rather than to cost-effective outcomes, a process that was taken to an extreme in the Soviet era. According to some, it has survived in the attitudes of post-Soviet local and regional councils:

> The problem with both parliament and council in Kiev is that they want to have total control over what the executive does, but want the executive to take total responsibility. (Interview with Kiev city official, March 1995)

The same view is expressed by officials in many Russian cities, and cited as one of the reasons why councils were discredited in advance of the government's 1993 campaign against so-called 'soviet power' (i.e. that of elected councils or soviets).

(4) Corruption as a recognized part of administrative life.

This appears to have been the case throughout most of the imperial period and much of the Soviet period (although during the latter, corruption, like so much else, was largely centralized). The collapse of the administrative–command system allowed a major expansion of corruption both in scale and scope, with some administrators acting as nodes in organized criminal networks which, profiting from the lacunae in business, commercial and administrative law, effectively took over the economic coordination functions previously carried out by Soviet ministries, even with some continuity of personnel.

These characteristics do not of course represent anything like the whole of local administration in Russia and other former Soviet republics. However, they are characteristics which preceded the democratic experiments of the late nineteenth and early twentieth centuries, and might have been gradually marginalized had the latter been given more time in which to become rooted. Instead the idea of democracy was appropriated and in many respects discredited (at least at the local level) by the practices of the Soviet regime, so that citizens of post-Soviet countries have probably less experience or expectations of democracy of citizenship than their predecessors had at the turn of the century:

> We are starting from less than zero. What existed one hundred years ago has to be built from scratch. Whatever problems people have, with bad public services, for example, they will try to get round by their own efforts. They have no faith in any collective action or representation, nor in any legal rights. (Interview with Kiev city official, March 1995)

The Distortion of Democracy

The reforms of Alexander II in the 1860s significantly increased local autonomy and local democracy (the two have often been quite separate concepts in Russian history, and continue to be so), notably through the establishment of local councils – it is easily forgotten that Russia had nearly sixty years of a degree of limited local democracy and mass private property before 1917. However, the effectiveness of these was hampered by a conflict of interests between the emerging middle class who dominated the municipal councils (dumas) and the peasants who dominated the rural assemblies (zemstvos) over the appropriate form of local taxation (Rieber, 1982).

Councils were not generally seen as legitimate governing institutions in their own right. The powers of municipal dumy were trimmed back when they took decisions of which central government disapproved. In the case of St. Petersburg, the most highly developed city council, the government reduced its electoral base following one such decision

(Rogger, 1983).

After the October Revolution, despite the Bolsheviks' slogan of 'all power to the soviets' (local councils of workers', peasants' and soldiers' deputies'), local councils were a means of centralizing power. Thus it was in the name of the soviets that the democratically–elected Constituent Assembly was abolished in 1918, after which the Soviets were themselves closed to members of other parties (Fainsod, 1953). From then on the soviets increasingly became instruments of central government. The 'leading role' assigned to the party by Article 6 of the Soviet constitution rendered any independent political (or executive) role for the soviets superfluous in theory and impossible in practice. In the late 1920s local government was marginalized by the top–down structures of the Five-Year Plans and this trend continued throughout the Stalin period. Regional administrations and party organizations became primarily concerned with helping enterprises fulfil Plan targets, set from above. Local government in the traditional sense was marginalized, although it has been argued (Cattell, 1968) that the very marginality of local councils meant they had a degree of autonomy in those matters which remained within their control. In the post-war period, the Soviet Union saw a major expansion in the responsibilities of local government, although successive moves towards decentraliz-ation were balanced by compensatory centralizing measures (Hill, 1977).

Under the Soviet system three parallel hierarchies ran from the Kremlin down to the smallest village, taking in central government, republics, regions, cities, city districts, districts in regions and villages (collective and state farms). These three hierarchies were:

(1) that of legislative or representative power (from the Supreme Soviet down to the village council), for which one-party elections were held according to the principles of democratic centralism;
(2) that of the executive, from the USSR government through republican and city administrations down to district level. The main institution at sub-national level was the executive committee (*ispolkom*), a collegial/functional management board which existed at regional, city and district levels;
(3) that of the party, which was organized along the same territorial lines as the other two hierarchies, which it effectively shadowed.

The system was designed to ensure party control whilst maintaining a democratic facade. The councils were large and unwieldy rubber-stamping bodies which met every few months to approve the decisions taken by the executive in their name. The executive consisted of party appointees, approved by the councils. The respective roles of the legislature and executive were largely irrelevant, since the party organization was the real centre of power and decision-making at all levels of government. The system could not work without the party, and was designed so as not to be able to do so. Three reforms of the late 1980s set the scene for a highly complex sequence of events relating to local government in Russia in the early 1990s:

(a) the decision by Gorbachev to separate the party from the representative and executive hierarchies of the state, thus giving elected councils and their executives a stronger identity;
(b) a significant devolution of power to elected councils. This complemented a parallel decentralization of power to state enterprises and their managers (previously the enterprises had been run directly by sectoral ministries);
(c) the abolition of Article 6 of the constitution in which was enshrined the 'leading role' of the party. This allowed non-party candidates to stand for election in councils at local, regional and republican levels (Walker, 1993).

At each level of government, administrators were to attempt to re-establish the party principle of the 'single vertical line' (*'ediniy vertikal'*) over lower-level authorities within their domain – although they were apt to be averse to higher-standing authorities applying the principle to them. This echoes the Soviet principle of 'dual subordination' whereby decision-makers at each level are entirely answerable not only to their own bosses, but to their bosses' bosses (Scott, 1958).

The paradox of the Soviet system was that of a multi-level dictator-ship – administrators at each level being responsible for everything and for nothing, in theory wholly in command of lower-standing authorities and wholly beholden to those above. There was thus a strong centrifu-gal element to be unleashed as soon as central power weakened sufficiently. It has been argued (Gazaryan, 1992) that the demands for republican and regional independence which arose in the late 1980s were voiced first by apparatchiks eager to free themselves from vertical control and establish a small-scale Soviet regime on their own territory. When democrats took over they found themselves at a disadvantage. As McAuley (1992) has argued, political reform succeeded in breaking the power of the party, but did not establish a new political order, the new political authorities being very weak in terms of control of economic resources. Many democrats proved not averse to participating in this updated version of the old political order, in the process of which political reform itself was held back.

The enduring impression of local government in Imperial Russia and the Soviet Union is that of a colonial system. The Soviet model represented a more control-intensive version of the imperial/colonial model (Hill, 1977). In Russia after 1990 initial democratization (as elsewhere in the former Union) soon came to be regarded as entailing the creation of a workable system of local and regional government, and was, from late 1991 onwards, gradually discarded in favour of a gubernatorial/prefectorial system of administration, more akin to the Tsarist system than the Soviet, but with greater centrifugal pressures than either, as administrators at different levels struggled with each other to gain control over local property and resources.

Other former Soviet republics such as Ukraine and Moldova (see Chapter 4) have experienced a similar shift from representative to executive power, although far more ambiguously than in Russia. This does not reflect greater efficiency on the part of democratic organs in the two other republics mentioned. It may however reflect the following factors:

(1) that the Russian Federation was the setting of, and the heir to, the main institutional power struggles surrounding the collapse of the Soviet Union – most notably in the Russia versus USSR stand-off in August 1991. The need to re-establish the shattered central power in Russia was thus greater than in the other republics, and the issue of this process is not yet entirely clear. This may be one of the reasons for the Chechnya events.
(2) the struggle against the Union in Ukraine and Moldova was associated with nationalist movements which, as soon as they had achieved their objective, were faced with secessionist movements on their own territory, with which they were obliged to compromise; this prevented them from realizing the goal of what might be termed 'executive centralism' which at least some among the ruling elites of both countries had hoped to introduce.

The need to seek a compromise with the secessionists (in Transdniestria and Gagauzia in Moldova, and in Crimea and, potentially, the Donbass, in Ukraine) reflected not only the scale of the secession demanded (proportionately much greater than that of the few outright secessionist regions in Russia) but, more importantly, the political, moral and even military support all the secessionist movements in Moldova and Ukraine received from Russia (although more explicitly from successive Russian parliaments than from the federal government), and the link with both countries' economic dependence on Russia.

In the preceding sections I have attempted to set out the reasons why transition towards local democracy was likely to be especially problematic in the former Soviet Union, not because no such tradition had existed, but because that tradition had been thoroughly distorted by the institutional legacy of Soviet democracy.

Given that the rise and fall of local democracy in Russia have been described by the author elsewhere (Campbell, 1994a), the remainder of this chapter focuses instead on how the legacy of the Soviet period complicates the workings of local government in practice in two Russian cases, in both of which both administration and elected representatives were pro-reform and pro-democracy from 1990 onwards.

Cases in City Government

(1) St. Petersburg

The case of St. Petersburg has been dealt with in detail elsewhere (Rutland, 1991; Duncan, 1992; Campbell, 1993; Campbell, 1994b) so only its main elements will be dealt with here. In the local and regional elections of March 1990, Leningrad (as it was until June 1991) elected the most radical democratic council in the USSR (the other major gains being Moscow, Sverdlovsk and Kiev).

Almost immediately, the democrats encountered the two main operational problems of post-soviet local government: (a) the apparent inability of the representative power to work effectively or to agree an appropriate balance of power with the executive, and (b) the lack of practical power in the hands of either the city council or the executive.

The latter may be viewed with irony from a Western standpoint. Local councils in the UK, for example, not infrequently find grounds to complain that marketization and the spread of quasi-governmental agencies have led to 'fragmentation' at the level of service delivery, making strategy and coordination difficult. In Russia the Soviet system bequeathed an even more fragmented local government system: municipal bureaucracies are skeletal in nature, most services being provided by arm's length organizations (*glavki*) many of which were and are subject to multi-subordination, being accountable to district, city, region and central government simultaneously. In the past this complex web of accountability was held together by the discipline of the 'party card' – all service directors being party members. In the absence of the party system, the multi-subordination of service organizations often means they are accountable to no-one in practice (interview with M. Manevich, Leningrad City Council Economic Reform Committee, March 1991).

Were the problems generated by this system not enough, conflict became endemic between commissions of the council and corresponding committees or departments of the executive (even though the latter included many new democrat appointees). Within the executive itself there were major conflicts between departments such as that of economic reform (under Anatoly Chubais) and industry (under Bolshakov). The tension between economic reform/finance and industry/economic development in fact persisted long after both had left, being resolved in March 1994 when Chubais's former deputy, Alexander Kudrin, became first deputy mayor in charge of a combined finance and economy department, the most powerful in the city administration, allowing for the first time a clear link to be made between resource allocation and performance by other departments (interview with Anatoly Zelensky, deputy chair of the Finance and Economy Department of the St. Petersburg Mayor's Office).

Unable to choose a leader from within their own ranks, the city council invited the celebrated USSR deputy Anatoly Sobchak to become chair of the council. This led to a long-running conflict between Sobchak and the more radical Shchelkanov, chair of the city executive committee, with radical council deputies becoming increasingly hostile to both (interview with Marina Sal'ye, Member of Leningrad City Council Free Democrats, April 1991).

After Shchelkanov had unsuccessfully tendered the resignation of the entire executive committee for the eighth time (in April 1991), the consensus moved in favour of establishing a 'strong mayor' system in the city. Sobchak, like other leading 'mainstream' democrats (notably Gavriil Popov, chair of Moscow City Council, and Boris Yeltsin, then speaker of the Russian Parliament), was much in favour of strong executive rule (Sobchak, 1991). In retrospect, some councillors saw the alliance of these three figures and their allies as having the aim of recreating a new version of party domination via a 'party of power' based on the executive branch of government at all levels (interview with Aleksandr Shishlov, St. Petersburg Small Council, October 1993). Ironically, given the bitterness of the power struggles with the city council that were to characterize Gavriil Popov's short period as Moscow mayor (before being replaced by his deputy, the current mayor and presidential pretender Yuri Luzhkov), the Moscow city council approved a version of the strong mayoralty that gave the mayor sweeping powers except over the budget. Leningrad city council was more cautious and debated 112 amendments to the original draft, many of them originating with the Free Democrats, who most distrusted Sobchak's ambitions. In the event, Sobchak, knowing that he would receive an overwhelming mandate from the population in the forthcoming mayoral election (timed to coincide with the Russian presidential election, 12 June 1991), approached the Russian parliament with a mere half page setting out sweeping generalized powers for the mayor, and this was formally approved, making nonsense of the council's decision (interviews with S. Udalov and M. Gorny, Leningrad City Council Commission on Local Self-Government, May 1991).

The position was further complicated by Parliament's passing of a Law on Local Self-Government which specified different competencies for the representative and executive branches at local level, the former having sole right to approve budgets. According to the President of the Association of Russian Cities (V. Kirpichnikov, interviewed in April 1994), it would have been better to adopt a northern European-style of system where the council possesses both full authority and full responsibility regarding the actions of the executive. Instead the Law was seen to institutionalize the conflict between the two branches of government, leaving as it did the executive to take full legal responsibility for decisions taken by the council.

Conflict continued between council and mayor right up to December 1993, when (reportedly at Sobchak's behest) President Yeltsin formally abolished the city council, the last such abolition in the wake of the 'October events' of that year (on which the city council had adopted a characteristically cerebral position – against the Russian parliament on policy, but in favour of it as an institution).

The abolition was followed by elections in March 1994 for a new city duma (with the power only to approve rather than initiate or veto decisions) which received only derisory support – the turn-out for almost half of the fifty seats was too low to be valid and the elections for these had to be repeated in September 1994. No fewer than seven warring democrat factions were represented, demonstrating the continuing failure to create local politics with any relevance to more than a small minority of voters. The city could be regarded as having little or no separation of powers, and a mayor's office with almost unchallengeable power (Gorny and Shishlov, 1994).

A similar analysis moved the president's representative in St. Petersburg, Sergei Tseplyaev, to attempt to redress what he saw as the city's 'democratic deficit' via the establishment of an assembly of voluntary organizations. At the same time he attempted to raise the profile of federal, rather than mayoral, power by re-grouping and re-housing federally-subordinated organizations on one site so that he could coordinate them more effectively (interview with S. Tseplyaev, Presidential Representative for St. Petersburg and Leningrad *oblast'*, September 1994).

In the case of St. Petersburg, the city's proximity to the West combined with an increasingly high profile in terms of foreign investment, and its highly educated and cosmopolitan population, meant that the failure to build a more balanced political order did not seem to prevent the city from maintaining its position as a centre of progressive change. In cities where these conditions were less pronounced, the price of the failure of political reform (beyond the initial objective of breaking party control) may have been more costly.

2. Ekaterinburg

In some respects Ekaterinburg may be regarded as a smaller (population 1.5m) and more isolated version of St. Petersburg. The city is dominated by military and heavy industry, much of it linked in the past with that of Leningrad. It is said that in the Stalin period many of the deportees from Leningrad ended up in Sverdlovsk, the latter city's strong pro-democratic traditions being linked to its proximity with the Gulag, of which many local inhabitants had direct experience. Sverdlovsk provided the power base for Boris Yeltsin's career, and is said by some to have been prepared as a bolt-hole for the Russian president if the events of either August 1991, or October 1993, had gone the other way. Sverdlovsk was one of the three large Russian cities to elect a large democrat majority to its city council in March 1990.

Three years later, an opinion poll held in Ekaterinburg (formerly Sverdlovsk) in March 1993 found that no fewer than 74 per cent of the city's residents believed that the city was ruled by 'mafia groups who had bought up local officials' (Zhitenev, 1993). This compared with 14 per cent who thought the city administration was in control, and only 4 per cent who thought the city council was in control. The findings of Zhitenev's team were published by independent Ekaterinburg publishers Novaya Gildiya in September 1993, but most copies of the pamphlet were seized in a police raid on the publisher's offices the following month. Far from representing popular hysteria, the pamphlet had been able to include as its preface an open letter (of 15 January 1993) to Boris Yeltsin from the president's own envoy to the region, V. Mashkov, which appealed for help against 'the active and growing influence exercised over local authorities by primitive criminal warlord leaders'.

Whatever the underlying reasons for the city's achieving a reputation for ungovernability, in the sense of collapsing law and order (the same proximity to the former Gulag that helped reinforce the progressive vote also means that 'all freed criminals pass through the city'), Ekaterinburg and the surrounding Sverdlovsk region provide one of the best examples of how the Soviet legacy complicates local government structure and functioning.

Relations between the city council and the city executive committee were difficult almost from the beginning, with much of the problem being ascribed to personality differences (as with Sobchak and Shchelkanov in Leningrad). This contrasted with relations at the oblast or regional level, where there was said to have been a high degree of cooperation between the two branches. This reflected a greater concentration of radical voters and deputies at city level, whereas at regional level the party economic management networks are more strongly represented, leading to a less radical and more pragmatic approach. In the first round of this conflict, in 1990, the regional council supported the city council and the executive committee were dismissed and replaced by people more in line with the council's preferences, the new executive being led by Arkady Selnitsky. However, following the same curious logic of events as in St. Petersburg and Moscow, the appointment of a more pro-reform executive led not to a diminution of conflict with the radical council, but rather to its escalation.

Selnitsky, like many other 'heads of administration', did have a legitimate grievance in that, as described above, the law held the executive, and not the council, responsible before the law for the council decisions it implemented. Selnitzky drew up a document which set out legal grounds for the executive having the right to question the legality of council decisions, which might otherwise have brought the city executive into conflict with the courts and the regional authorities. City deputies apparently found this idea difficult to adjust to, seeing such constraints as a dilution of their mandate (interview with Anatoly Ishutin, Deputy Mayor for the Economy, Ekaterinburg, September 1993).

This led to a cycle of conflict between the city council, led by its radical chairman Yuri Samarin, and the executive authorities at city and regional level. The conflict came to a head when, in April–June 1993, Samarin finally lost a vote of confidence in the city council amid scenes referred to as amounting to theatre of the absurd (*Oblastnaya gazeta*, Ekaterinburg, June 1993), with Samarin claiming that the session which voted to end his chairmanship had not been quorate and that his enemies had been pressing the electronic voting buttons of absent deputies (not an uncommon practice in Russian councils of the period in question). Evidence was sought from security cameras. This appeared to show, although not beyond doubt, that Samarin had been wrong. Samarin was accused by some of having helped to discredit democracy by his use of what might be termed 'gesture politics', although others saw the affair as underscoring the weak position of councils and the inadequacy of the current political management arrangements. Samarin was at least elected, whereas heads of administration at district, city and regional level were (after the end of 1991) all appointees of the head of administration at the next level up.

Regardless of the rightness or otherwise of his stand, it was significant that Samarin fell victim indirectly to the practice, prevalent at the time, of multiple mandates. The city council contained deputies who were also deputies of city-district (raion) councils and of the regional (oblast) council, and it was these two levels that were seen to combine in order to depose Samarin (interviews with I. Dyakonov, chair of district council and of Ekaterinburg City Council Commission on Education and Culture, and with members of the Ekaterinburg City Council Commission on Local Self-Government, September 1993). Both the regional and district councils tended to represent more pragmatic managerial interests; city districts had been targeted by Samarin for abolition, in favour of decentralization down to neighbourhood level (interview with E.V. Animitsa, Professor of Local Government, Urals Economics Institute, September 1993), which the districts naturally opposed. The radicals themselves had lost much of their earlier enthusiasm for disputes, or had moved on to new activities – as elsewhere, an increasing number became employed by the executive they had previously been in conflict with.

From the point of view of economic reform, the loss of the city council's influence (or rather its failure to exercise any effective influence) was probably of marginal importance. From the point of view of political reform, the implications may have been more serious in a city lacking the favoured economic position of St. Petersburg. According to Mark Ukk, a former long-term political prisoner and advisor to the city council on human rights;

> Those who carry out the gangland killings are merely pawns in a much larger commercial and political game in which regional state security agencies play a not inconsiderable part ... The machinery for dictatorial rule is still there, contrary to what people think... with most people being completely divorced from politics, only small forces would be needed to seize power. The ultra-nationalists in Ekaterinburg have at their disposal about 2,000 armed irregulars, although of much greater importance is their network of 200–300 supporters among the intelligentsia. The political void in the city is such that, if the time were right nationally, there would be nothing to stop them taking over, regardless of the lack of active support for their ideas. (Interview, Ekaterinburg, September 1993)

For its part, the city administration appeared to place a high premium on minimizing social instability. Whilst the authorities in St. Petersburg or Moscow might be sufficiently confident to risk repeated predictions of social 'explosions', the caution of those in the more isolated Urals is understandable. In order to ensure low prices, the city kept control of 30 per cent of retail outlets. In order to stave off food shortages in a region which is low on agricultural produce, it came to an arrangement with the growing banking sector, making licensing and land allocations conditional on banks' providing cheap credits to the (90 per cent privatized) food wholesale trade. No privatization was to be considered for municipal or communal services (interview with Ishutin). At the same time the city boasted high growth (700 new companies a month during 1993) in the private commercial sector, which helped to absorb some of the labour from the collapsing large state enterprises that had formed the basis of the city's economy. The latter, however, contained large reserves of hidden unemployment, and were frequently at a standstill (with workers on leave without pay) for months at a time during 1993–5.

The city administration found itself in a difficult position in relation to the regional administration. There is a natural conflict of interest between large cities and higher-standing authorities, in this case the regional administration, which have the function of channelling resources out of the city into the smaller regional towns and districts (the same phenomenon could be seen to occur in Romania, for example), and which are proportionately more strongly represented at the level of the region than are the large cities. Half of the districts in the region were said to be subsidized by the region, which placed pressure on the largest city, which had budgetary problems of its own.

There is also the tradition, from the Imperial and Soviet periods, of the region being a level of government in the full sense of the term, as opposed to 'self-government', the term used to describe councils and administrations at city, town or district level. This status difference, combined with hierarchical superiority and control over resource allocation and a large-versus-small town element, provides sufficient explanation why relations between regions and cities in Russia (like those between cities and counties in Romania) often involve a degree of conflict.

In the case of Ekaterinburg there was, until late 1993, a further conflict of interest between the city and Sverdlovsk region of which it is the capital. The regional governor, Eduard Rossel, was leading a campaign to upgrade the region's status to that of a republic (Campbell, 1994a, and see Chapter 9 below), as part of a wider strategy of bringing the Urals regions together in what could be seen as a sub-national confederation. For his part Rossel saw this as:

> The only way out of the game of divide and rule which began when the region was reduced in size in 1933, and which continues to be played on us to this day ... We can build a civilised form of government here, even if Russia as a whole can't ... If we do not, there will be civil war. (Speech to Kursk veterans, 21 September 1993)

There was little enthusiasm for this project at city level. This was because, if successful, it would significantly increase the hold of the region over the city – 'republics' as opposed to regions have the right to a constitution of their own, within the framework of the Federation, and therefore have the right to design the local government system on their territory as they see fit. As it was, the republic was abolished as illegal by presidential edict in October 1993, although much of the inter-regional system of cooperation that Rossel built up in the Urals remains in place, and Rossel, although sacked as governor, remains an influential figure within this system.

The city had, arguably, some suppressed ambitions of its own – it is the largest city in Russia not to have Federal status – the two largest cities (Moscow and St. Petersburg) have regional status in their own right. They are thus independent of the regions in the heart of whose territories they are situated. Ekaterinburg's claim to a higher status was partly recognized under the Soviet regime, in which, on account of its industrial importance, it had had a separate 'line' in Gosplan documents, separate from the line representing Sverdlovsk region.

For their part, the seven districts (raions) within the city were anxious about their status. This in part stems from the fact that the raion is a managerial unit invented under the Soviet regime to be coterminous with party organizations. This has provided Moscow and St. Petersburg city authorities with the political excuse to dispose of what is (from the city-level point of view) an unwelcome source of countervailing power. In fact the raion's managerial rationale (based on economies of scale) as opposed to natural community boundaries (whether within cities or outside) is reminiscent of English districts, London boroughs and Parisian *arrondissements*.

The Ekaterinburg raiony were liable to complain at the way in which local enterprises were dumping much of their various types of social provision on to the raion, whilst the city delegated the messy day-to-day problems downwards to be resolved locally. In addition to their technical and social responsibilities, raiony tended to carry out many coordinating or progress-chasing functions that might have been carried out by party structures, but often had not been – such as calling together organizations involved in building maintenance for joint problem-solving. As in the case of the rural raion described in the chapter on Moldova, raiony may be regarded as keeping services running in the transition period, by operating in the grey area between new and old styles and structures of administration. Raiony had grounds for complaint in that they carried out these varied functions without their status, responsibilities or budget being clarified from above. As elsewhere, there is considerable uncertainty over which buildings and resources used or serviced by the raion are its property, and which belong to the city (or region). As a result, the raions of the city had formed an association which met monthly to decide which matters should be referred collectively for the city administration's attention (interview with Aleksandr Lashchev, Chair of Kirovsky raion).

Both the raions and the city face the problem of poor tax recovery. Of the tax to be collected locally, 70 per cent was said to go uncollected. People were said to be used to receiving services, but not to paying taxes. Enterprises received tax-breaks in exchange for those services they still provided. However, when they become corporatized as joint stock companies (as most did), they tended to withdraw from service provision, and the scale of local tax extracted from them did not meet the cost of the extra services for which responsibility was transferred to the city (interview with Vladimir Yatnov, head of the Urals Region Department of the Urals Economics Institute).

3. Sverdlovsk-44

To complete this picture of the web of administrative relationships in which the city of Ekaterinburg is situated, it is worth drawing attention to more tangible aspects of the Soviet inheritance, namely the closed towns of the military-industrial complex. A large number of closed settlements were said to exist within the region around Ekaterinburg, but the most significant is the still closed city of Verkh-Neyvinsk, now re-christened Novouralsk, but generally known by its code name of Sverdlovsk-44 (it is actually more than fifty miles from the former Sverdlovsk). Sverdlovsk-44 is one of the ten purpose-built closed cities of the Atomic Energy Ministry. It is still characterized by maximum security, including a physical perimeter surrounding the entire town of 150,000 people. It continues to enjoy a highly privileged standard of living by former Soviet standards, with few identifiable social problems, and high incomes derived from the main employer, the uranium *kombinat* which now supplies a guaranteed market in the US (a measure of the secrecy observed in the past was that use of the word 'uranium' was banned even for engineers working with it – the term 'product' had had to be used instead).

Like so many other territorial units in Russia, Sverdlovsk-44 is beset by concerns about its status. Sverdlovsk Region is keen to absorb it formally in order to have access to the considerable wealth that could be distributed to hard-pressed towns elsewhere in the region. As it is, the town is an extra-territorial entity, being grouped with the other nine towns under the purview of the Atomic Energy Ministry.

Almost all of these far-flung nuclear towns are economically less fortunate than Sverdlovsk-44, which therefore carries the main burden of a voluntary system of re-distribution between them. This system is however less onerous than Sverdlovsk Region's demands for resources would be, were the town to have its status 'normalized'. The subsidy to the other towns is seen as worth providing to maintain the special status of the group of ten. As it is, the town deals directly with the Ministry of Finance, without going through the intermediary of a region (as Ekaterinburg and all other cities apart from Moscow and St. Petersburg have to). Thus it attains the ideal of many local administrators in Russia, that of having discretion over all taxes collected on its territory, rather than sending shares up to the region and the federation for redistribution – this after all formed part of the 'Urals Republic' project, to upgrade the region in order to reduce the share of taxes going to the centre to subsidize other regions and republics which paid a lower share of tax.

A further reason for maintaining closed status is that thanks to its physical border and tight security, the town is almost entirely free of the crime and associated social disorders that characterize other towns and cities in the region. The town is negotiating with its neighbours and with the region to expand its borders to cover 25,000 hectares as opposed to the current 9,000 hectares (interview with Sergei Moskalyov, Chair of Sverdlovsk-44 Town Council, September 1993).

The general impression provided by the chair of the council was that there was little of urgency to do, apart from subsidize business-start-ups and safeguard the town's way of life. This idyllic view was not shared by a former vice-chair of the council:

> There is no one you can work with in the council, they let the factory – which runs the city administration in effect – take all the decisions, just as they do in most smaller towns. There are too many people like our councillors, always in power and never deciding anything. All they and the administration are good at is selling out the people in order to stay in power. There is no point being in politics now ... I will return to politics from business when there are enough of us, people who have built up capital and acquired real power, then there will be real politics, rather than power for its own sake deciding nothing and leading nowhere. (Interview with Vitaly Komarov, September 1993)

City government throughout Russia and the former Soviet Union is still prevented to a greater or lesser extent from dealing with the tangible problems that it faces by the accumulated institutional legacy of the Soviet period. This, rather than any problem of ideology or 'mentality', is the cause of the degree to which democratic rule has failed to live up to expectations. A statement made in relation to Kishinev in Moldova demonstrates quite concisely the difficulty of carrying out simple operations in the post-Soviet institutional environment:

> At the moment the city's authority is still very weak – we can't even get the snow cleared from the streets. In the old days, if the snow wasn't cleared the person in

charge of roads (who would of course be a Party member) would be summoned by the Party hierarchy. He would be quaking in his boots before that meeting. They would tell him that if the streets weren't cleared by the next day he would lose his Party card. Losing your Party card meant losing your job, your career, your home, and all your other privileges. Of course we don't want the Party back, but we do need some mechanism of authority. If we demand to see service managers, they tell us, the city authorities if you please, that they're too busy to see us, and if we demand that they see us, they ask us who exactly we think we are. (Interview with acting mayor of Kishinev [Chişinaŭ], February 1994)

References

Campbell, A. (1993), 'Local Government Policymaking and Management in Russia: the Case of Leningrad/St. Petersburg', *Policy Studies Journal*, vol. 21 no. 1, pp. 133–42.

Campbell, A. (1994a), 'Local and Regional Power in the Russian Federation', in A. Coulson (ed.), *Local Government in Eastern Europe*, Aldershot: Edward Elgar.

Campbell, A. (1994b), 'Three Cases in Russian Local Government: Nizhny Novgorod, St. Petersburg and Moscow', in Coulson, *op. cit.*

Cattell, D. (1968), *Leningrad: A Case Study of Soviet Urban Government*, Praeger.

Duncan, P. (1992), 'The Return of St. Petersburg', in G.A. Hosking, J. Aves and P.J.S. Duncan (eds), *The Road to Post-Communism: Independent Political Movements in the Soviet Union, 1985–1991*, London: Pinter.

Fainsod, M. (1953), *How Russia is Ruled*, Cambridge, MA: Harvard University Press.

Gazaryan, A. (1992), 'The Role of Local Government in the Transitional Period', paper presented at ESRC project workshop on local government in Eastern Europe, University of Birmingham.

Gorny, M., and A. Shishlov (1993), 'Organizatsiya vlasti i upravlenie v Sankt-Peterburge', *Severnaya Palmyra* (St. Petersburg, Strategy Centre), no. 4, pp. 1–21.

Hill, R. (1977), *Soviet Political Elites*, London: Martin Robertson.

McAuley, M. (1992) 'Politics, Economics and Elite Realignment in Russia: A Regional Perspective', *Soviet Economy* vol. 8 no. 1, pp. 46–88.

Rieber, A.J. (1982), *Merchants and Entrepreneurs in Imperial Russia*, Chapel Hill, NC: University of North Carolina Press.

Rogger, H. (1983), *Russia in the Age of Modernisation and Revolution*, Harlow: Longman.

Rutland, P. (1991), 'From Perestroika to Paralysis: the Stalemate in Leningrad', *RFE/RL Report on the USSR*, 22 March, pp. 12–16.

Saltykov-Shchedrin, M., (1870/1980), *The History of a Town*, London: Meeuws, originally published in 1870.

Scott, D. (1958), *Russian Political Institutions*, London: Allen & Unwin.

Sobchak, A. (1991), *Khozhdenie vo vlast'*, Moscow: Novosti.

Walker, R. (1993), *Six Years That Shook the World*, Manchester: Manchester University Press.

Zhitenev, V. (ed.) (1993), *Mafia v Ekaterinburge*, Ekaterinburg: Novaya Gildiya.

3. Political and Economic Issues in the Re-creation of Lithuanian Local Government

Artashes Gazaryan and Max Jeleniewski

The Soviet Type of Government: A Short Introduction

All administrative-territorial units, i.e. the republics, regions, cities and settlements, in the Soviet Union were looked upon by the Centre and regarded themselves first of all as producers. They 'produced' houses and services, as well as meat and milk, coal and oil, and tractors. Fulfilling the state orders for production was the main task for a local administration at any level.

When the idea of the necessary effectiveness of centralized planning and the 'socialist mode of production' had become discredited, the counter-idea of guaranteed prosperity under a regime of total economic independence of 'producers' arose. The buzz words of the day in the middle 1980s were 'regional self-financing', 'self-supporting [territorial] management' and 'territorial independence'.

The main obstacle to economic independence of the administrative-territorial units appeared to be the legislative domination of the strong centre in Moscow, which had the power to divide and re-distribute the national products of the republics. Naturally, the question of political independence for areas with comparatively high productivity began to be raised. It is not accidental that the republics with the best living standards, such as Lithuania or Estonia, became leaders of the movement for national self-determination, and not Tadzhikistan or Kyrgyzstan.

In the Soviet Union the local social and industrial infrastructures were, in principle, managed in such a way as to meet demands set by the nation as a whole. Meeting the demands of the local community was not regarded as an objective. The needs of local inhabitants were looked upon as a necessary evil, requiring central planning bodies to allot a certain minimum of resources to meet them.

The elected bodies of the local authority used to exist purely for the sake of appearance. They never made any real decisions. Councillors were in practice appointed by the committees of the Communist Party; elections were just a formality. The city and regional party organization borders always coincided with the borders of administrative-territorial units of so-called self-governments or Soviets.

Party committees could make any decisions, and it was obligatory for them to make decisions in all local cases requiring decisions, but they were not accountable for this decision-making to the population. Their decisions were aimed not at meeting the demands of local inhabitants, but at the implementation of orders given by the party. Thus the committees, consisting of professional 'politicians', tackled local problems and made decisions, but it was not local self-government. The local executive bodies did not perform the functions of self-government, either. On the one hand they were obedient servants of the central state government; on the other hand they were masters of the local government and of the residents of the local government territory, within the limits allowed by law and the party organs.

Politicians in the party machinery at all levels were expected to be loyal to the party leaders. On that condition they could issue orders and exercise control over local executive bodies and other state institutions. After the 'reconstruction', the most active of the newly-elected council members usurped the role of the executives, formerly played by the party professionals. But, unlike the 'politicians' of the party, who were strictly subordinated to party discipline and were responsible to the political authorities, the new politicians were not controlled by anybody. They were responsible only to the public through elections.

Economic Dimension of 'Territorial Independence' and the Role of Local Authorities

Initially, the struggle for political independence in the Baltic states followed the struggle to secure the economic interests of certain 'territories'. Although, later, economic aspirations on the national level in the Baltic States have not, as in the Soviet era, determined local priorities, they have influenced the understanding of 'territorial independence'. Local self-governance was mainly conceived as serving economic prosperity, not the organization of public services or democratic development.

In 1990, just after the declared independence of the country, a law on local government was passed in the Lithuanian parliament, the 'Seimas'. This Law on the Basics of Local Government was the first step in a decentralization process. The principle of economic independence for local governments was stated clearly in the law. According to the law there would be local democratically elected authorities on two levels: the so-called 'lower' and 'higher' level (Figure 3.1).

Figure 3.1: Administrative-territorial units of local self-government in Lithuania in 1990–1994

CENTRAL GOVERNMENT

Regions (44)	Cities (11)
Governments of lower level (529 Units)	

POPULATION

The lower level embraces rural territorial units (426), settlements (22) and towns (81). The higher level embraces regions and cities. According to the law, local governments of both levels had the same social-economic rights and were responsible for solving the same problems of the population. The government's decisions on the distribution of state property rights between levels of government actually granted the local authorities of the higher level the right to allocate all municipal property. The law implementing the division of municipal property, however, came into effect only in 1995.

Conflict between the state and local authorities soon became apparent. The state authorities sought a local basis for managing the national economy, the local authorities wanted to use local resources for the sake of local residents only. In the first two years of independence, a conflict arose between the 'ultra-patriots' in the central government and the so-called 'old communists' at the local level. Often, in fact, the local politicians had nothing in common with the Lithuanian Communist Party. But what had recently been a popular striving towards 'territorial economic independence' came to be labelled 'local egoism' and 'blocking of reforms'.

Nonetheless, the first postwar government of an independent Lithuania, adhering to the popular slogan of 'territorial independence', accorded some respect to the power of local authorities. The second government, however, led by the former reformist and nationalist Communist Party First Secretary of Lithuania, Algirdas Brazauskas, was not very fond of the institution of local democracy, and consistently tried to turn local governments into organizations directly subordinate to the central machinery. The government succeeded in receiving from the Supreme Council the right to dismiss mayors and other local executives who disregarded instructions from Vilnius. In July 1993 the Lithuanian parliament passed an Act establishing central government representatives on the local level, whose only function was to supervise and control the actions of local authorities.

Quite often local governments were accused by the central government of adopting decisions which violated one or another legislative act. That served as an argument against their independence. Sometimes such failures were inevitable, given the legal illiteracy of the newly-elected local leaders; sometimes they were dictated by the sheer impossibility of following two different, contradictory acts, laws or decrees at a time. It should be noted that the central government was also violating the law, and pleading 'objective necessity'. Analogous actions on the part of the local governments were described as 'sabotage by ex-communists', as the government had no other excuses for its failures in the implementation of economic reforms.

From the above it is clear that in the course of 1991 to 1993 the central government did not succeed in implementing the Law on the Basics of Local Government. The economic independence of local governments did not materialize. Some old state structures survived in local government, despite the law. No property was transferred to local governments: enterprises, land and real estate stayed in the hands of the central state. The privatization process was run by the central government using the local government as executive offices. Local government budgets were drawn up by the central government. In fact, there was no special attention to local needs.

So there are two main dimensions for any discussion of local government in Lithuania in the first three years of independence. First, there is the economic dimension: the local governments did not own any resource but were only managing the former state socialist property, such as land, infrastructure, and so on. Second, there was the political dimension: Lithuania was governed at first by right-wing leaders (the Landsbergis administration), while at the local level the opposition reigned. This particular cleavage disappeared however when these right-wing leaders lost power at the centre in November 1993. Now it looks as though the situation is reversed: the former Communist Party is in power in the centre, not really taking initiatives to decentralize, and local governments are trying to survive. In general, during this first period after independence there was no room to discuss public administration reform or development of local democracy.

Structural and Political Weakness of Local Democracy

In the Law on the Basics of Local Government of 1990 the former Soviet idea that the mayor and other members of a city administration could not be members of the city council was preserved. The mayor is the chairman of the administration and this position means he acts as a chief executive.

Except for those issues that are within the exclusive competence of the elected council, the administration, consisting of unelected people, could formally adopt any political and administrative decision. However, any decision of the administration could at any time be cancelled by the council. This used to happen quite frequently, as any single councillor who disliked the decision of the administration might demand to discuss the issue at a session of the council. In this way an organizational matter can be politicized, and decisions taken about it can be altered in the process.

In some cases city councils adopted the decision on the division of the responsibilities and delegated some of their rights to the mayor or the administration, thus reducing the number of conflicts. Even in those cases, however, the right of 'veto' remained, and the councillors actively used it against the executive, which was blamed for any failure to turn the good intentions of the councillors into a good life for the electorate.

The ill-defined status of the executive power, the absence of a contract system and legal guarantees created ideal conditions for witch-hunts. Any employee, whether elected or appointed by the council, could be dismissed at any moment without an explanation, just because a majority of councillors did not like him any more. As early as 1991 the mayors of four of the five largest cities and of some other cities and regions were relieved of their posts. This process continued in subsequent years. The situation in the regions was not very stable either.

At the same time, councillors have not, for practical purposes, been accountable to voters. The electorate, as a rule, is depoliticized and disorganized. The first election campaign was characterized by bitter invectives against the Soviet regime. To become a local council member during the first local elections, it was enough to proclaim oneself an enemy of the 'bad' system and support the 'good life' exemplified by the West. There was also no question of councillors being answerable to parties, as they were elected on a personal basis. They could be non-party, or they could join a new party every month; it did not alter their status and did not interfere with their position in the system.

A study of the working of the Siauliai City Council, for example (Clark, 1995), found that in 1994 only 21 of the 58 deputies belonged to political parties. The mayor, Alfredas Lankauskas, was an independent, elected by the voters of the non-party deputies. In its attempts to cope with the city's acute economic difficulties (Siauliai housed a Soviet military base and military-related all-Union factories), the City Council, according to Clark, initially found no civic body or organized interest group with which it could work. Only the Association of Industrialists had, by mid-1994, lobbied the council, and their interests were in getting subsidies for the large, Soviet-era, electronics plants, not in restructuring. Eventually, the mayor was able to enlist the support of an association of small businesses, representing the new, small firms of the area, created from scratch, to develop plans for a free economic zone.

It may well be that this pattern will increasingly be observed across Lithuania, as local governments' interests in local economic revival overlap with those of the emerging class of 'new' entrepreneurs. It must be borne in mind, however, that the latter generally – as Clark notes in the case of Siauliai – want to pay as little as possible in taxes. It is noteworthy that, in Clark's account, it was the Mayor of Siauliai who took the initiative in contacting the entrepreneurs, and not vice versa.

The local elections of 25 March 1995 showed a strengthening of the role of parties in local elections, apparently brought about by a change in the electoral rules (see below). A real integration of local and national politics is suggested by the interpretation placed by the media on the outcome: a sharp setback for the ruling party, the leftist Lithuanian Democratic Labour Party and a strong recovery for the conservative Homeland Union (*OMRI Daily Digest*, 27 March 1995). The turnout, at 42.5 per cent, was low, though not below that in many Western local elections.

Hitherto, however, the new arrangements at the local level have rarely been conducive to the maximum democratization of the society. Many democratic i.e., anti-communist, leaders among those who came to power acted, in many respects, just like the former 'apparatchiks'. In the administration some people who worked for local governments under the old regime survived, but many new and inexperienced people were also brought into local administration. The political control of the city councils over the work of the executive bodies was weakened by the contradictions in the legislation, conflicts among the politicians and their poor understanding of many practical issues. Both political inexperience amongst elected councillors and administrative inexperience amongst the staff of the executive cadres have been sources of difficulty.

Representation of Ethnic and Political Minorities

One of the specific features of Lithuania in the first years after independence has been the notion of democracy as the power of the majority, in the name of the majority and only for the benefit of the majority, 'suppressing the resistance' of all others. At the Soviet census of 1989, 81.5 per cent of the population of Lithuania were ethnic Lithuanians. So the dominant aim of politics in this period – that of rebuilding an independent state – has been closely intertwined with the re-assertion of the ethnic identity of that majority.

The priority given to the main ethnic group was perhaps natural in this extreme situation of state reconstruction, when the instinct of self-preservation of an ethnic group in its struggle for independent existence demands the total mobilization of all the resources for solving its problems. Any decision inimical to the perceived political, economic or cultural interests of the 'winner-nation' becomes not only unpopular, but practically impossible. The minorities are forced to accept their fate without protest. General ethnic conflicts are unlikely so long as the minorities are scattered over the territory of a state more or less proportionally. As a minority group in each electoral district they just disappear from the political map. However, if the geographical distribution is uneven, the same majority system of direct elections, which paints one region with one ethnic colour, could paint the neighbouring region with a different one, annihilating their half-tints and exaggerating the differences. If the interests of these different local majorities are contradictory, we may well face a conflict, which then appears ethnic.

The majority of Russians, Ukrainians and Belorussians in Lithuania were against the independence of the state, mostly, perhaps, because they were employed at big enterprises belonging to the Union and strongly dependent on all-Union resources and the all-Union market. They were afraid, with good reason, of losing their jobs. Lithuanians, on the other hand, were seeking state independence and hoping for better economic conditions, once they were able to make independent use of their advantages (real or imaginary) outside the Soviet Union's planned economy.

There were no signs of inter-ethnic conflict, it is true, but at the same time there was no guarantee that ethnic minorities would be involved in public life. The Lithuanian Law on Citizenship, passed in 1989, made all people permanently living and working in the country at that time eligible for citizenship. All residents, irrespective of their citizenship, were able to participate in the elections to the Supreme Council and local councils in 1990. But in practice it was very hard for a non-Lithuanian to get elected at the national level and in most regions. So members of different ethnic groups were equal in their right to vote, but not in their chances of being elected. So far, at the national level, only the Polish community has succeeded in creating its own political party and winning some seats in the Seimas.

At least until the local elections of March 1995, local representation of ethnic minorities was low. In Vilnius City, where half of the population is non-Lithuanian, deputies of non-Lithuanian nationalities constituted 11 per cent of the total number in the council. The 12 per cent non-Lithuanian component population in Siauliai was not represented on the council at all. Among 54 members of the Klaipeda City Council, 53 councillors were ethnic Lithuanians, representing in this respect only 64 per cent of population, and only one, who never speaks, was Russian.

In the March 1995 local elections, however, the Polish minority made its presence felt more strongly at local level. The Polish Electoral Alliance captured 55 seats. This was only 4 per cent of the total, but in Vilnius – the major concentration of the ethnic Polish population in Lithuania – they won 19 of the 27 seats (*OMRI Daily Digest*, 27 March 1995).

Even before the 1995 elections, however, there were already some regions with a majority of Polish or Belorussian residents, where the council members were almost entirely of non-Lithuanian origin. Representing the position of the non-Lithuanian population (for example, on issues of introducing the Lithuanian language or relations with neighbouring countries), they found themselves in opposition to the central authority, and in some cases expressed a desire for autonomy. These councils were disbanded in the autumn of 1991. Residents were allowed to elect new councils but the level of participation was low. In the Electoral Law of 1994 it was laid down that only political parties could participate in elections; independent candidates could not. Therefore, of the non-Lithuanian ethnic groups, only the Polish minority can participate in elections, since they alone have established a political party.

In this way the elected bodies, formed by the ethnic majority only, have tended to become hostages of this majority and virtually unable to make any decision favourable to the minority. The best thing that a tolerant majority nationality may do in a post-totalitarian period is not to be aggressive towards the minorities. But an explicit representation of ethnic minorities would provide a better guarantee of their interests.

The ethnic problem in Lithuania is mostly related to the language issue. A new independent state was being built by Lithuanians using the Lithuanian language – for meetings, discussions, publications and so on. From the beginning, local council meetings were transmitted by radio, and much information was published in local newspapers in Lithuanian only, which was problematic for many residents. As a result, the Russian-speaking population was initially excluded from participation in the management of public affairs, and this may become a tradition. But the fact that most residents belonging to other minority nationalities have accepted Lithuanian citizenship and speak Lithuanian by now may help to change this in the near future.

The other problem is that the political structure inside the local councils has little in common with the political preferences of the electorate. The national political unity of the majority during the first term of local governments did not last long. Most city councils split up into many small factions and individuals, mostly without any electoral basis. It was expected that at least this would change after the elections for local government in 1995. But the political parties are small in membership (10–40 persons in a city with population of 200,000) and often consist mostly of councillors. The programmes of these parties are very similar and often seem to amount to mere slogans. People seem to identify them only by the names of their leaders.

Local Government Reform

With local elections coming up, a great number of new laws were passed in Parliament in 1994. These laws greatly affect local governments. First of all, there is the new Law on Local Municipal and Regional Government of the Republic of Lithuania, which was passed in mid-1994. This law replaces the 'old' one of 1990. The law comes into force on the first day after the election of local councils. These elections, held in accordance with the new Law on Elections to Local Councils, took place in March 1995. Further important laws are the Law on the Attribution and Transfer of State-Owned Assets to the Ownership of Local Governments, the Law on Administrative-Territorial Division, the Law on Districts (or '*apskritys*', as districts in Lithuania are called) and the Law on Civil Servants. Except for the last one (1995) and a new law on local finance (expected in the fall of 1995), all these laws were passed in the second half of 1994. So in the year 1995 Lithuania has a new system of territorial governance.

Figure 3.2: Local government structure 1995 –

CENTRAL GOVERNMENT

Districts (10 *Apskritys*)
Self-Governments (56 *Savivaldybes*)
Units (*Seniunija*)

POPULATION

What are the main innovations in the new laws?

The present two-tier system of local self-governments is replaced by a one-level system of self-government, called '*savivaldybe*' (of which there are 56). These areas are left with the same territories as the former regions and cities. So the system of self-government in Lithuania consists of the territories of 12 cities (11 former and 1 new), and the 44 regions. The 'lower level' of administrative-territorial units of local government as described in the law of 1990 are abolished; instead, the councils will have the right to establish smaller units, called '*seniunija*'. The managers of these units are to be appointed by the mayor and these managers will have very restricted powers under a statute authorized by the mayor.

At the same time, ten new, large districts are established by the Law on Administrative-Territorial Division and Law on Districts. These districts are '... an integral part of the central government' (Article 1 in the Law on Districts). The district governor is appointed by central government, without election. Some of the central government's tasks are transferred to the districts, some other activities stay in the ministries, but these are supposed to be coordinated by the districts. On the other hand the districts will take over some responsibilities from local governments, mainly in the sphere of social welfare, education, health care, planning, monument protection, land exploitation and agriculture. But actually the law is not clear on how this will be organized. Each of the districts unites the territories of several local governments.

The institution of Government Representative has been kept, for the time being. This means two unelected bodies control the elected local governments.

In this way the 'democratic pie' of 100 per cent self-governance on the level of territories is replaced by the 'state order hamburger', with state control on the top through the districts, the local units at the bottom, and local self-government in between (see Figure 3.2).

Apart from the territorial changes the new Law on Local Municipal and Regional Government provides some other main changes in comparison with the former law of 1990. The Mayor and the Deputy Mayor now have more direct political responsibility. They are elected, 'by secret voting', from the city council itself. The Mayor, Deputy Mayor and some councillors can establish a board which has to be based on a majority of councillors. In this way there is a good chance that the number of conflicts between city council and city board, which used to frustrate the local governments, will diminish. The chairmen of the city council committees are elected by the council on the proposal of the Mayor. The law leaves open the possibility that these committee chairmen will constitute the city's board.

The Mayor appoints an administrator, who is the chief executive of the city administration. In the former law on local government this position was taken by the Mayor. The administrator is directly responsible to the Mayor and organises all the spade-work for the council and the board meetings and the preparation of documents adopted. He is responsible for the staff and internal order in the administration. Where the Council decides to establish lower administrative units (the *seniunija*), the Mayor also appoints the unit managers. They are responsible directly to him.

The Mayor is directly responsible for carrying out tasks delegated by the central government. These responsibilities are: civil registration, enterprise registration, also perhaps national parks management and organization of municipal police, fire protection and other functions 'delegated by the law'. In the law there is no clear description of what kinds of functions are delegated.

It is curious that in the new law some of the basic functions carried out currently by local governments – such as water supply or street lighting, etc. are not mentioned as local government tasks.

Local authorities still lack the power to determine the level of revenue for their own budgets. This remains fully under the control of the parliament and the central government. They fix the level of income for each local government annually. The money is transferred to local governments through the State Tax Service Bureau. So far there have been no truly local taxes in Lithuania. But local governments may fix the levels of local levies, such as a fee for permission to use a car in the city centre. These and some other modest revenues make up the 'extra-budget funds'. The state grants may be shared and used, in accordance with the new law, only for implementation of targeted programmes. For cities in general the amount of grants is fixed during the course of the year. An example of a city's budget is given in Table 3.1. This shows the budget of the city of Klaipeda, the third largest city and a major Baltic port.

The Ministry of Finance proposes to the government the percentage of local tax collected that is to be allocated to each city for each of the three important taxes: personal income tax, enterprise profit tax and value added tax. As can be seen in the budget of the city of Klaipeda, these taxes make up 94 per cent of the income of the town. This used to be done completely without consultation with the different local governments; however, in 1995 the cities do have some ability to influence the percentages, if not the total sum. In this way the government can decide to leave for one city 100 per cent of private income taxes and 30 per cent of enterprise profit taxes, and for another city quite the opposite, or plan a smaller 'direct' income from taxes and compensate by a bigger grant (see Table 3.2). However, there is no certainty that the cities will get the full amount planned for them. In 1994 the city of Klaipeda received only 65 per cent of the enterprise profit tax income because of poor performance in collecting the taxes by central government. The fact that local governments do not possess any assets, on the other hand, makes it very difficult for them to borrow. In this way local governments have little scope for planning capital investments in their cities. It is hard to pursue an independent economic strategy.

Table 3.1:   Budget of Klaipeda City in 1994 (206,000 inhabitants) Figures in Litas: 1 $US = 4 Litas

Expenditure	Budget
Municipal government	1,496,590
Public order	3,512,700
Education	33,337,560
Health care	29,425,090
Social welfare	3,017,940
Housing & housing construction	27,695,300
Sport & culture	6,268,300
Others	975,640
Public transport (loss)	2,740,000
TOTAL	108,469,120
Income	
Private income tax (PIT)*	20,513,000
Enterprise profit tax*	69,000,000
Tax for fixed assets	2,340,000
Value added tax (VAT)*	12,733,000
State levy/fines	2,033,000
Other income	1,850,730
Net total	108,469,730
State budget grants	0
TOTAL	108,469,730

* Income set by central government through fixed percentages of revenue collected in the city.

Source: Klaipeda city administration.

Table 3.2: Percentage of tax the city receives from the total sum raised within its jurisdiction 1994

CITY	PIT	VAT
Vilnius	9.2	6
Kaunas	80	18
Siauliai	55	22.3
Klaipeda	20	11.9

Source: The administrations of the above cities.

In accordance with the constitution adopted in 1992, local governments in Lithuania cannot be the owners of land, which may only belong to either the state or a private person. Other kinds of immovable property may be owned by local governments according to the Law on the Attribution and Transfer of State-Owned Assets to the Ownership of Local Governments. At the moment local governments are doing inventories to prepare for the change of ownership. However, it is to be expected that discussion of this will take time since the division of responsibilities between districts and the local government is not yet clearly defined. Nonetheless, this could be the first step in real decentralization.

Some Comments on the Recent Transformation

Developments in Lithuania seem at the moment to be moving in the right direction. Nonetheless, there are some basic defects in the legislation. In general, the weakest point of the new law on local government – and this is inherited from the old law – is a poor description of municipal services as the main designation of all the activity of the local authorities. The law says a great deal about the structure of power and decision-making, but it fails to say what the aim of all of this is. And there are no criteria for effective local government, apart from the requirement to carry out the law and governmental decisions.

It should be pointed out that about 84 per cent of the citizens of Lithuania live in 'communities' of more than 40,000 members (see Table 3.3). With the present model of local democracy, it is doubtful whether the full participation of all parts of Lithuanian society in decision-making can be realized. In this way the concept of local self-government, despite the positive developments in the recent legislation, could lose ground to the two surrounding levels of non-democratic administration.

Table 3.3: Population size of Lithuanian local self-government communities, by per cent of population living in them, 1989

Population-size	% of Population
2,000–5,000	0.2
5,001–20,000	0.0
20,000–40,000	15.9
40,000–100,00	43.0
> 100,000	40.8

Source: Government of Lithuania.

The uncertainty about the 'functions delegated by the State', the heavy financial dependence of local governments on central government funding, the ambiguities deriving from the new, non-democratic district level and the future 'battle' over municipal real estate between districts and municipalities will lead to a lot of confusion in the first two years (1995 and 1996) of the new local governments. The mix of functions of local government for which local authorities are responsible to local people and 'delegated' functions may result in a weak local government, which will undertake only limited tasks on its own. There is a danger that local governments will spend more time and energy on thinking about how to carry out central government decisions than about meeting real local demands.

A more encouraging development, however, is the Seimas's adoption, after long discussions, of what we judge to be the right definition of local self-government. Article 1 of the law prescribes that 'local municipal and regional government .... shall have the status of local government institution as well as the real power to act freely and independently according to the constitution and the laws of the Republic of Lithuania. Local government shall bear responsibility when regulating and carrying out public affairs according to its needs'. This gives some hope that the gaps in the laws and ambiguities in regulations may be covered by more constructive legislative decisions in the future, and that local democracy in Lithuania will develop in the best traditions of European public administration.

The reform of local government in Lithuania is a slow process, as is the case everywhere in Central and Eastern Europe. Changing the practices of 50 years (or more) of the old top-down approach, which did not take local needs into account, cannot be achieved overnight. Earlier developments in transition countries like Spain and Portugal have shown that the pace in the beginning is often unsatisfactorily slow. It takes time for people working in local government to see for themselves the positive aspects of reform.

At the same time, in spite of all the old and new problems connected with the development of local democracy in Lithuania, it should be noted that significant progress has been achieved in this sphere. Instead of totally formal and absolutely obedient councils, actual and active bodies of representative power have appeared. The public is growing accustomed to its own responsibility and a new structure of local authority, in the absence of the absolute monopoly of the Communist Party.

Gradually some understanding of local self-government is forming. This makes it all the more necessary that the conditions within which the cities have to work are clear. In this respect there remains much to be done in the coming years. It appears that the activities of newly elected councils and the work of local administrations will be more closely related than in the past to local problems and the development of local services. This will bring them closer to the public and to democracy.

Reference

Clark, Terry D. (1995), 'A New Grass-Roots Partnership', *Transition* (Prague), vol. 1, no. 3, pp. 34–6, 51.

4. Local Government and the Centre in Romania and Moldova

Adrian Campbell*

Introduction: A Third Category?

There is a temptation to classify countries undergoing transition according to the degree to which they are, or are likely to become, 'Western'. This is misleading, firstly, because it assumes a homogeneity among 'Western' governmental systems and business cultures which is, to a large extent, fictitious. Secondly it assumes the transition to be a universal one, whereby all the countries involved are seen to be following the same route of development, but at different speeds. This idea has been at least partly undermined by, among other phenomena, the emergence of 'Russian capitalism', involving rapid development along a trajectory that does not appear to lead towards any conventional picture of Western 'normality', but moves nonetheless. Although the alternative temptation, that of the recourse to historical explanations, is perhaps equally dangerous, there seems to be a good case for seeing the development of the transitional countries as being strongly influenced by their starting-point and their past history, such influences affecting not only their speed of development, but also the direction of that development.

It is in this context that one may attempt a classification of the local government systems of Central and Eastern Europe. A first category might include countries such as the Czech Republic, Hungary and to a lesser extent Poland, whose systems, although inevitably characterized by conflict, are operating within a broadly pluralist conception of centre–local relations. A second category might include the Russian Federation where history has bequeathed a system capable of simultaneously realizing extremes of centralism and regional autonomy, but one which has a well-established logic of its own.

In the third category, to which Romania and Moldova may be said to belong, the underlying logic is less clear. Both are marked by a strong tendency towards centralization, but this may be regarded as reflecting uncertainty rather than confidence within central government.

A Different Type of Transition

In several countries of East–Central Europe, transition, for all its complexities, may be viewed as requiring the elimination of anomalies which had been imposed and maintained by external forces, the withdrawal of which was a sufficient precondition for political and economic transition to begin. In Romania, Moldova and also neighbouring Ukraine (with which some features are shared), the reality was far less straightforward.

Romania had a longer history of independence prior to the Second World War than had some of the other countries in East–Central Europe, but its experience in more recent decades was marked by a particularly oppressive regime, and one which (if initially imposed by Soviet power) acquired a curiously home-grown character. Unlike the other regimes in the region, its overthrow thus required a far from 'velvet' revolution:

> ... Romania embarked upon its way towards reform in totally different conditions, as compared to all the other countries in transition ... It was only in Romania where a totalitarian, unipersonal, despotic and absurd communist regime existed ... based on the principle of excessive centralism ... The violent revolution meant ... the disintegration in a few days only ... of the hierarchical structures and of the balance of values which ... led to a total political and social void. That is why Romania started to move towards transition with a considerable lag, over two years being necessary for the settling and stabilizing of society and economy within a structure able to be reformed. (Cosea, 1994a)

In other words, the state was seen to need to be re-created before it could be reformed, a quite different type of transition from that of Poland, Hungary or the Czech Republic.

Secondly there was, in the initial phase in Timisoara, an ethnic (Hungarian) dimension to the revolt, something that was absent elsewhere in Central and Eastern Europe. Thirdly, the political revolution was not 'rounded off' in the same way as elsewhere, in the sense that although democracy was introduced, whole sections of the *ancien régime* remained in place. The new president, Ion Iliescu, was the only one of the Gorbachev-generation of reform communists in East–Central Europe to gain long-term power.

In Moldova and Ukraine the revolution was still further removed from those of Central Europe. In neither case was the change driven by economics to any marked extent, but rather by the pursuit of self-determination (even if nationalism was then used as an instrument for greater power by some leading party functionaries, most notably Leonid Kravchuk in Ukraine).

In Ukraine it was widely assumed that independence would of itself bring prosperity (an argument widely accepted at the time by the Russian-speaking minority, of whom a majority also voted for secession from the Soviet Union). When the opposite occurred, and 1992–4 saw Ukraine become dubbed as the economic 'basket case' of the East, the arguments for closer association with Russia were strengthened.

The nationalists, now forced back on their Western Ukrainian power-base (which had been under Soviet rule only since 1944) fought back openly with the argument that no degree of economic collapse could justify in any way compromising the achievement of the country's independence (interviews, Kiev, September 1993). The majority remained unswayed by this, and elected Kuchma, the favoured candidate of the Russian minority and of Moscow) as president in 1994.

In Moldova a not dissimilar sequence of events took place, but with the compromise being made at a much earlier stage. The revolution was focused on the issue of national and cultural self-determination. A leading role in the Moldovan Popular Front was played by the Alexei Mateevici Literary and Music Club (Aves, 1992, p. 40), which in 1988–9 fought a successful campaign to have Romanian, the language of the majority, rather than Russian, recognized as the republic's official language, and the return of the Latin script.

A campaign to re-unite with Romania followed, but when this called forth strong opposition from non-Romanian minorities (both the Russian minority in the Transdniester region and the Gagauz [a Christian Turkish people] in the south threatened to secede), a more gradualist approach was pursued by the newly-elected president, Mircea Snegur, a pragmatic communist party official, who was broadly sympathetic to the Moldovan Popular Front (Aves, 1992, p. 62).

As with Romania, the *ancien régime* in the former Soviet republics had been of a far more comprehensive nature than, say, in Poland or the Czech Republic, where the ruling elite proved relatively detachable, and a new elite relatively easy to recruit. With the possible exception of Western Ukraine, where nationalism provided an unbroken source of opposition, the Soviet system in Moldova and Ukraine was, as in Russia, culturally, if not ideologically, pervasive. This had been compounded by the degree to which both republics, and Moldova in particular, enjoyed a standard of living in Soviet times of which many, if not most, Russian provincial towns would have been envious.

Geo-Political Uncertainties

Uncertainties and conflicts within the governmental systems of Ukraine, Moldova and Romania may be seen to reflect ambiguities in their geo-political identities or roles. Romania has ambitions to join the EU in the medium term and NATO in the longer term, but has a history of ambiguity in its relations with the rest of Europe, having participated on both sides in both world wars, and having pursued, in the Ceausescu period, a foreign policy that was broadly independent of Moscow and resistant to simple categorization. The three countries now occupy a potentially significant position between Russia (or rather, Russia's southern 'interests') and Western Europe, and between Europe and competing spheres of influence of Turkey and Iran. Romania's involvement in the oil industry (it has lost much of its traditional Soviet market for oil installation equipment) links it, at least potentially, with current power struggles between Russia and Turkish or Western interests over control and routing of oil supplies to Europe from Central Asia and the Caucasus.

The two former Soviet republics have a more direct interest, namely the search for alternative sources of fuel to ease the potential or actual stranglehold Russia possesses over their energy supplies. In November 1994, Moldova signed a five-year agreement on the purchase of oil as well as forms of economic cooperation (Basapress, Kishinev, 4 November 1994). Ukraine had already signed such an agreement, with effect from January 1994, to import from Iran the equivalent of earlier Soviet oil supplies, although implementation has been delayed by technical difficulties, which President Leonid Kuchma cited as being among the main reasons why executive power needed to be strengthened in Ukraine (Radio Kiev, 7 December 1994). This and broader areas of diplomatic and economic cooperation were the object of an Iranian parliamentary delegation's visit to Kiev in December 1994 (Itar-Tass, 6 December 1994).

Potentially of greater significance is the relationship of the three countries to each other, which is influenced by complex issues of ethnicity and national boundaries. President Kuchma recently complained to President Iliescu about the continued absence between Romania and Ukraine of:

> any political treaty, the first clause of which would be territorial integrity and the inviolability of borders. (Radio Kiev, 7 December 1994)

At issue are the potential Romanian claims on the Black Sea coast of Bessarabia and the district of Northern Bukovina (including the cities of Khotin and Chernovtsy) which were taken from Romania and ceded to Ukraine in July 1940, as a consequence of the Molotov–Ribbentrop pact.

Relations between Ukraine and Moldova are better – the presence of ethnic Ukrainians in secessionist Transdniestria and elsewhere does not appear to affect relations significantly, any more than does the presence of a sizeable ethnic Romanian population in Kherson oblast, adjoining Transdniestria. However, there remain two territories (Northern Bukovina and Southern Bessarabia) which were transferred to Ukraine from Bessarabia (i.e. Moldova) in November 1940, following the latter's annexation by the Soviet Union (Nebelchuk, 1993).

Relations between Romania and Moldova are more problematic. Already by December 1991, when Moldovan independence was declared, enthusiasm for reunion with Romania (which had been actively campaigned for since 1988) began to recede, not only because of strong opposition by non-Romanian-speaking ethnic groups, but also because of a fear of becoming a peripheral province in a Greater Romania – which had been the fate of Bessarabia/Moldova during 1918–40. Moldova has made the alleviation of the conflict in Transdniestria a more pressing priority than any prospect of union with Romania. Statements made by President Iliescu of Romania in October 1994, referring to future unification with Moldova, were openly criticized by Moldovan Prime Minister Andrei Sangheli, on the basis that they threatened the improved prospects for lasting peace in Transdniestria, which necessitates a broader concept of 'Moldovan' identity, covering all the country's ethnic groups.

For their part, Romanian leaders come close to denying the legitimacy of Moldova as a sovereign nation (although not in strictly formal statements), and wholly reject the idea of a separate 'Moldovan' national identity (Interfax, 21 October 1994). The problem is not unlike that of Greece and Macedonia – for if there is a separate Moldovan national identity, what does this mean for the Romanian province of Moldavia, for which in Romanian the name is the same, 'Moldova'? Hence the Romanian preference for referring to their eastern neighbour as Bessarabia – although in accepted usage the name Bessarabia excludes Transdniestria.

Uncertain Transition and Centre–Local Relations

The factors outlined above all influence relations between local government and the centre in the countries concerned. It could be argued that in each case anxiety and uncertainty over the form and role of the country as a nation state are reflected in local concerns, whereas in more stable countries, a clearer boundary may be seen to exist between national political concerns and the relationship between central and local government. This is of course an imperfect and over-generalized view of the characteristics of the state in the three countries, but one which does serve to clarify differences between the latter and some of the other countries undergoing transition.

Although similarities between the case of Ukraine and those of Romania and Moldova have been hinted at above, the size and complexity of the issues involved in Ukraine's local and regional government (see Campbell, 1994a) preclude detailed consideration here. The remainder of this chapter therefore consists of a discussion of local government in Romania and Moldova, the background to centre–local relations in both countries, and further discussion of the ethnic and historical antecedents of national uncertainty which, it is argued, complicates centre–local relations in each case.

Romania

Ethno-historical influences

The ethnic question in Romania has been well-publicized since the mid-1980s. Before referring to it in more detail, it is worth recording what appears to be a widespread Romanian perception that the importance of the issue is exaggerated abroad, and, more significantly perhaps, the perception of some that the issue is not primarily ethnic but that, like the 'anti-semitism without Jews' that periodically surfaces in Eastern Europe, it is to a large extent a vehicle used by anti-liberal elements against their liberal opponents, regardless of the latter's ethnic origin.

Officially 7.12 per cent of the country's 22.8 million population are ethnic Hungarians (Farcas, 1994), who constitute a largely territorial minority, concentrated in northern and western Transylvania, notably in the cities of Cluj, Oradea and Timisoara. The other minorities make up around 10 per cent of the population, but these are largely non-territorial. Two historic minorities, ethnic Germans and Jews, have largely emigrated, whilst Russians, Ukrainians, Bulgars and Greeks have largely been absorbed. The number of Gypsies is probably under-estimated (the official figure is 1.7 per cent), given the degree to which they remain social pariahs.

The kingdom of Romania was formed in 1859 by the unification of the sovereign principalities of Wallachia and Moldavia, which had been under Turkish suzerainty prior to the Treaty of Bucharest in 1812. The name of Romania implied an unbroken link back to the province of Dacia, conquered by Trajan and settled by Roman subjects. The term 'Romanian' had in fact been in popular usage to describe both people and language from at least the fifteenth century although at that time the language was officially referred to as Moldavian (Nebelchuk, 1993). Romania's main historical precursor was the kingdom of Moldavia of the fourteenth to sixteenth centuries, which bordered the Dniester, the Danube, the Black Sea and the Carpathians, before falling under Turkish domination. Romania's national day commemorates not the union of 1861, but the conquest and incorporation in 1918 of Transylvania, previously an Austro-Hungarian province, in which Romanian speakers were a majority. The three provinces had only once before been united as an independent state, in 1600 under Michael the Brave of Wallachia (Krikhan, 1993). Transylvania reverted to Hungary in 1941 under pressure from Nazi Germany, but was re-conquered from the Hungarians by Romania in 1945, after the latter had changed sides in the war.

However strong the linguistic and ethnic basis of Romania's statehood, the history of its foundation means that there are strongly divergent regional identities in Moldavia, Wallachia and Transylvania, to the extent that a federal arrangement might be expected to be more appropriate than the centralized unitary state. It is this regional diversity, linked to very different historical and cultural influences, rather than simply the presence of a significant ethnic Hungarian minority, which may be the cause of the Bucharest government's perceived unwillingness to decentralize power, on the basis that this could lead to fragmentation of the state. Professor Mircea Malitze, previously Romanian foreign minister during the 'liberal' period of the 1960s, propagates a view with which the current Romanian government would very likely concur (interview, March 1993):

> the popular idea of the 'Europe of the Regions' is not only simplistic but very dangerous, particularly if applied in the Balkans. We need to understand this if we are to avoid a repeat of the Yugoslav case.

The local government system

Romania's local government system owes its main features to two laws passed in April 1864: the Communal Law, and the Law on the Creation of County Councils. The system established at that time drew on local historical precedents – the county had been a major feature of the Moldavian system from the sixteenth century and before, as had the institution of the local *judet* or judge, the name later applied to the second tier or county.

The main influence on the system from 1864 was, however, French. The *judet* or county was a state administrative sub-division, although a legal person and property-holder in its own right. It was presided over by a council, from whose ranks a chairman was elected. Mayors were also elected, but considered as state functionaries. Decisions and members of the councils could be suspended by the prefect, who was appointed by central government (Local Democracy and Development, 1994). In the 1920s further laws set out to devolve more power to the lower-tier authorities, and also to establish a hierarchy of 'government territorial organs – deconcentrated ministerial structures coordinated by the prefects (*ibid.*). Under the dictatorship of 1938–45, the commune and the province became (temporarily) the only units of elected sub-national government whilst the counties became purely administrative units of central government. After a brief period of democracy in 1945, a Soviet-style system was introduced, complete with its traditional features of dual subordination, and consequent drift to greater and greater centralism (*ibid.*).

The present local government system of Romania was established in Law 69 of 1991, and has much in common with that of the period 1864–1938. Most importantly it retains the overlap between local government and local state administration at the regional level which characterized both the Napoleonic and the Soviet models. The upper tier consists of 41 *judete* (counties) while the lower tier consists of 2,688 rural communes, 238 urban communes (*orase*) and 78 cities (*municipii*). The city of Bucharest has its own two-tier system, with one overall city authority and six city districts each with the status of a city (*municipio*). The lower-tier authorities all have elected councils and mayors. The county councils are indirectly elected from the commune and city councils on their territory. Each county council elects one of its own number as chair. Mayors, who are in charge of the executive and of the implementation of council decisions, are directly elected at large, and are not members of the council, except in the case of Bucharest, where the city-wide 'mayor-general' also chairs the city council.

Each county has a prefect who observes the legality of council and mayoral decisions, and looks after state and ministerial interests and functions on the county's territory. The Law 69 which re-established this system (which is broadly that which characterized pre-communist Romania) appears to make a clear distinction between functions and scope of authority of prefect, county council, mayor and local council. Prefects' involvement in local decisions is intended to be confined to monitoring; there is supposed to be no hierarchical subordination between county councils and local councils, only different competencies; and there is supposed to be a clear division between the policy-making role of councils and the implementation role of mayors (Campbell, 1994b).

All these distinctions appear to be blurred in practice. Councils are often seen by mayors to be unwilling to take responsibility for major decisions (a common complaint of mayors in Eastern Europe and the CIS); mayors as a result become over-loaded and councils fall into 'oppositionism' to the mayor (Young, 1994, p. 23). Councils do not always trust mayors; the county councils appear to have assumed for themselves the role of overseeing the distribution of resources between lower-tier authorities on their territory, and prefects appear to have considerable informal power over both the county councils and over local enterprises and organisations which are said to see the prefect as the natural heir to the regional party boss (Campbell, 1994b, p. 82).

That the system set up by Law 69 left much to be desired may best be illustrated by the intricate web of appointments and mandates it established: local councils and mayors both have a mandate from the local population, the deputy mayor is elected from among the members of the council, whilst the secretary (the head of the mayor's administration) is a government employee, appointed by the prefect. Prefects are appointed and controlled by one of the most powerful ministries, the Department of Local Public Administration. Services are provided by arms' length organizations known as *regii autonome*, of which the management are accountable to different levels of government, in some cases simultaneously (echoing the multiple or conflicting accountabilities of service organizations under the Soviet system). County councils appear to be torn between the influence of the local councils which elect them, and the prefects, with whom they have to work on a day-to-day basis.

The main dysfunction in the system is the lack of a law on local finance to complement the organizational arrangements set out in the 1991 Law. The latter referred to such a law being in preparation, the assumption being that the system of authorities and competencies being established could not operate without appropriate new financial procedures. No such law has since been passed, although there have been many rumours over the past four years that its passing is imminent. This has led to considerable confusion. Almost all taxes are collected by the state and then re-distributed downwards. This allows the counties (and perhaps even the prefects) to influence the distribution of funds to the local level, even though this contradicts the spirit of Law 69, which emphasizes complementary, not hierarchical, relations between levels. As a result only a small percentage of the budget is under direct local control. Share-taxes are handled in very much the same way as subventions, and these transfers together counted for 79 per cent of local revenue (Local Democracy and Development, 1994, pp. 11–31). There is much dispute about the figures and little clarity. Bucharest City Council, for example, claims to receive only one-sixth of what it needs to run services in line with government recommendations (interview with Deputy Mayor, December 1994). The Department of Public Adminstration, on the other hand, states that 55 per cent of tax income returns to the lower tier (interview with Secretary of State for Local Public Administration, October 1994), whilst rumours circulate that the published figures are a notional exercise in which the Ministry of Finance allegedly adjusts figures to balance the books. What is beyond doubt is the lack of an appropriate formula around which more coherent negotiations could take place. As it is, the transfer system:

lacks clearly defined and transparent rules and explicit criteria for the distribution of transfer resources ... from the central administration to the judete and, subsequently from the judete to the municipii, orase and commune ... contributes to maintaining a legal institutional confusion in the structure of local administration by granting the judete, in financial matters, the role and competencies of a quasi-intermediary level government. (Local Democracy and Development, 1994, *loc. cit.*)

Observers tend to link the non-appearance of the promised law on finance with the fact that the local elections of February 1992 (fought on the basis of Law 70 of 1991 on local elections), saw major gains for opposition parties (notably the Democratic Convention) who won mayoral and council elections in the vast majority of the major cities and towns.

This was a sudden development in a system where, during the two years after the revolution, prefects and mayors had all been appointed from above (Savulescu, 1994). It is not surprising and perhaps understandable that the government appeared to see this sudden change as threatening not only to itself but to the idea of social and political stability guaranteed by gradual reform. The Department of Public Administration was accordingly perceived to mount a campaign to rein in the potentially disruptive force represented by the new mayors. At the very least it appeared to be sanguine about reports of prefects exceeding their authority. As one commentator has put it (Farcas, 1994, p. 170):

The government is aware of the necessity to delimit the authority of prefects from those of local councils and mayors but considers that the control of the prefects over the administration of local affairs should increase rather than decrease.

The role of the centre

The Department of Local Public Administration, with just over 200 staff, is considered by some to be one of the most tightly organized and powerful ministries in the Romanian government (interview with a consultant to the Romanian government, January 1995). The Department has four directorates.

The First Directorate is concerned with control of state administration at local level. Most ministries have deconcentrated divisions and inspectors in each county and these are hierarchically subordinate not only to their ministries but also to the local prefects, who are themselves hierarchically subordinate and accountable to the Department of Local Public Administration, whose authority therefore cuts across that

of most of its fellow ministries. The Second Directorate is concerned
with coordination and support (but not control) of elected councils and
mayors. The Department's officials emphasize that these elected
authorities are not hierarchically subordinate to each other or to the
prefect, but only to the law (interview with head of directorate, October
1994). The Department is planning a major programme of legal and
financial training for local government staff and councillors across the
country. The Third Directorate is concerned with the appointment and
control of prefects and their staff. The Fourth Directorate is concerned
with legislative affairs (including the drafting of new laws) and with
external or foreign affairs, including external training.

The Secretary of State, Octav Cozmunca, is a figure of long-standing
influence, whose authority is perceived to be proportionate to the
extreme rarity of his public appearances. In an interview with the
author, in October 1994, Mr Cozmunca emphasized three themes – the
need for only gradual decentralization if the ultimate reforms are to
succeed, the practical limits to financial devolution and the need for
centrally-monitored consistency and legality in local decision-making:

> We are accused of conservatism and rigidity, but we are in fact flexible. Our aim
> is to strengthen local autonomy, gradually, and to see that laws are implemented
> ... If people are not observing the law, then the prefect has to intervene, laws have
> to be observed across the whole country ... Some mayors ask for all financial
> resources to remain at the local level, but this is simply not possible – ministries
> and the general fund need to be provided for – many communes could not support
> themselves without re-distribution, and no-one surely wants to increase discrep-
> ancies between regions and communes ... We now have strategies for further
> decentralization elaborated with each government ministry, to be backed up by
> special legislation and appropriate controls. Some want this to happen overnight,
> but it would take ten years to attain Western levels of decentralization – although
> if we ran our local government system like you do, we would be accused of
> *dirigisme* ... Now after months of debate we have finally passed to parliament the
> draft law on accelerated privatization of state-owned capital. We are only at the
> beginning and we need to take the right decisions for our citizens.

The government's position thus has its own clear logic, which could be
interpreted as meaning that too hurried a political decentralization may
impede the effectiveness of administrative and economic decentralization, and that the resulting collision between different local interests
and between local interests and the centre may threaten both the long-
term reform programme and the integrity of the nation state.

A diametrically opposed view is expressed by Adrian Moruzi, Mayor of Brasov and President of the Federation of Municipalities of Romania, a charismatic figure in the opposition and a renowned orator:

> The delayed reform: the nest of oligarchy.
> The Government: executive political exponents of old/new bureaucracy policy.
> The Prefect: the perfect conservative political connection between government and big state-owned companies' managers in the policy of delay.
> Financial centralization as financial base of this monstrous coalition. (Headings in Moruzi, 1994)

The absence of a law on finance is complemented by the lack of any law on municipal property, so that the latter has no legal or practical existence – as one mayor put it, in a comment from the floor at the conference on Land and Decentralization, Bucharest, September 1994:

> We don't even own our own offices, we are still the unofficial occupiers of former Party buildings. We can't let central government just go on distributing property by itself.

One mayor claimed, in an interview with the author in September 1994, that the issue of property was at the heart of the conflict between municipalities and the centre:

> What the government does not want is for local authorities to have any role in the privatization programme that is about to start. Ideally a large proportion of state property would be devolved to local authorities to sell and distribute to the public. What they want is to manage the sell-off centrally in such a way that the best assets are disposed of to whomsoever they choose (thus monopolizing contacts with foreign investors), and leaving the population to buy whatever's left ... Of course there would be some corruption if privatization were controlled by local authorities, but the wider the dispersal of assets at the start, the less important such corruption would be as a proportion of the total ... By this method we would be more likely to build a propertied middle class, rather than having property concentrated in the hands of the ruling elite as is likely to happen with their method.

1994: The stakes are raised

The conflict between local authorities and the centre began to take a different turn towards the end of 1994. By this time two local authority associations had become well-established – the Federation of Munici-palities, to which all the larger towns and cities (those designated as *municipii*) belonged, and the Association of Presidents of County (*judet*) Councils. A federation of Romanian small towns – *orase* – had also been organized. The first two associations became major points of contact for the international aid agencies, and with bodies such as the Council of Europe, all of whose activities in Romania were stepped up markedly in 1993–4, once the principle of Romania's eventual entry into the European Union had been agreed.

The Association of Chairs of County Councils has enjoyed far better relations with the government, who have been seen by some as cultivating the counties in order to isolate the Federation of Municipalities (interview with an aid agency consultant, September 1994), whilst the aid agencies pursued a policy of trying to bring the two associations closer together. This was difficult because municipalities saw the county councils as responsible for what was perceived to be wholly arbitrary redistribution of government subventions to the local level (Campbell, 1994b, pp. 83, 94). Nonetheless, relations between the two associations were becoming noticeably close during late 1994, with members attending meetings of each other's association, and with an agreement to form a joint foundation to facilitate the receipt and effective use of foreign aid.

The alleged aim of the government was further to undermine the position of elected mayors in advance of the local elections of 1996. It was said (interview with a city mayor, April 1993) that the lack of clarity over finance and control of services was maintained so as to direct public discontent against mayors, who had fought their electoral campaigns on the basis of the 1991 Law according to which they had assumed they would be in a position to influence developments for which they would be held accountable.

In parallel with this there was a sudden increase in the numbers of mayors dismissed by prefects for alleged malpractice. By November 1994, the total who had been dismissed or had resigned since 1992 had reached more than 130 (Savulescu, 1994, p. 4). In some cases mayors had resigned on account of the unexpected difficulty of the role, whilst others had indeed acted in a corrupt fashion. However, the sheer numbers thus indicted, compared with a perceived leniency towards corruption in other areas of state activity, raised suspicions, particularly when eleven mayors belonging to the Federation of Municipalities were sacked in late 1993 and early 1994.

Finally, in August 1994, the President of the Federation, Adrian Moruzi, the mayor of Brasov, was accused of corrupt practice (albeit on an insignificant scale). Suspicions regarding this development were not eased when the prefect who had compiled the allegations was elevated to a higher position, that of presidential adviser. Moruzi was eventually dismissed in February 1995, but reinstated after a court decision the following month found him not guilty, thus ending more than six months of speculation about his future, seen by many as crucial to the effectiveness of the Federation. The courts did however uphold the dismissal (in January 1995) of the mayor of Sibiu, who had been the Secretary of the Federation of Municipalities.

The Department of Local Public Administration has always insisted that the allegations and subsequent dismissals had been motivated by purely legal considerations. A further action taken by the Department seemed to be calculated to weaken the Federation whilst at the same time seeking to establish a new relationship with it.

The action in question was the re-designation (in December 1994 and January 1995) of no fewer than 24 small towns as *municipii*, thereby making them automatically members of the Federation. Here it is important to bear in mind that small towns are far more likely than their larger counterparts to be controlled by pro-government parties. Thus the Federation's membership was increased almost overnight from 56 to 80 towns or cities, with most of the newcomers being more conservative than the Federation's existing members. Since some of the new *municipii* were towns of only a few thousand inhabitants, there seemed to be no theoretical limit to how many towns could be thus re-designated and brought into the Federation, radically altering its political colour in the process (discussion with members of the Federation, January 1995). This could be interpreted as meaning that the government had finally decided to end the impasse on decentralization, but was seeking to ensure that this would not lead to an automatic increase in the power of the opposition.

A further sign of the government's adjustment of its approach could be found as early as May 1994, in a document setting out priorities for central and local institutional reform (Government of Romania, 1994) – the programme of reform referred to by the Secretary of State cited above. The document re-states the arguments referred to earlier that it had been necessary to re-invent the state before reforming it, and the need for subsequent reforms of central and local administration to be carried out as part of the same programme. The two main local associations are cited by the document as having played a significant role in the design of the planned reforms, hinting at a degree of cooperation behind the scenes which belies the public rhetoric of conflict. The document refers to the clarification of local finance, and the handing-over of property to local authorities as being provided for in the programme, although there appears to be an upgrading of the role of the county to that of an 'organ of local leadership' (Government of Romania, 1994, p. 3), which seems to go beyond the county's role as described in the 1991 Law. A major programme of training for all local government officials is referred to, and has since become government policy, although its implementation appears to have been hampered by what was perceived by some to be too much emphasis on central control of the programme.

By 1994, the perception began to grow amongst international aid agencies that Romania was dragging its feet on reform in general and on local democracy in particular. Romania's international agenda of integration into the Council of Europe (it had signed the European Charter of Local Democracy in 1991) and other cross-national bodies was beginning to clash with its policy of gradualism regarding, amongst other things, local administrative reform. An awareness of this apparent discrepancy perhaps underlay the Romanian government's decision to lend its full cooperation to an international conference on Local Democracy and Development in Romania, held in Bucharest 28–30 October 1994.

The organizing committee of the conference brought together the government, the local authority associations, the European Union, the Council of Europe and the World Bank, and participants also included governmental representatives of the UK and US and local authority representatives from Poland and the Czech Republic. Unusually for events of this type, all the international and foreign agencies provided summing-up statements unambiguously critical of the Romanian government's record on local democracy. The Council of Europe's most detailed criticism was reserved for the recent dismissal of eleven mayors, on the basis that this should have been dealt with legally rather than administratively, an argument which the Romanian government seems subsequently to have accepted, hence the re-instatement of Adrian Moruzi, referred to above.

The government's defence of its record was grounded in the argument that acceptance of local democracy in theory did not mean that it could be immediately implemented, because decades of centralism had bequeathed a lack of professional competence at the local level, an argument put to the conference by the President (Iliescu, 1994):

We have inherited over-centralized structures in which local initiative was crushed. Even if we have democratically-elected local authorities, their activities are still too timid, insufficiently adapted to the demands of reform, and sometimes parasitized by corruption and incompetence and the most detestable bureaucratic behaviour.

The argument appeared to be that local democracy was desirable but not an end in itself, and that local authorities were not yet ready to carry out their appointed role. This view was vigorously developed by the Minister for Public Works, whilst the representative of the department of Local Public Administration defended the actions of his ministry by stating – largely correctly – that it had drawn up the 1991 Law in accordance with the European Charter. He added, however, that the problem was that mayors would not observe the Law.

A more conciliatory note was sounded by the President of the Council for Coordination, Strategy and Economic Reform, who implied that the economic and administrative reform agendas could not be pursued in parallel (Cosea, 1994b, p. 13):

Naturally it is expected that the preoccupation of the Government should concentrate on aspects of economic reform. Privatization, microeconomic restructuring and macroeconomic stabilization have represented absolute priority for the Government and the Council of Reform. The programmes for administrative reform, both central and local, initially occupied second place on this priority list.

He also stressed that the reforms now in preparation required full collaboration between the different levels of government and cited the conference itself as proof that this could be achieved. He was, however, careful to add (*ibid.*, p. 3) that:

The local authorities are only accountable for what is happening in the localities to the local electorate. However, the Government is accountable to the whole electorate for what is happening throughout the country ... local activities, solutions and problems are only components of the national ones. The Government will continue to coordinate the way in which local problems are solved.

Delegates from the local authorities appeared unappeased by these arguments, and repeatedly voiced concerns over the problem of local finance, and their perception that power was becoming increasingly centralized. As one mayor put it from the floor of the conference:

We cannot have every hospital run by the Ministry of Health, and every village run by a prefect.

The overall conclusion to be drawn from the events of this period is that the Romanian government can be regarded as serious in its professed aim of greater decentralization (a reform of April 1995 involving the attachment of many of the *regie autonome* service organisations to towns and cities seemed to confirm this), but that it would pursue this aim in a way that would minimize the potential of local authorities to pose a political threat, and which would keep intact central government's machinery of coordination, monitoring and control.

Moldova

Ethnic composition of Moldova

Moldova has a population of 4.4m, of whom, according to 1989 figures (Nebelchuk, 1993, p. 27), 64 per cent are Moldovan (i.e. Romanian-speaking), 14 per cent Ukrainian, 13 per cent Russian, 3.5 per cent Gagauz, 2 per cent Bulgarian and 3 per cent other nationalities. Prior to 1941 Jews had accounted for 7 per cent, and Germans for 3 per cent, both groups largely disappearing subsequently. Significantly, the Slav population is not primarily a Soviet-era phenomenon – by 1858, the Ukrainians already made up the same percentage of the population as now, whilst the most rapid growth of the Russian population was in the 1920s, when Moldova was part of Romania (*ibid.*, p. 15). The figures for 1897 show Bessarabia to be a patchwork of nationalities: Moldavian/Romanian 47.6 per cent, Ukrainian 19.6 per cent, Jews 11.8 per cent, Russians 8.0 per cent, Bulgarians 5.3 per cent, Germans 3.1 per cent and Gagauz 2.9 per cent (Berg, 1918/1993, p. 75).

The Slav population is heavily concentrated in the capital Chisinau (Kishinev), and in Transdniestria, the strip of Moldovan territory (about 12 per cent of the country's land area) on the east (that is, left) bank of the river Dniester. Slavs also make up a large proportion of the population of large towns such as Balti in northern Moldova. In Transdniestria, Slavs are concentrated in the towns, notably the country's second city, Tiraspol, and also Benderi, the flashpoint for the conflict of 1992, which, like Tiraspol, lies alongside the Dniester, although on the western side. Slavs predominate in the service sector and in the Soviet-era industries of the larger cities. The countryside, home to the fruit- and wine-growing wealth of the country, is overwhelmingly Romanian-speaking. On the right bank, there is a fairly clear division between the regions to the north and south of Chisinau, the north being considered more 'European'. In the south (as in the south of Romania) the Turkish influence is more visible, not least in the Gagauz districts towards the southern border with Ukraine.

The origins of the Moldovan state

Moldova's ethnic composition and its frontiers are the product of a highly complex history, and it is necessary to describe this history in some detail in order to appreciate the dilemmas currently confronting reform of the country's administrative structure. The Dniester, which had once been the eastern frontier of the Roman Empire, became, in the eighteenth century, the border between the Russian and Turkish Empires. Under the compromise of the Treaty of Bucharest, of 1812, which gave independence to Wallachia and Moldavia, the latter was partitioned (Russia had originally wanted all of it) and the territory of Bessarabia – that part of Moldavia which lay between the Pruth and Dniester rivers (i.e. broadly corresponding with present-day Moldova) was handed over to the Russian Empire, whose troops had occupied it since 1806 (Saunders, 1992).

Russian rule allowed a degree of autonomy (set out in a decree of 1818) to the province of Bessarabia; there was no serfdom (the same applied to other new provinces of this period, such as Finland) and the local Romanian-speaking nobility remained powerful in rural law and administration. The main change was the development of Kishinev as a provincial capital and an administrative and commercial centre, oriented towards the growing market of Odessa and southern Russia (Berg, 1918/1993, pp. 62–74). Between 1812 and 1861 the city's population grew from 7,000 to 93,000 (*Kishinev*, 1984, p. 204). This marked a contrast with Bessarabia's marginal cultural and political position when it had been ruled direct from the Moldavian capital Iasi. The Kishinev city Duma was established in 1818, initially consisting of five members drawn from the city elite. An executive organ or *uprava* was established soon afterwards. From 1871 onwards, a larger body was elected from a broadened franchise. The new Duma was empowered to elect its own *uprava*, carry out a wider range of functions and set and collect taxes. The budget was subject to the approval of the provincial governor. Over time the provincial author-ities tended to exert greater powers of veto over Duma decisions in practice (*ibid.*, p. 188). This was reflected in the fact that appointment of the head of the executive (*gorodskaya golova*), who was elected from among the members of the Duma, was subject to ratification by the Russian Ministry of the Interior, and from 1892 had the status of a national civil servant (*ibid.*, p. 206).

The history of Transdniestria in this period was quite distinct from Bessarabia. The main city Tiraspol had been founded by Catherine the Great as a fortress guarding the left bank of the Dniester from the Turks. The incorporation of Bessarabia after 1812 led to Tiraspol's growth as a commercial centre between the former and Odessa, which was still a lower-status town than Tiraspol within Kherson province (Hill, 1977, p. 9).

In December 1917, the *Sfatul Tserii*, or Bessarabian parliament, proclaimed the province the 'Moldavian Democratic Republic', leading to a declaration of independence in January 1918, and a declaration of conditional union with Romania in March 1918. Romania annexed the territory in November 1918, which led to an unconditional declaration of union (Nebelchuk, 1993, pp. 139–42). In the meantime, across the border, Tiraspol's status had also changed. In 1924 it became part of the newly-formed Moldavian Autonomous Soviet Socialist Republic (MASSR), and its capital from 1929. The MASSR, which formed part of the Ukraine SSR, included present-day Transdniestria and a somewhat larger territory to the East. The real purpose of the MASSR was, however, to provide a structure for the re-incorporation of Bessarabia at a later date (Hill, 1977, p. 11). This was provided for in the secret supplementary protocol of the Molotov–Ribbentrop pact of August 1939, and put into effect in July 1940, when Bessarabia and the neighbouring territory of Northern Bukovina were ceded from Romania to the Soviet Union. Bessarabia was to be merged with the MASSR, to form a full-status Moldavian Soviet Socialist Republic, with Kishinev, not Tiraspol, as the capital.

In the process both Bessarabia and the MASSR were partitioned, with both losing substantial territory to the Ukraine SSR. Bessarabia lost three of its nine districts (the extreme north and the Black Sea coastal districts), whilst the MASSR lost eight of its fourteen districts, leaving only the narrow strip of present-day Transdniestria. Romania seized the territory as part of the Axis invasion of the Soviet Union, but lost it on its surrender in 1944, when it was re-incorporated into the Soviet Union.

Under Soviet rule the Romanian local government structures that had been introduced into Bessarabia after 1918 were dismantled and replaced with those of the standard Soviet type: 40 districts (*raiony*) to which were subordinated 15 towns, 50 urban settlements and around 850 rural settlements. In addition there were five cities with district status, and the capital Kishinev with its urban districts. This structure remains in place, although since 1991 its status is officially temporary and the districts are referred to as *judete* and the district-status cities as *municipii*, although the old terms are also in use.

Moldova's development as an independent state since 1991 has been overshadowed from the outset by the attempted secession of Transdniestria and of the Gagauz region, and an account of these events and their aftermath is essential before considering the local government system in more detail.

The 'Dniester Republic'

As mentioned at the start of this chapter, the impetus for Moldovan independence from the Soviet Union came largely from the Romanian-speaking population, and was fought initially around the issue of language – notably the rejection of the Soviet fiction of a Moldavian language separate from Romanian and the demand for the return of Latin script instead of Cyrillic (although, ironically, Romanian used the Cyrillic script prior to the nineteenth century). The related demand for reunification with Romania caused concern among the non-Romanian population. In September 1990 (one month after the Gagauz had taken a similar step) the Slav majority in the eight districts on the left bank of the Dniester proclaimed the establishment of the 'Dniester Soviet Republic' (later called the 'Transdniestrian Moldavian Republic'), a lineal descendant of the pre-war MASSR, with its capital at Tiraspol. The Kishinev (now Chisinau) government's popular boycott of the referendum on the maintenance of the USSR as a single state (17 March 1991) was ignored by the local councils on the left bank, where 650,000 votes were cast in favour of preserving the USSR (*Europa Year Book*, 1993, III, p. 1957). In the meantime, city and district councils in Tiraspol, Dubossary and Ribnitsa had started to train paramilitary formations which were said to be supplied and supported by the locally-stationed Soviet 14th Army (Nebelchuk, 1993, pp. 73–4).

In late 1991 left bank councils used their new militias (soon to be joined by Russian Cossack detachments and other 'red–brown' volunteers) to take over or supplant police forces on their territory. By March 1992, there was open military conflict between the separatists and the newly-formed Moldovan army. Over 700 were killed in fighting which, after negotiations involving Romania, Moldova, Russia and Ukraine, ended in a peace agreement of July 1992, by which Transdniestria was accorded an undefined special status within Moldova, peace-keeping forces from the two sides and from the Russian Federation were deployed and negotiations began for the withdrawal of the 14th Army.

The peace left Moldova in a weak position, since the total of 10,000 Russian troops and 8,000 Dniester fighters now stationed on the left bank (Socor, 1993b) was now larger than the entire Moldovan army, whilst in economic terms Moldova remained dependent on Russia for more than half its external trade. By refusing to withdraw the 14th Army until the Dniester question was settled, President Yeltsin was seen to be allowing the Dniester Republic *de facto* legitimacy. Whilst negotiations remained deadlocked, the Dniester regime tightened its grip, refusing to allow the return of 50,000 refugees to the left bank, banning the use of Latin script, restricting access to mass media and putting pressure on left bank residents to take up Dniester citizenship as well as failing to implement electoral laws, thereby allowing distortions or abuses of electoral practice (Socor, 1993a).

The 14th Army moves centre-stage

During 1994, however, the 14th Army began to adopt a markedly more neutral position. Its commander, Lt-General Lebed, gave up his seat in the Dniester parliament in protest at Dniester fighters' participation in the Moscow revolt against Yeltsin in September 1993 – the far right had declared their aim to be to re-build the Soviet Union beginning with the Dniester Republic. Lebed was also highly critical of the human rights record of the Dniester authorities, notably their outlawing of the Latin script in all left-bank schools (Basapress, 7 November 1994).

On 21 October 1994 an agreement was finally signed in Moscow for the withdrawal over three years of the 14th Army, and this was followed in November by the unilateral withdrawal of half of the four-battalion Russian peace-keeping force, which served to pressure both parties towards a settlement. The agreement over the 14th Army had the effect both of inflaming the rhetoric of the separatist authorities, and also of moving them nearer the negotiating table. The Dniester vice-president, Alexander Karaman, declared that the withdrawal, and the hand-over of 35 per cent of the army's equipment to Moldova (the other 65 per cent returning to Russia), would lead to an arms race between the Dniester Republic and Moldova (Basapress, 25 October 1994), although it was noted that the withdrawal would leave the separatists facing a Moldovan army four times larger than their own.

It was not therefore surprising that talks between Chisinau and Tiraspol on the status of the Dniester region began to take place in earnest in October and November 1994, with Russia and the CSCE (Conference on Security and Cooperation in Europe, now re-named the Organization for Security and Cooperation in Europe or OSCE) as observers. There were however some stumbling blocks in terms of what a special status for the Dniester region might involve – not least the Dniester authorities' stated wish to have their own army and foreign policy (Itar-Tass, 1 November 1994).

The talks were upstaged by the 'school war' of October–November, 1994, in which parents, notably in Benderi (Tighina) and surrounding villages, defied the Dniester authorities' ban on the use of Latin script, a ban which in at least one case was upheld only with the assistance of Dniester Cossack detachments. Protesters responded with a series of protracted blockades of railways and main roads in the Benderi district (Radio Mayak, 25 October 1994), a tactic which was aimed not least at provoking the Moldovan government to give them more active support.

Before it could escalate further, the dispute appears to have been brought to a rapid close through the intervention of the Ukraine railway authorities, who issued Chisinau with an ultimatum that if the blockade on the Dniester were not lifted within 24 hours, all fifty Moldovan trains stranded on Ukrainian territory would be impounded and auctioned off. Within hours the blockade was lifted and a compromise agreed in Benderi; namely that, of the two most disputed schools in the city, one would be assigned to the Russian-speaking population, and the other to the Romanian-speaking population and would be allowed to use the Latin script (Yurii Selivanov in *Segodnya*, 10 November 1994).

The same period saw what appeared to be a final breakdown in relations between the 14th Army and the Dniester authorities. On 5 November 1994, the president of the Dniester 'republic', Igor Smirnov, issued a decree on fighting serious crime, allowing measures such as 30-day 'administrative arrest'. Lt-General Lebed not only ordered his troops to ignore the decree, but denounced it as an attempt to introduce 'odious communist measures', arguing that it would be used against opponents of the regime, and that the underworld had been given advance warning (Basapress, 5 November 1994). He also accused the Dniester authorities' leaders of being 'a criminal group which is profiteering by the arms trade' (NTV, Moscow, 7 November 1994). The decree may even have been prompted by Lebed's investigations into the two-way underground arms trade between Transdniestria and Crimea, and the alleged role of the Dniester authorities in the trade.

In this respect, Lebed was praised by Mircea Snegur, the President of Moldova, who had personally warned President Yeltsin about the negative consequences should Lebed leave the command of the 14th army, since only he could be trusted to prevent leakage of arms into the hands of the separatists (Basapress, 9 November 1994). Lebed himself was soon expressing concern over the practicalities of withdrawing the 14th Army, in that official withdrawal of the army would de-stabilize the region since it would leave behind an armed force, no longer under military orders, made up of half of the officers and 80 per cent of other ranks who were 'local residents'. Lebed also said that the Dniester authorities and their forces had stepped up observation of the 14th army, in order to profit from the leakage of arms and equipment that would occur once withdrawal commenced – the Dniester authorities had openly laid claim to the 65 per cent of equipment officially designated to return to Russia in the event of withdrawal (Itar-Tass, 26 November 1994). The position was not entirely clarified by a speech by President Snegur of Moldova at a CSCE Summit a few days later in which he appeared to refer to the withdrawal of the 14th Army as actually having taken place.

The multi-ethnic state

More significant, however, was President Snegur's description, in the same speech, of the Dniester conflict as being 'political' rather than 'ethnic' in nature, a matter of 'separatism' rather than 'self-determination' (Hungarian TV1, 6 December 1994). This view ties in with the Moldovan government's view of the country as a multi-ethnic state, rather than an alternative (or potential province of) Romania. Since early 1993, the Moldovan parliament had in fact dropped the once-popular concept of the 'two Romanian states' in favour of a multi-ethnic concept of the nation. A whole series of laws passed in the period 1991–2 (Nebelchuk, 1993, pp. 32–46) underpin this view, granting citizenship to all those resident in Moldova since 1990, and recognizing Russian as the official language of 'inter-ethnic communication', to complement Romanian as the state language, and extending this provision to the Gagauz language in areas where its speakers were in the majority.

A shift in the balance of power within the Moldovan parliament during 1993 set the seal on the multi-ethnic approach. In the earlier period, progress in terms of solving regional disputes and building new institutions had been held back by the control of key committees by the pro-Romanian Popular Front and Congress of the Intelligentsia, who opposed Moldovan statehood in the hopes of achieving re-unification with Romania. After 1992 they lost much of their control to pragma-tists, such as the new speaker Petru Luchinschi, like Snegur a former Communist Party leader, who were impatient to solve the Dniester and Gagauz questions and to consolidate Moldovan independence around the multi-ethnic principle (Socor, 1993b, p. 2). This approach found support from a large majority of the population in the election of February 1994, which gave Snegur's Agrarian Democratic Party a large majority and marginalized the pro-Romanian Popular Front and the Congress of the Intelligentsia.

To an extent, the widespread support for the Agrarian Democratic Party and its allies reflected practical realities – the need to win back, via Moscow, the markets Moldova had supplied in the past (it claimed to have provided 40 per cent of the fruit and 70 per cent of the wine consumed in the USSR), and the loss of which in 1991 had left a gaping hole in the economy, as well as the need eventually to win the Dniester districts back into the Moldovan unitary state. It may also be seen to reflect a genuine belief in a separate Moldovan national identity in which the mixture of Romanian, Russian, Ukrainian and other influences had created a culture quite distinct from that of neighbouring Romania. This view may be supported by casual observation, and appears to be shared by some Romanians on the other side of the border (whether they choose to stress the positive or the negative aspects of the perceived difference).

Either way the Romanian connection could be seen to have weakened since 1991 from the point of view of potential unification. In a meeting in Bucharest, President Snegur found it necessary to assure President Iliescu that relations between the two countries had not 'cooled', whilst for his part Iliescu emphasized Romania's respect for Moldovan independence, 'taking the political realities of the region into account' (Infotag, 5 December 1994).

Overall, the Moldovan government's handling of the Dniester question must be said to provide (to say the least) a positive contrast with comparable disputes in the former USSR such as Nagnorny Karabakh, Abkhazia and Chechnya, and its non-dogmatic policies regarding the ethno-linguistic dimension of the state could also be contrasted favourably with those of Ukraine or the Baltic States. In a recent interview, the speaker of the Moldovan parliament, Petru Luchinschi, expressed satisfaction that Romanian nationalists in Moldova, whom he (somewhat harshly) termed 'the party of war' had been shown to have little support amongst voters, enabling a peaceful settlement to be reached (*Sankt Peterburgskie Vedomosti*, 4 February 1995):

> I recently spent a few days with the speaker of the Dniester parliament, G. Makarutsa, in the Aaland Islands. This province forms part of the unitary state of Finland, but has a considerable degree of local autonomy. Moldova by its constitution is also a unitary state. And we are trying to find just such a formula for the existence of the Transdniestrian region in this framework ... It is scarcely worth it for the Transdniestrians to insist on full statehood. The Aaland islanders, for their part, have long understood that what is really important for them is how the state budget is distributed.

The Gagauz question

The problem of the status of the Gagauz minority in Moldova has many aspects in common with the Dniester question, which has overshadowed it on account of its greater scale and intensity. The Gagauz are a Christian Bulgaro-Turkish tribe, whose ancestors migrated into the area from present-day Bulgaria in the early nineteenth century, receiving various incentives to do so from the Russian Imperial authorities (Nebelchuk, 1993, p. 24). From the beginning they have thus been more closely identified with the Russian-speaking population of the region rather than the Romanian. Much of the Gagauz-settled territory of Bessarabia was in the southern districts ceded to Ukraine in 1940, leaving the remainder concentrated around Komrat, near the Ukraine border in south-central Moldova.

In 1989 the Gagauz organized strikes against the proclamation of Romanian as the state language of Moldova, and in August 1990, fearing re-unification with Romania, they proclaimed a separate 'Republic of Gagauzia' in the district around Komrat, anticipating a similar declaration in Transdniestria by one month – in fact official Moldovan sources regard the Gagauz action as the result of 'orthodox communist' Gagauz leaders being influenced by Transdniestrian separatist agitation (Nebelchuk, 1993, p. 25). In October 1990 the

Moldovan government declared a state of emergency in Gagauzia, and sent in 50,000 armed volunteers to prevent the elections taking place for the parliament of the self-styled republic, but failed to stop them because of intervention by the Soviet 14th Army (*Europa Yearbook, loc. cit.*). The latter also appear to have assisted the Gagauz in setting up their own police force or militia. The Gagauz voted in favour of keeping the USSR together in the referendum of March 1991, despite the Moldovan boycott, and their leadership declared its support for the August 1991 coup (Nebelchuk, 1993, p. 26).

The stand-off between Moldova and the self-proclaimed Gagauz republic (now with its own elected president, Stepan Topal), continued until after the Moldovan parliamentary elections of February 1994. These, as described above, consolidated the policy of Moldovan multi-ethnic statehood. Gagauz voters had participated in the elections, on the side of Snegur's Agrarian Democratic party and its allies, on the basis that this would lead to resolution of the republic's status. There followed a long series of diplomatic negotiations involving President Snegur, parliamentary speaker Luchinschi, the president of Gagauzia and the latter's five 'district executives'. After some delays parliament passed, in January 1995, a law conferring special juridical status (involving a degree of budgetary autonomy) on Gagauzia as a region within the Moldovan unitary state. Assurances had been given by Peter Buzaji, the vice-president of Gagauzia, that the rights of the 17 non-Gagauz minorities on the region's territory would not be affected by the law, and that the Gagauz would consider their being proportionately represented on the region's 'power bodies' (Infotag, 16 November 1994).

Historical and symbolic factors in the choice of local government system

The shape of Moldova's local government system was a subject of political controversy from 1991 through to the end of 1994. A more rapid resolution of the issue had not been possible because of three factors.

Firstly, no new system could be effectively agreed on or implemented as long as the Dniester and Gagauz questions, which pre-dated independence, were resolved.

Secondly, much of the interim period was characterized by a degree of inertia on account of the dominance at the time of pro-unification factions and parties who saw little urgency in building a Moldovan state separate from Romania. They did prepare a draft law on local government, however. The draft proposed a system very much along the lines of that of the period of Romanian rule, 1918–40, and could be seen as geared to facilitating re-unification. But by the time this draft was ready the balance of power in parliament had become uncertain, and pro-Romanian forces had weakened, so that the law, although debated more than once from January 1991 onwards, was not submitted to a vote (*Izvestiya*, 31 January 1991).

This leads to the third factor, which was the historical symbolism underlying the choice of local government system. As the earlier section on the origins of the Moldovan state demonstrates, the key period in the development of the country's institutional structure, and of the development of its capital city, was the century of Tsarist rule, with Romanian-style structures being introduced temporarily at a later date, before being swept aside by the Soviet-style system after 1944. The structures of the Soviet period were different from those of the Tsarist period, but nonetheless had what might be termed a 'family resemblance' to them, and to some extent acquired legitimacy as their successors. The result was that in 1991 Moldova was faced with a choice between the *judet* or county-based system of the Romanian tradition, or the *raion* or district-based system of the Soviet period. Although it might appear fanciful to ascribe the choice between the two to symbolic historical considerations, this appears to be the case. The Romanian system was gaining ground as an alternative to the Soviet-era status quo during the period of the pro-Romanian nationalist ascendancy of 1990–91, but was shelved during the period when the latter came to an end, and was finally discarded in favour of an amended version of the existing structure when the concept of a multi-ethnic independent Moldova was consolidated towards the end of 1994.

An emphasis on Romanian identity, beyond the (qualified) status of Romanian as the official state language, would automatically exclude a large part of the population. This may seem curious given the very different approach adopted in the Baltic States, for example. In the latter case, however, the influx of large numbers of Russians had been more specifically a post-1945 phenomenon, and the states concerned had stronger separate national identities. In the case of Moldova, the Romanian connection also provides a major source of difference from the Baltic States. Moldova's experience as a Russian province, and as a Soviet republic (after the Stalinist era), was by the standards of other territories with similar history a relatively prosperous one, whereas as a Romanian province it had had a marginal status, being seen as not quite as Romanian as it should have been, as a result of more than a century of Russian influence. In this context the decision not to change the local government structure radically may be seen as implying a qualified affirmation of the non-Romanian aspects of Moldova's national identity.

Debates over the structure of local government

The draft law on local government referred to above was drawn up by the pro-Romanian Popular Front, and presented to parliament in January 1991. It aimed to abolish the existing structure of 40 *raion* districts and ten cities with district status, and replace them with a structure of between seven and ten *judete* or counties and two cities of county status, Kishinev and Tiraspol. The mayors of the two cities would also be members of the government, and would be appointed by parliament on the recommendation of the prime minister. The counties would be run by appointed prefects who would also be members of the national government. District and town councils (*soviety*) would be abolished. The former districts would be run be *pretore*, appointed by, and subordinate to, the prefect. Towns would receive new councils, with an elected mayor (*primar*) and mayor's office (*primaria*), as would the communes which would replace the existing village councils (*selskiye soviety*).

The draft was in some ways a characteristic product of post-Soviet local government thinking, combining as it did an emphasis on the province or county as the main unit of territorial government by the centre, together with an expansion of the legal rights (but not the functions) of the lowest tiers, giving them the status of legal persons, the ability to draw credits and engage in their own contracts and financial, business transactions.

The draft was justified on the basis that it would cut the numbers of administrators employed in the regions by half. The district structure was seen as extravagant for a country the size of Moldova (although it would be seen as a skeleton administration by Western standards). It was also justified on the basis that it would be a break with the structures of the Soviet period (in particular the district councils or *soviety*) and would allow the government to press through reforms and overcome the resistance of interest groups such as local bureaucrats, collective farms and state enterprise managers.

These arguments were put to parliament, where a number of

opposing arguments were put. Firstly, that the structure would destroy the representative power of the soviets elected democratically only the previous March (1990), which had already had many powers such as tax inspection, police and local newspapers taken away by central government, and would lead to administrative chaos just when the state budget was under unprecedented pressure. Secondly, and most importantly, it would introduce a 'command-administrative' regime with an unacceptable amount of power in the hands of the prefect, and therefore in those of central government, of which prefects would be members. Significantly, it was also asserted (*Izvestiya*, 31 January 1991) that:

> Bessarabian peasants still recall what it was like to live under the harsh rule of pre-war prefects and *primari*.

Although the above might be written off as a standard piece of Soviet parliamentary rhetoric, the draft law did appear to touch on real and widespread concerns regarding potential unification between Romania and Moldova. Whether these concerns were entirely justified is another matter. As the deputy mayor of Chisinau in an interview of February 1994 commented:

> How often we have heard about how Romanian officials used to beat recalcitrant peasants here before the war – but I have yet to see any evidence that it actually happened ... whereas the deportations of hundreds of thousands by the Soviet authorities after the war is well documented.

Either way the law was seen by a significant number of deputies to be an attempt radically to transform Moldova on Romanian lines. A vote was taken to refer the draft to a working party (*Izvestiya*, 31 January 1994). There is one underlying irony, namely that the model which proposed that the country should be divided into eight *judete* drew on the precedent of Bessarabia having been divided into nine *uyezdy* under the Russian Empire (interviews in State Chancellery, Chisinau, January 1994) – the *uyezd* being a unit within an *oblast*, or province: as such it corresponded closely to the Romanian *judet*.

For the purposes of this chapter, it may be commented that the uncompromising centralism that characterized the draft law reflected the uncertainty of central government over the ambiguous identity of the country, and the consequent wish to hammer a new identity and structure into place as quickly as possible. In the event, this very ambiguity arising from the country's history guaranteed that such a clear-cut, one-sided vision of its future would not find acceptance.

Following the shelving of the draft law, the Moldovan government issued a directive (Pravitelstvo, 1991a) in July 1991, setting out a local government structure for the transitional period until a more radical reform might be adopted. The transitional system amounted to a moderate de-Sovietization of the system, whilst keeping the main structure intact. It confirmed the abolition of the presidiums of the councils at each level; confirmed the existing levels of district, town, and village councils; and replaced the Soviet-era *ispolkom* or executive committee with a body of the same name – executive committee of the district council – but with a separately elected chairman. The town and village councils would have mayors (*primari*), rather than executive committees. The status of the cities (including Chisinau and its five city-districts) was largely unaffected, except for similar changes in terminology. The directive attempted to elucidate the fine balance between the authority of central government and the districts, and between the districts and the towns and villages. These were the subject of some revisions to the directive two months later (Pravitelstvo, 1991b) which emphasized the district's power to dismiss town and village mayors if they failed to observe the law. It also stressed that the chairman of the district executive committee's role in coordinating organizations of ministerial subordination on the territory of the district could be exercised only with the express agreement of the ministries involved, and that any conflicts that arose would be decided at the level of central government.

From the above-mentioned points, one may observe that the chairman of the district executive committee was being regarded as the linchpin of this temporary structure, and had acquired something of the status of a Romanian prefect, albeit on a smaller scale and with more carefully delimited powers in practice. How the structure actually worked is best explained through reference to specific examples, and these are set out in a later section.

A further draft law was drawn up as the successor to the transitional system (Lege, 1993). It was compiled by deputies and by officials of the State Chancellery, a ministry which brought together a number of corporate functions within the government, and within which is located the unit concerned with coordination and monitoring of local authorities. It represented a more considered and democratic version of the earlier draft law, drawing on a broad range of foreign systems, notably those of Romania and Holland (interview in State Chancellery, January 1994).

It proposed a Romanian-style structure of *judete, municipii, orase* and *commune*. In place of the existing 40 districts, 10 cities and 961 towns and villages, it proposed 8 *judete* (counties), 12 *municipii* (cities), 56 *orase* (towns) and 1008 communes. It differed from the earlier draft by its proposed establishment of county councils. Each county council would elect a standing delegation (as in Romanian practice), but at the level of cities or towns the standing delegation would be made up of members of both the executive (mayor and deputy mayor) and the council (3–5 councillors). The prefect would, as in Romania, appoint the secretaries (chief professional officials) of county and city or town administrations. Local services would be clearly subordinated to city, town and commune executives and councils, whilst local ministerial organizations would be coordinated by the county. The county council would be independent of central government and of the prefect, who would be a government functionary. The rationale of the system – the author was told in the State Chancellery in January 1994 – was that it would allow for a more effectively decentralized system than the smaller units of the current system (40 districts and 10 cities), the implication being that the district was too small a body to provide proper local coordination:

> At the moment every mayor ends up coming to Chișinaŭ – in a bigger district or county, administration would be more truly local.

Discussion of this and two other related draft laws was postponed by parliament during 1993, and eventually presented to the incoming parliament after the February 1994 election. This parliament proved unwilling to opt for radical change of this type, particularly whilst the separatist questions described above remained unresolved. Finally, as moves towards normalization in Gagauzia and Transdniestria got under way in the Autumn of 1994, parliament did, on 19 October 1994, finally pass a law on local administration. The new law avoided any major upheaval, dividing the country as before into 40 districts which would include 40 towns and 900 villages, very much as before. Four cities would have republican status – Chisinau (Kishinev), Balti (Beltsy), Orghei (Orgeyev) and Tiraspol. One curious innovation which was received with some disquiet was that the mayors of these four cities would not be elected, as those of the towns and villages would continue to be. Instead they would be nominated by the President of the Republic, out of those elected to the city council, thus contradicting Article 109 of the constitution which declared that local officials were elected, not appointed. Some concern was also expressed that the law recognized villages many of which had less than 1000 population, and would be more efficiently administered if merged to form communes (Basapress, 19 October 1994).

To conclude this review, the following sections provide examples of how the Moldovan local government system works in practice. The summary that follows is based on interviews carried out in January–February 1994 in two districts, two towns and four villages. It does not apply to cities of republic status, such as Chisinau or Balti.

The district and the town

The district or town division of competencies is at first sight a surprising one. Districts are responsible for coordination and management of the local infrastructure and economy, including any organizations subordinate to ministries, with the exception of primary education, primary health care and social welfare and communal services (in the sense of cleaning, repairs and so on), which form the main three areas of competence for town mayors. Districts therefore cover construction, roads, energy supply, communications, post, and production for local consumption (meat processing etc.).

The mayors are to a very significant extent subordinate to the executive committee. Until late 1994, they were still district appointees, although the transitional law foresaw that they would be elected at some stage. However, mayors have typically been elected chairmen of their respective councils before being nominated – it is impractical to appoint a village mayor who does not have some personal legitimacy. The district committee, which is accountable to central government as well as to the district council, will typically have 11 members, and will meet once a month, whilst the district council will meet quarterly. The centre of power is the chairman and the four deputy chairmen who are functionally differentiated and directly accountable to the ministries covering the areas they manage – finance, general affairs (health education, social welfare) construction, agriculture (the first deputy chairman in rural districts). The district employs directly only 33 people, of whom 17 are officials.

The role of the district appears to rely considerably on the brinkmanship and 'fixing' abilities of the chairman and the small district staff (notably the accountant). The district is expected to maintain services which are not primarily subordinate to the district, solve problems of supply from local enterprises, find jobs for rural school-leavers, assist villages in balancing their books despite irregular resource flows and rapid inflation (837 per cent from December 1992 to December 1993), and at the same time present all financial information in the precise and detailed form desired by the Ministry of Finance, which, in the circumstances, is often difficult. Despite these pressures, the chairman is a more powerful figure than in the past when the party secretary would chair the council and would dictate decisions to the executive.

The impression is a paradoxical one, the chairman of the district executive committee, the quintessential 'fixing' role of the Soviet era, being employed, in effect, to 'hold the line', so that macro-economic stabilization policies pursued by central government can be maintained without engendering social collapse. The survival of the role may reflect a recognition that, at the level of the rural district, a proper market economy cannot be expected to emerge or operate in the early years of the transition period, so that the brinkmanship and networking skills of the old regime are required to keep the district functioning, and help ensure that public support for macro-economic reforms is not undermined. The Ministry of Finance exerts close control on funding (most of the budget is ostensibly made up of specific grants relating to the district-level functions of the various ministries) whilst leaving it understood that figures and budget headings have to be manipulated on a day-to-day basis so that inflation and the public spending squeeze do not bring individual communities or services to a standstill. The district chairman interviewed prided himself on the continual 'firefighting' involved, and his implied remit of finding the best fit between government prescription and rural realities.

This district's careful balance between centralization and decentralization was a response to the problems which occurred in an earlier period, that of 1989–90, when towns and villages had acquired greater autonomy and had allowed their expenditure to exceed their income. This autonomy had been clawed back via a 'decentralization' of the finance function, whereby accountants were placed in every town and village, but remained wholly under the control of the district finance department, who required them to restrain spending within prescribed limits. Here it was a matter not only of meeting the targets set by the Ministry of Finance, but also of making sure that providers of local services belonging to central ministries and only partially accountable to the district, were paid and did not withdraw their services from individual villages or towns. In addition the district had the task of using its influence to see that services (such as road repairs) were provided evenly across all towns and villages – complaints seemed to result not from the quality of services, but from any perceived inequities involved in their delivery.

Village mayors appeared relatively satisfied under the district system, town mayors and staff less so. The reason is that village mayors rely heavily on the collective farms (now joint stock companies) with which they and their councils had been synonymous under the old system (see below). Town mayors and councils have no such buffer to fall back on – the economic power in the towns lies with a few large enterprises (typically agro-industrial, and wine-related) which tend to ignore the town authorities and deal directly with the district, where they perceive the real power to lie. This means that any appeal to enterprises to provide extra resources for public purposes (and this need regularly arises) has to be mediated through the district chairman or another member of the committee. In the villages, mayors are able to build up the 'extra-budgetary' funds (beloved of mayors throughout the former USSR) through appeals to the collective farm joint stock companies, who have every incentive to assist the mayor in meeting village needs, since the more contented local residents are, the less likely they are to opt out of the collective company (very few did in fact opt out in the early years of transition).

Whereas the district committee will usually know what decisions are being taken in relation to the town (for example, the local representative of the Ministry of Justice allowing changes in the retail profile of local shops), the town authorities may be the last to know, and lose credibility among the population as a result. Towns also bemoan the fact that most of their money comes from higher-standing authorities. Their attempts to rectify the situation by, for example, income generation through charges – such as, for grazing animals on municipal pasture – tend to fail because a majority of the local residents involved fail to pay, recognizing that the town has no real mechanism through which to enforce its demand. As in Romania, much of the day-to-day work falls on the secretary, half of whose time is said to be taken up with filling in 'mechanistic' forms to send back to central ministries. In the remainder of the time, the secretary is able to carry out the role that councillors might have been expected to fulfil, namely that of listening to complaints by members of the public, and then using informal influence with local service enterprises to settle the matters concerned.

Villages and joint stock farms

The institution of the village mayor as separate from the collective
farm dates back only to 1991, before which the collective farm
management and the village administration were one and the same.
Mayors of villages (typically 2000–3000 inhabitants) have few staff –
frequently only themselves, one assistant, the local army recruitment
clerk and the accountant, who does not report to them but to the district
and the ministry. Village mayors are beset by problems of equity in the
privatization of land and property and its distribution to local residents,
planning permission, domestic disputes, unemployment and the
maintenance of primary school and health services. They typically have
little money for virement, and therefore rely heavily on the support of
the management of the local collective farm, which now usually has
joint stock status, with most local residents as shareholders – the shares
being in the form of land they own and work themselves, whilst the
company provides transport and other services, which raises barriers in
terms of overheads against any farmer wishing to withdraw from the
company.

The squeeze on budgets is such that most of the local services –
schools, medical units, roads and so forth – are directly supported by
the company, and it is by, or through, the company that technical
services such as sewerage, electricity and water are provided, often at
little or no cost to individual users (they might, for example, pay for
their consumption, but the costs of repairs and maintenance will be met
entirely by the company). Sports and cultural facilities will usually be
built with company money, although the (generally opulent) houses in
the villages will usually be built by the residents themselves, although
presumably with assistance from the company in terms of access to
low-priced materials etc. In addition the company may guarantee work
to all local residents – so that workers from the countryside who have
lost their jobs in the restructuring of city enterprises return to their
villages where their unemployment will in this way become 'hidden',
although local initiatives between mayors and companies do typically
result in commercially viable small-scale manufacturing or service
enterprises being set up in villages.

It comes as no surprise, therefore, that the company openly partici-
pates in most decisions taken by the mayor and council. The general
impression is that decisions are made in negotiation between the mayor

and the director of the company, with the mayor then winning over the council to the view already agreed on. Some mayors do not relish this position, seeing their authority hemmed in by the company on one side and central government on the other, the latter's squeeze on budgets and competencies forcing the mayor into the arms of the former if residents' needs are to be addressed at all. Districts are in a similar position, although with more practical power to make deals in order to get things done. They will trouble-shoot for villages, their inclination to do this necessarily balanced by the perceived need to maintain an equitable spread of resources and services across the district, and (through direct control of village budget-spending) to prevent villages from departing from norms set by central ministries, notably the Ministry of Finance. Some saw the mayor's role as untenable in the long term, since it combined a high level of accountability upwards with a large amount of everyday responsibility downwards to local residents, and had little formal or practical authority.

From the brief review of issues at the local level, it can be said that centralization in practice leads to a range of somewhat messy compromises and informal decision-making. The institution of mayor, (and of district chairman, for that matter) is able to attract people of high calibre, but, it appears, fails to make sufficient use of them, by forcing them into rather weak brokering modes of operation. In the background is a considerable degree of uncertainty over what authority means in the post-communist transition, and who should possess it. This is combined with a still chaotic mixture of old and new laws which the government is said to expect to be obeyed, even when two laws contradict each other (here one may note the contrast between the inflexible position of the Ministry of Finance in relation to local autonomy, and the more facilitative, advisory approach adopted by the local government section of the State Chancellery, which appeared to see itself as partner to the local authorities it monitored).

The weakness of the institution of the mayor is such that the League of Mayors set up in 1990 (when mayor and chairman of the executive committee were one and the same) has largely faded from view, although it may have been a greater potential asset than central government were prepared to recognize. As the President of the League of Mayors said to the author in an interview in February 1994:

In the beginning we had 90 per cent of all mayors attending meetings of the League, including those from Gagauzia and Transdniestria. The network of mayors could have been used to help defuse those conflicts, but government and parliament did not choose to proceed in that way, and the rest is history.

Conclusion

This chapter has attempted to show that local government systems are closely influenced by historical and ethnic tensions in the structure of the state, particularly where the state is unitary in nature, but where historical regional identities are characterized by a high degree of divergence. Where these conditions coincide with attempts to implement post-communist transition, there will be conflict between the democratic agenda and that of economic reform, since the central authority will wish to concentrate decision-making on both the design and implementation of reform at the centre, for fear of the historical and ethnic differences combining with the social repercussions of economic restructuring to destabilize the unitary state. Also, in such cases, there will be difficulties in applying international 'best practice' in local government, since the decisions regarding the shape and functioning of the local government system will be largely determined by political considerations (as they may be in most countries), and geared to the resolution of problems derived from the specific history of the country.

Postscript

On 27 March 1995, a referendum held by the Dniester authorities found a large majority of left bank residents to be in favour of the continued presence of the Russian 14th Army. Demonstrators in the left bank territory appealed to the Russian Duma to support the decision. Pro-Russian separatists were very probably emboldened by the escalation, in late March, of the Russian Duma's activity in relation to the Russian enclaves of the Crimea in neighbouring Ukraine. In Kishinev the referendum was criticized by both President Snegur and speaker Piotr Lucinschi as an unconstitutional act, and the capital city once again saw large demonstrations in favour of union with Romania (Ostankino News, 27 March 1995).

Notes

* This chapter draws largely on material gathered via the author's participation in projects for the British Know How Fund (Romania) and the United Nations Development Programme (Moldova).

All the interviews listed here were carried out by the author. Those conducted in Romania in 1994–95 were carried out in conjunction with Dr John Watson of the Development Assistance Group, University of Birmingham. In an attempt to avoid confusion, a distinction is made here between 'Moldova' (the present name of what was the Soviet Republic of Moldavia) and 'Moldavia' (the province of that name in neighbouring Romania). In Romanian the name for both is 'Moldova', although Romanians routinely refer to the state of Moldova as 'Bessarabia', the name it had when it was a province of the Tsarist Empire.

References

Aves, Jonathan (1992), 'The Evolution of Independent Political Movements after 1988', in G.A. Hosking, J. Aves and P.J.S. Duncan (eds.), *The Road to Post-Communism: Independent Political Movements in the Soviet Union, 1985–1991*, London: Pinter.

Berg, L.S. (1918/1993), *Bessarabia*, Kiev: Universitat.

Campbell, A. (1994a), 'Regional and Local Government in Ukraine', in Andrew Coulson (ed.), *Local Government in Eastern Europe*, Aldershot: Edward Elgar, pp. 115–27.

— (1994b), 'Local Government in Romania', in Coulson, *op. cit.*, pp. 76–101.

Cosea, Mircea (1994a), 'The Policy for Privatization and Restructuring of the Armaments Industry in Romania', in NATO, *Privatization in NACC Countries, Colloque 1994*, Brussels: NATO, pp. 17–21.

— (1994b), statement presented to conference on Local Democracy and Development, Bucharest, October.

Farcas, Mihai (1994), 'Basic Information on Local Government in Romania', in E. Lowther (ed.), *Local Government in the CEE and CIS, 1994*, Budapest: Institute for Local Government and Public Service.

Government of Romania (1994), 'Programme for Institutional Reform of the CCSER', paper presented at G-24 High-Level Meeting in Romania, Brussels, 19 May.

Hill, Ronald J. (1977), *Soviet Political Elites: The Case of Tiraspol*, London: Martin Robertson.

Iliescu, Ion 1994, 'Allocution du Président de la Roumanie Ion Iliescu pour l'ouverture de la Conference à La Democratie et de développement local en Roumanie', Bucharest, 28 October.

Lege (1993), *Lege (Project) privind administratia locala*, draft law on local government, prepared by State Chancellery of Moldova.

Local Democracy and Development (1994), Local Democracy and Development: Romania, International Conference, Introductory Reports, 28–30 October.

Kishinev (1984), *Kishinev Entsiklopedia*, Kishinev.

Krikhan Anton, (1993), 'Introduction' to Berg, *op. cit.*

Moruzi, Adrian (1994), 'Everyday Questions and Remarks in Post Communist Romania', paper presented at UK Government Know How Fund conference on 'Decentralization', Warsaw, November.

Nebelchuk, V. (1993), *Respublika Moldova*, Kiev: Universitat.

Pravitelstvo (1991a), Pravitelstvo Respubliki Moldova, Postanovlenie no. 357, 22 July.

— (1991b), Pravitelstvo Respubliki Moldova, Postanovlenie no. 533, 25 September.

Saunders, David (1992), *Russia in the Age of Reaction and Reform*, London: Longman.

Savulescu, Victor (1994), 'The State of Decentralization in Romania: Legislation and Reality', paper presented at UK Government Know How Fund on 'Decentralization,' Warsaw, November.

Socor, Vladimir (1993a), 'Isolated Moldova being Pulled into Russia's Orbit?' *RFE/RL Research Report*, 6 December.

— (1993b), 'Moldova in 1993', *RFE/RL Research Report*, 13 December.

Young, Ronald (1994), 'Towards Local Autonomy: Paper for a Dialogue', Satumare: Europrint.

Part II. Studies in Democratic Development: East-Central Europe

5. Hungary: Into the Second Reform Cycle

Kenneth Davey

Introduction

Hungary has been, and remains, the pacesetter in local government reform in Central and Eastern Europe. Its reorganization of local administration in 1990 and 1991 went further and faster than in any other ex-socialist country, leaving it the first (and perhaps the only) fully operational system of local government.

This *avant garde* position was reinforced in 1994 when Hungary entered a second cycle of reform. Detailed proposals for amendment of the Local Government Act were prepared by the government and subject to wide public consultation ahead of the national elections. These were designed to correct the deficiencies in the 1990 system in the light of four years' experience. A substantial number of these proposals were adopted by the newly elected parliament in September in time for implementation during and after the municipal elections held in December 1994 (themselves delayed for three months to allow the changes to be made). The residue remain under active discussion.

Some of the changes made in September 1994 were substantial. They were made by a new parliament in its first month of operation and required a two-thirds majority, since the Local Government Act is regarded as a 'fundamental law' under the constitution. They reflect, therefore, a wide measure of agreement on the need for change arising from the experience gained. The deficiencies they addressed arose from the political pressures of the immediate post-communist period, and related to issues which have dogged local government reform in neighbouring countries as well. This process of revision in Hungary deserves discussion within the wider context of decentralization in the region.

The 1990 Reforms: The context

The Hungarian reorganization of local government in 1990 was driven by much the same dissatisfactions with the communist system as elsewhere. Causes of bitter resentment included

- the absence of autonomous legal identity and property ownership on the part of municipal bodies;
- the forced amalgamation of smaller self-governing settlements into larger territorial units;
- the lack of free political competition for municipal office;
- subordination to arbitrary direction and intervention by government and party officials operating through the county-level institutions;
- lack of independent revenue raising power and reliance on arbitrary and unpredictable resource allocations by central and county government.

Hungary differed from its neighbours, however, in its more gradual transition to a mixed economy and relative tolerance of political debate in the 'soft communism' era of the 1980s. This had two important consequences for the 1990 local government reform. Firstly, fiscal reform creating the basic tax structure of a mixed economy took place ahead of the political revolution. This meant that a new system of local government could be accompanied immediately by a new structure of central–local financial relations, including both the assignment of local tax bases and the sharing of national taxes. Indeed, important elements of the new structure which came into effect in January 1991 were anticipated in the 1990 budget. Czech, Polish and Slovak local authorities, by contrast, had to work for three years under transitional financial arrangements, while national tax reforms were put in place.

Secondly, the introduction of pluralist democracy was openly debated in Hungary in the late 1980s together with the restoration of local government autonomy. The Hungarian Institute of Public Administration, a research and policy analysis arm of the Ministry of the Interior, undertook wide comparative research of Western systems of local government and formulated proposals for new legislation based on the principles of legal separation from the state and competitive election. The author attended a meeting at the institute as early as 1988 to review a draft local government law.

The Legislative Process

The result of the HIPA's preparations was that comprehensive legislative proposals for local government reform were ready as soon as a democratically elected parliament took office in May 1990. The director of the institute, Dr Imre Verebelyi, and his deputy, Pal Kara, became Administrative State Secretary and Deputy Secretary of the Ministry of the Interior, respectively. By September 1990, a new Local Self-Government Act and a Local Elections Act had been enacted, and mayors and councils had been elected in 3100 towns and villages.

Other ex-socialist countries, such as the Czech and Slovak republics, Poland and Romania, exhibited similar speed in constituting and electing autonomous local authorities in 1990. The Hungarian reforms were ahead of the field in two vital aspects, however, both attributable to their longer and more systematic preparation. Firstly, the two 1990 Acts establishing local self-government and regulating local elections were followed quickly by other legislation providing its operational framework – laws assigning powers and functions, financial resources and ownership of property. By mid–1991 virtually all these elements were in place, although the actual transfer of state property took longer to implement.

A Two-tier System

The second characteristic of the Hungarian reform was that it created a far more comprehensive system of local self-government than that of its neighbours. In the Czech and Slovak Republics and in Poland, for example, the 1990 legislation created a primary tier of elected municipalities, but left the introduction of a higher tier of local government open for further consideration (still unresolved in 1995); the gap was filled by retaining a deconcentrated state apparatus at the equivalent of county level. This did not happen in Hungary.

The emphasis of the 1990 Local Self-Government Act, as of parallel legislation in neighbouring countries, was on the primary level of local government. 'Settlements' had the right to constitute their own elected body and claim municipal status; this reversed the previous process of amalgamation and the number of authorities virtually doubled. All municipalities were accorded mandatory duties such as the maintenance of basic education and the provision of potable water, together with a general competence to do anything for the benefit of their citizens not specifically illegal or accorded to other agencies. All municipalities had equal taxing powers and were entitled to a formula block grant and to earmarked grants for particular types of investment. Municipal decisions were subject to external review only on the grounds of legality.

Where the Hungarian Act differed was in creating (or reviving) simultaneously an upper tier of county self-governments. It was no mean achievement. The county, though of great historical significance, was synonymous in 1990 perceptions with Communist Party domination and manipulation of local administration. Many parliamentarians wanted to wipe the county from the Hungarian map. Familiar with British patterns, Dr Verebelyi proposed a separation of tasks between county and municipality, enabling a strictly non-hierarchical relationship between tiers. Even so, it took six weeks of debate to persuade parliament to retain the county tier. The price was a severe emasculation of its powers and status. County assemblies were to be elected indirectly by colleges of municipal representatives; the county government was given no independent taxing power, only grants pertaining to its responsibilities and some share in the fees it collected or revenue from its limited stock of property. County government was given responsibility for services with large catchment areas like secondary schools, hospitals and social care institutions, but only on a residual basis; the municipality in which they were located could lodge a pre-emptive claim to their ownership and management, together with corresponding elements of grant; many did so.

The retention of county self-government, in however weak a form, had two major impacts on the reform as a whole. It enabled transfer of responsibility for the services with supra-municipal catchment areas to local government. This was a marked contrast to the situation in the Czech and Slovak Republics and Poland where secondary education, social care institutions, hospitals and similar institutions have remained in the hands of deconcentrated agencies pending establishment of upper tiers of local government which are still beyond the horizon. Secondly, no major apparatus of state administration like the Polish voivodships or the Czech and Slovak districts remained in being at county level, merely a collection of small, separate and specialized agencies.

The 1994 Amendments

Both parliamentary and municipal terms of office expired in 1994. In the year preceding fresh elections the Ministry of the Interior promoted a wide debate about amending the 1990 Local Self-government Act and published specific proposals, some in the form of dual options. A number of conferences were organized by the ministry, local authority associations and political parties. The opinions of international gurus (including the present author) were sought. The hope was to obtain a wide measure of agreement on changes ahead of the national elections.

The ministry failed to get the outgoing parliament to legislate before its dissolution. It did succeed, however, in persuading the newly elected parliament to give immediate attention to the proposals when it convened in September 1994, and to postpone the municipal elections to December to allow the amendments which affected elections to take effect.

The Socialist Party won an overall majority in the 1994 parliament, but opted for a coalition with the Free Democrats, whose leader became Minister of the Interior. This gave the coalition the two-thirds majority required for amending fundamental laws like the Local Self-government Act. It also gave disproportionate influence to the Free Democrats who had won the greatest support in the larger municipalities in 1990.

The debate over the amendment bill was highly controversial; the opposition (largely the previous governing coalition headed by the Hungarian Democratic Forum) demanded the same degree of all-party consensus as had surrounded the passage of the 1990 Act (at that stage a necessity as the government had not possessed a two-thirds majority). It was thought to be anxious to postpone the municipal elections until 1995, by which time inevitable rises in administered prices would have eroded the new government's popularity. The coalition averted this by deferring those amendments which were highly contentious and did not affect the operation of the municipal elections.

On this basis a shortened version of the amending bill was enacted in September 1994 and implemented in the December elections. The amendments were still substantial in number. Several were mainly legal clarifications, but major changes of substance were also made. These are described below.

County government

The hostility towards county government softened considerably between 1990 and 1994. There were a number of reasons. Experience had demonstrated the weaknesses of relying on a plethora of small rural authorities to provide services, particularly in secondary education, health and social care. There were recriminations between central municipalities and surrounding villages over the running of services such as secondary schools. Villages accused the town of discriminating against their residents; the town accused the villages of failure to contribute to the cost of a common service. This led to support for the role of the county in running services with wide catchment areas.

There were criticisms, too, of the multiplication of 'decos' - specialist field offices of central government ministries at county level. This mingled with suspicion of empire-building by the commissioners of the republic, discussed below. This gave rise to a desire to reintegrate decentralized agencies with county government, both to promote coordination and to reduce overheads.

Two major changes in the role of the county were made in the 1994 Act. Firstly, provision was made for direct instead of indirect election of county assemblies; this took place in December 1994. This gave the assemblies and their presidents a more direct mandate and potentially greater political clout.

Secondly, the Act specified more clearly the responsibility of county governments for services beyond municipal capacity, including secondary education, libraries, social care, specialist medical care, education and care of the disabled, museums and child protection. The right of municipalities to take direct responsibility for these services was preserved, but with greater restriction; the majority of users had to be within their jurisdiction and the county assembly would have to be satisfied that the rights of other users would be preserved. This amendment represented an important shift of emphasis. It is not yet clear whether it will result in much actual change in management; central municipalities have already been vested with ownership of the assets attached to these services such as school buildings, and changes are likely only in the case of voluntary surrenders.

The amending Act also specifies more clearly the responsibility of the county governments for the coordination of regional planning, tourist planning and coordination, regional employment policy and vocational training, and the protection of the built and natural environment. A special inter-governmental committee on regional development is to be established, coordinated by the county government. These are potentially important roles, but still nebulous. The extent of coordinating authority over the activities and decisions of municipalities or central government agencies is unclear and the planning processes undeveloped. The changes, nevertheless, give county government a higher profile and reverse its marginalization.

Budapest

Budapest has a fifth of the national population. To illustrate its dominance, a third of all income tax payers live in Budapest, paying nearly double the national average amount.

The 1990 Act preserved a two-tier structure in Budapest with a Capital City government and 22 districts. Unlike their counterparts in Prague or Bratislava, the Budapest districts are separate legal entities with their own budgets, property and staff. The majority of members of the City Assembly are elected directly, but a minority are nominated by the district councils. The division of tasks and resources between the tiers was left to separate legislation.

Since 1990 there has been considerable friction between the Capital City and the districts and dispute over property and competence. One district, an island in the Danube, held a popular referendum to consider secession from Budapest; this was overwhelmingly voted down by local residents who feared major increases in the charges for city-wide utilities such as telephones, public transport, water and sewerage.

The amendment proposals included an option abolishing the independent legal status of the districts. This went too far for parliament. However, the 1994 Act defined the division of tasks between tiers more clearly and with a heavy bias to the authority of the Capital City. The City retained its responsibility for the city-wide infrastructure of water supply, heating, sewerage, public transport, public lighting, flood control, main roads, drainage and waste disposal. It had the right to run services serving more than one district such as secondary schools, hospitals and specialist health services; as in the case of the counties, this provision may have only limited application where buildings have already been transferred from state to district ownership. Perhaps most importantly in terms of change, the Act gave the City the right to issue decrees setting city-wide policies on issues such as development planning, architectural standards, water and air quality, the renovation and disposal of public housing (governing rehabilitation and disposal), and parking.

Election of Mayors

Like its neighbours Hungary retained executive mayors in the 1990 reform. Like their neighbours also, Hungarians agonized over whether mayors should be appointed by the councils or elected by the public at large. The arguments are well known and universal to strong mayor systems. Election at large gives a mayor a mandate for strong integrating leadership and makes him or her highly accountable to the public for municipal performance; the risks are excessive power and destructive conflict with the council. The choices were debated throughout Central and Eastern Europe in 1990. The twin republics of what was then Czechoslovakia went in opposite directions; Czech mayors are appointed by councils, Slovak mayors elected at large.

Hungary chose a compromise in 1990. In municipalities with populations below 10,000 mayors were elected at large (as indeed were councillors since ward systems were introduced only in municipalities above this size). In municipalities above 10,000 inhabitants mayors were elected by the council (not necessarily from their own membership). There was, of course, some rationale in the distinction: individual candidates for office were more likely to be known to the electorate in small communities.

Appointment of mayors by councils in 1990 did not totally eliminate conflict between them. Individual political parties rarely had overall majorities on councils, so that party allegiance did not necessarily provide mayors with secure support. Some mayors were unseated by their councils. In the pre-election debate on local government reform in 1994 there was a strong lobby for electing all mayors at large; the need for strong but accountable executive leadership to tackle economic and environmental problems was advanced as a reason for change.

This proposal was accepted by the new parliament. It particularly suited the Free Democrats who controlled the Ministry of the Interior within the new coalition; their Socialist majority partners accepted it as part of the price for Free Democrat participation in the government. Election at large was thought to favour incumbent mayors; voters were expected to favour the devil they knew. The majority of incumbents in the larger towns were Free Democrats; the parliamentary election results suggested that they were more likely to survive under direct election, since their party would probably win fewer seats in the councils than in 1990.

And so it turned out. The majority of incumbent mayors were re-elected in December 1994, but now faced councils in which their parties had reduced representation. It is far too early to assess the impact of the change in system. Conflicts between mayors and councils have not been slow in emerging, however. The election of deputy mayors has provided an instant battleground, and has reached an impasse in some municipalities.

External control

The 1990 Act restricted external supervision of local government to appellate jurisdiction over state administration functions (largely regulatory powers), and the review of legality. As already mentioned, only a small apparatus of state administration was retained at county level.

The implementation of the 1990 Act nevertheless aroused major controversy. The supervisory powers were vested in eight commissioners of the republic, each responsible for a region combining two or three counties. These posts were given high rank in the government hierarchy and filled by supporters of the Hungarian Democratic Forum, the leading party in the ruling coalition. The coalition fared badly in the 1990 municipal elections, and the main opposition parties, the Free Democrats and the Young Democrats, controlled most of the larger municipalities. The commissioners were accused of empire-building and of highly partisan use of their supervisory powers against opposition-held municipalities. They could not override municipal decisions within their autonomous sphere, but only refer them to the courts. Many references were made to the courts; in the substantial majority of cases the Commissioner's objection was overruled and the municipality upheld.

The defeat of the HDF and its partners in the 1994 national elections sealed the fate of the commissioners of the republic. The Amendment Act abolished their post. Supervisory powers were vested in county offices of state administration. Headship of these offices was filled by public advertisement and competitive selection, with a strict emphasis on legal qualification and political neutrality.

Administrative Leadership

The 1990 Act created executive mayors. It accompanied these with posts of chief administrator known as 'administrative notaries'. These were to be professional administrators who must either be lawyers or graduates of the High School of Public Administration. The Act required all councils to appoint an administrative notary; village authorities too small to do so independently were required by law to combine with neighbours to employ one and operate a common administrative office.

The administrative notary is responsible under the law for running the municipal office under the general directions of the mayor, and for giving legal advice to the mayor and council. The exercise of most regulatory functions such as award of planning permission, building regulation approvals and licensing is also vested personally in the notary, who is independent of mayoral direction in this respect.

These provisions represented another of the compromises made in the 1990 legislation. State administrative functions were delegated to local government, but subject to professional rather than political exercise. Executive power was vested in elected mayors but with the support of a professional administrator with certain entrenched duties and powers.

Conflicts between mayors and administrative notaries were bound to occur – and so they did. There were three main battlegrounds. If administrative notaries considered municipal decisions illegal they were obliged to record their opinion in the minutes, thereby inviting external intervention; this was not popular with the elected officials. They were responsible for the effective operation of municipal offices, but had no disciplinary authority over the staff, who were hired and fired by the mayors. They made regulatory decisions according to their interpretations of the law which did not always accord with the preference of the mayor or the council.

These disputes led in several cases to councils dismissing their administrative notaries. Such decisions were usually overturned on appeal to the courts or industrial tribunals, but it was difficult in practice to reinstate a notary who was completely at odds with mayor or council.

The position of the administrative notary was widely debated in the pre-election period. The mayors' lobby tended to demand reductions in their powers, with regulatory decisions being subject to municipal direction, and the obligation to record legal opinions rescinded. The professional administrative view, particularly influential within the Ministry of the Interior at civil service level, prevailed. The Amendment Act left the administrative notary's powers intact. They were in fact strengthened; an amendment specified that the notary should exercise the employer's disciplinary rights in respect of municipal staff.

Unresolved Issues: Inter-municipal Cooperation

The main amending proposals deferred by parliament in 1994 concerned inter-municipal cooperation. They are still on the table in 1995. Small villages took full advantage in 1990 of their right to constitute independent municipalities and secede from the unions which had been imposed by the communist administration. Of the 3,100 municipalities 2,900 have populations below 10,000, and 1,500 have fewer than 2,000 people; some barely exceed 100 inhabitants. The proliferation has continued during the past four years.

As already mentioned, the Act required cooperation between small villages in employing an administrative notary. In the areas of functional responsibility it is up to small local governments to make their own arrangements for overcoming their limitations of size. The law permits villages to combine into associations to discharge all functions or only specific tasks. They may set up a joint council, representing the member villages in proportion to populations, to unify their budgets and operate services collectively. They may also join together to contract a particular agency to deliver a specific service on their behalf.

These provisions are essentially voluntary, however, and few villages have exploited them since 1990. There has been considerable resistance to inter-communal cooperation, despite the consequent inability of villages to render services.

Hungary is far from the only country to possess a plethora of small municipalities: 33,000 out of 36,000 French communes have populations under 2,000. They are served by a wide range of both multi- and single-purpose joint agencies maintaining roads, water supplies and social and educational services on behalf of member communes.

The architects of the 1990 Act were well aware of the French models. But inter-communal cooperation in France and similar countries has not developed within a purely voluntary framework. The French structure has developed historically with strong prefectorial intervention, financial incentives and coercive legal provisions. Cooperation between a group of neighbouring communes may be imposed on reluctant partners if two-thirds of the communes or communes with two-thirds of the population support it.

There has been increasing debate in Hungary over the need 'to make small local authorities cooperate'. The Ministry of the Interior's draft amendments to the Act provided that inter-municipal associations could be imposed upon a group of neighbouring municipalities by a resolution of the county assembly if a majority of them were in support. It also provided that parliament could legislate separately (that is, without the need for a two-thirds majority) to make associations compulsory for the discharge of specific mandatory functions; these include water supply, primary education, basic health care, public lighting, maintenance of local roads and cemeteries.

The Ministry's draft proposals also sought to restrict the right of a local community to secede from an existing municipality and constitute a new local authority. Under the draft bill, this right would be restricted to populations over 500 which could demonstrate ability to maintain a primary school and a general medical practice without loss of standards. The secession must leave at least another 500 people in the residual territory which must not suffer loss of service or financial viability from the split.

There was no consensus over these proposals nor a sense of urgency. They were deleted from the Bill passed in September 1994, and left for later consideration by parliament.

Conclusion

The amendments of the 1990 legislation considered in 1994 – and in the majority of cases enacted – touched on issues which arose in the re-establishment of local government throughout Central and Eastern Europe: the relationships between tiers, the government of the capital city, election of mayors, the division of authority between elected officials and professional administrators, the extent and location of external supervision, the proliferation of small authorities and cooperation between them.

The restoration of democratic local government in Hungary in

1990–91 and its panoply of powers, assets and resources, was more thoroughly prepared and rapidly executed than in neighbouring states. The retention of county self-government, though in a weakened form, overcame the uncertainties about the upper tier which continue to surround local administration in countries like Poland and Slovakia, and enabled responsibility for services such as primary and secondary education, medical and social care to be devolved to locally accountable bodies.

This did not mean, however, that Hungary avoided or solved all the problem issues that have arisen in the process of local government reform. Some, including the basis of electing mayors, do not have single, correct solutions, only a perpetual tension between pros and cons. Others, for instance the conflict between closeness to the community and economies of scale, were exacerbated by the overwhelming sentiment in 1990 in favour of the autonomy of individual settlements.

Hungary has had the advantage, however, of four years' experience of the operation of its local government system in a completed state. The differing outcomes of national and local elections in 1990 have also meant that the interests of local democracy have been stoutly defended within the political arena, and that the new coalition is under pressure to practise what it has preached in opposition. Finally, both the vision and the analytical ability of Dr Verebelyi and his colleagues, so important in framing the 1990 reforms, have remained at the heart of government. The performance of local government has been closely monitored, problems diagnosed, and corrections prescribed and promoted in public debate.

The demand for a vigorous system of local government in Hungary has out-lasted the political revolution in 1990. Local government has become a powerful institution spending nearly 20 per cent of GDP. The radical devolution of functions, property and resources pushed through while political support lasted has ensured that parties and politicians have had to continue taking its rights and interests seriously. It was no surprise that the newly elected parliament in 1990 should have given priority to reconstituting local government in its opening session. It is significant that its successor, four years on, should also have devoted much of its first few weeks in office to fine-tuning the system.

6. Polish Local Government: Whither the Second Stage of Reforms?

Anna Cielecka and John Gibson

The contribution and significance of local government to the political and economic life of society can be manifold. It is, even in a Western context, underemphasized in the typical shorthand categorization of the main issues in the subject of local government – structure, functions, and finance – used by scholars. Clearly, the role of local or, rather, decentralized government in democratization, the building of a civil society, as well as in economic management is, as was argued in the Introduction, extremely important in Russia and other former Soviet states – especially where there is ethnic diversity and tension. In Poland, the issues are not so dramatic, but, given the unexpected difficulties and hardships of the economic transition from the centrally administered and dominated economy, local government has much to offer in its potential for more efficient service delivery and democratically sensitive regulation and decision-making. It is here appropriate to recall the main shortcomings of 'Local Poland' during the period of communist party rule (Gorzelak and Mularczyk, 1991):

- low effectiveness in meeting the economic, infrastructural or social needs of local communities;
- very low efficiency in economic terms, with inputs failing to produce adequate output;
- little or no accountability of local officials and councillors to their locality;
- poor quality of government, constantly marred by excessive freedom of interpretation for bureaucrats and arbitrary decision-making.

The restoration of genuine local self-government for the 2,375 *gminy* in Poland which took place in 1989 covered, however, a limited sphere of activities. Many functions remained with the central state administration and the decentralized arms of the state administration: the creation of (267) *rejony* and the supervisory role of voivods in the

49 voivodships had been much criticized even in the initial stages (see Appendix for a description of the structure of Polish local government). There has also been ambiguity with respect to the relative responsibilities of the voivods/*rejony* and local government. Thus, whereas the Local Government Act stated that 'the jurisdiction of the local council shall extend to all matters falling within the terms of reference of the commune, *unless separate legislation stipulates otherwise*' (Art. 18.1; emphasis added), the law on the operations of voivodships stated that all functions and areas of competence not explicitly allocated to local governments were to be considered the responsibility of the voivods (and, therefore, *rejony*). Following the Competence Act, of 540 delineated functions, 45 per cent were allocated to local governments as 'own functions', 17 per cent to local governments as 'delegated functions,'[1] 35 per cent to the district agencies and 3 per cent to the voivods.

The basic responsibilities of local government were:

- education – children's day care centres;
- culture, including public libraries;
- health and social care (for the elderly or disabled);
- municipal house building and management (but this did *not* include the power to set rent levels, which remained with the centre);
- planning and land development;
- water, electricity, and gas supply;
- local public transport;
- roads, bridges, traffic control;
- waste collection and disposal;
- public parks, markets, cemeteries and public buildings;
- recreational and sports facilities;
- local law and order, fire services.

The limitations of these *gminy* responsibilities could perhaps be reflected in their share of public expenditure at little over 10 per cent in 1990 – an especially low ratio in a country without large defence expenditures. However, even in 1990 this ratio rather understated the role of Polish local governments because of their considerable activity and responsibilities in 'communal enterprise', which, of course, as trading enterprises had profits, or where loss-making, still had large offsets to net expenditure, thereby understating the activity or employment under the jurisdiction of *gminy*.

However, the introduction of genuine local self-government in the form of *gminy* was seen by many of those responsible and those who took office after the May 1990 local elections as only a first step towards the building of 'local Poland'. There was considerable disappointment and frustration that so many responsibilities and powers remained in the hands of the central state, through either the voivod or the decentralized arms of the central administration – the *rejony* or one of a number of special administrations.

The possibility and desirability of enlarging local self-government's functional responsibilities was acknowledged quickly in the case of primary education. From 1991 local governments were permitted to take over primary schools on a voluntary basis if they wished until 1994 – although many were deterred by lack of clarity, emanating from the central administration, and uncertainty with respect to the conditions and amount of central financial support – and it was planned that from the start of 1994 all primary schools must be managed by local governments.

Pressure for Change

Of course, the ability of local self-government to assume much greater functional responsibilities was limited at the commune level by the small size of many of them outside the main urban areas: over 80 per cent of *gminy* – nearly 2,000 – had a population of fewer than 10,000.

But the exercise of local government gave rise to a certain confidence and the formation of various associations of representatives of local governments. They had, in the years since 1990, mounted steadily growing demands and pressures for a further re-allocation of functional responsibilities from the state to local government and, as part of this, the creation of a second (upper) tier of local self-government – the *powiaty* (districts) – which had been an important 'traditional' unit of local government in Poland until scrapped in the communists' 'local government' reforms of 1975.

The first three post-Solidarity governments have been criticized for slow progress in dealing with the issues of the extension and further reform of local self-government and also the linked need to reform the state administration (Taras, 1993). Some of these criticisms were, perhaps, unreasonable, because there were, of course, many other urgent matters demanding the attention and energy of administrators and politicians; and it is clear that many of the new political leadership, including Balcerowicz himself, were well-disposed to the development of strong local self-government.[2] But the Suchocka coalition gave the reform of public administration increased priority. Michal Kulesza was appointed plenipotentiary for administration reform.

A strategy document was presented by the Public Administration Reform Office in early 1993 and accepted by the government. The document was critical of the current structure of public administration because it was still based on what it saw as excessive compartmentalized departmentalism which militated against the integrated consideration of issues and also resisted decentralization of responsibilities towards local government. It identified the following areas as priorities for reform:

a) creation of a rational centre of decision-making inside the government;
b) clear demarcation between political and permanent administrative posts within the government machinery;
c) ensuring compatibility between methods of managing public administration and the market economy;
d) creation of a system of public procurement in order to ensure rationality and cost-effectiveness in public administration;
e) rationalization of structures aiming at the elimination of special territorial units of departmental administration;
f) creation of a second tier of local government – the *powiat* – in order to decentralize a wide array of powers;
g) the establishment of clear guidelines for recruitment and career development in the civil service;
h) the improvement of information and data systems in order to give both public administrators and citizens an information base for effective understanding and decision-making.

Thus the government presented a legislative package to the *Sejm* to help achieve a number of these goals. Most notably the package included

• the creation of a Prime Minister's Cabinet Office and a General Government Secretariat;
• the creation of a small and permanent apolitical core of civil service staff;
• the creation of a Public Procurement Office to supervise and monitor all government purchasing;
• the decentralization of a wide range of functions performed by the state administration to a new second tier of local government, the *powiaty*.

The *powiat* Proposal and the Pilot Programme

Three hundred *powiaty* were planned. They were to be directly elected and to have responsibility for health (the running of hospitals and clinics), education, environmental protection, public safety, public libraries, theatres, shelters for the poor and a further range of minor powers currently dealt with by *rejony*. Together these would result in local self-government almost doubling its share of public expenditure to nearly 30 per cent. The elections were to be held in May 1994 and the *powiaty* to begin operation in January 1995.

In advance of this general programme the government set in motion in July 1993 a plan to give all cities with populations above 100,000 *powiat* status by the beginning of 1994. This would effectively create a new local government structure in these cities. The rationale for this advance implementation was twofold. First, it was argued that these cities already had the ability to cope with the transfer of functions. Second, operation of *powiat* powers would help the government monitor the effects of the new powers on local government ahead of the general introduction in the rest of the country. It was planned that finance equivalent to existing costs of taken-over functions would be provided, but that grants would not be earmarked, thereby leaving cities with the freedom to re-allocate resources if they found this appropriate.

Participation in the pilot programme was to be voluntary – based on agreements signed between the central government, voivodship authorities and the local authority. A deadline for signing agreements was set for 30 October 1993. By the time of the September 1993 parliamentary elections, 29 of the possible 46 cities had signed agreements.

The Suchocka government also set up a Central–Local Government Commission to examine and advise on all issues relating to the interface between central and local government.

The September 1993 Parliamentary Elections: Developments under the new Government

However, the comprehensive victory of the post-communist parties – the Social Democrats and the Peasant Party, or SLD and PSL – in the parliamentary elections and their formation of the new governing coalition was immediately marked by an interruption to this path of reform. The smaller PSL conceded control of the main economic ministries to the SLD, but won control of the Prime Minister's post – taken by PSL leader, Waldemar Pawlak – and achieved a dominant position in the public administration, with the post of chief of the Council of Ministers' Office going to the PSL's Michal Strak. Pawlak immediately sent a fax to voivods ordering them to suspend the pilot programme. Subsequently, after a challenge by the Democratic Union, a government directive moved the deadline for signing agreements from 30 October to 20 December. But the government indicated in its earliest months that it wished to scale back the pilot programme. In the event, various changes were made to the previously outlined programme, with substantial retentions by the state of educational, health and cultural facilities. There was a significant scaling down of financial support below that previously allocated and spent under the state management, which led to many refusals to take over specific institutions by the towns, unwilling to have their own ongoing investment projects curtailed. Funds were also now to be channelled through various ministries, rather than aggregated and channelled through the voivod as previously envisaged. The new procedures for deciding and transferring funds have been criticized as extremely bureaucratic and inefficient (*Wspolnota*, 26 February 1994). In secondary education, the effective scaling back of the pilot programme was substantial: although 43 of the potential 46 towns eventually took part in the programme and 624 secondary schools were taken over, in 11 towns no secondary schools were taken over. Many more cultural institutions remained with the centre than had been envisaged before the September elections.[3]

There were other signs of a reduced willingness to decentralize. First, the new Education Minister stated that he wished to leave *gminy* the possibility of postponing the takeover of primary school management that was to have been completed by the start of 1994. Second, Strak proposed that the overhaul of administration, and the creation of *powiaty*, be postponed until the potential costs could be better understood and the political situation became more stable. This was accompanied by much hostile rhetoric from the PSL members of the *Sejm* towards the actual details of the *powiaty* proposals (and the planned reduction in the number of voivodships) and questioning whether they were appropriate or best.

Political considerations appear to have entered in a number of ways into the coalition's decisions with respect to local government (Sabbat-

Swidlicka, 1994a). Thus Strak accompanied his initial thinking on the desirability of postponing the *powiat* reform by arguing that a precondition for any further reform should be 'an outcome of the local government elections (then due to be held in May 1994) thanks to which a wider spectrum of political parties would be represented, (*Rzeczpospolita*, 29 October 1993). This is, of course, reflecting the fact that in the May 1990 local elections the post-communist parties did extremely badly and the elections were won in many cases by candidates sponsored by Solidarity citizens' committees (see Chapter 7 for a study of the aftermath of one such victory). A second example has been in the PSL's approach to voivod appointments. From the outset a desire was expressed to have the profile of voivods reflecting the outcome of the 1993 parliamentary elections. This 'spoils' approach to voivod appointments has been implemented with a steady stream of dismissals of incumbents and appointments of coalition–approved candidates with a record of membership in the post-communist parties in the months since the parliamentary election. Political considerations also entered strongly in a late attempt to change the electoral law prior to the 1994 local elections (Sabbat-Swidlicka, 1994b), and in relation to the transfer of schools to local government and the reform of education, the subject to which we now turn.

The Education Problem

It is worth giving specific attention to the education issue as it symbolizes most trenchantly the pressures against decentralization of responsibilities to *gminy*, the pilot programme cities, and (ultimately) *powiaty* being exerted on the new government. Primary and secondary education are also commonly 'located' in the local government sector in most Western countries, and education, therefore, provides a measure of how far the Polish system is moving towards the typical Western democratic model of local government.

The Polish education system, rather like many industries inherited from the communist period, is characterized by low levels of efficiency and productivity, and suffered from a striking structural mismatch to contemporary needs after 1989. This is perhaps most starkly illustrated by the fact that there are many teachers of Russian, for which there is now a very low demand – although it continues to be the most widely taught foreign language – and many fewer teachers of English, for which there is a very high demand.[4] The existing system also included a large number of vocational secondary schools, run by each ministry, designed to train skilled labour for each branch or industry. These schools did not provide a good general education and after 1989 became of increasingly doubtful relevance.

Polish education is marked by a shortage of schools and classroom space, and children are taught in two or three daily shifts. However, teachers work comparatively short hours and pupil: teacher ratios are very low. Teacher recruitment had, in addition, been rather arbitrary, and about half had not completed university. The worsening condition of the state budget after 1989 and a decline in the share of education to less than 9 per cent of the budget also led to a deterioration in the material conditions of schools and the education infrastructure – most schools incurred large debts and have unpaid electricity, heating and phone bills – and in the relative and real levels of pay of teachers. Teachers do have, however, as well as short working hours, a number of privileges, such as almost free first-class rail travel, given to them in a Teachers' Charter drawn up in 1982.

The Suchocka government decided to tackle the education problem and the Ministry of Education prepared a reform programme for the rationalization of organization and expenditure, which was linked to the improvement in both teachers' and schools' material conditions. The Suchocka government approved this programme in March 1993. It envisaged a system of secondary education with the Ministry responsible for regulation, including the setting of academic standards, school curriculum and required teacher qualifications, coordination, and supervision – the latter to be carried out in each voivodship by *kuratorzy* (inspectors). Administration and the management of schools, including the payment of non-teaching costs, was to be transferred to local governments, but with teachers' salaries paid from the central budget.

The plan's success depended crucially upon the reorganization of the teachers' grading system, salary scales and promotion system, according to qualifications and performance. In place of the existing system, whereby tenure was given after three years' service, tenure was to be given to new teachers only after 18 years' service; existing staff were given guaranteed contracts only until June 1998. Those without the new qualification requirements – a three-year teacher training for primary school teachers and a university degree for secondary school teachers – were given until the year 2000 to acquire them. Hours worked were to be increased from 18 to about 40 per week, 18 to 22 of which would be classroom teaching.

This plan for the teaching profession met great opposition from the near half-million teachers, especially the 300,000 membership of the previously communist-sponsored union, the ZNP. A dispute over pay in 1993 led to a teachers' strike, which – alongside disputes by other budget sector workers – led the Solidarity Union in May 1993 to propose the no-confidence vote, the carrying of which was the immediate cause of the dissolution of the *Sejm*.

The ZNP joined the post-communist SLD election coalition and 32 of its members were among the 173 SLD candidates who secured seats in the *Sejm*. This was bound to give the ZNP a significant voice in the question of education reform.

The ZNP's first action was to argue, successfully – as we noted above – against the compulsory transfer of primary schools by 1 January 1994, mainly on the grounds of school indebtedness and local governments' unwillingness to take them over. In fact, they feared that the takeover would reduce their bargaining power, and that local governments would have greater incentives for reform, reducing privileges embodied in the Teachers' Charter.

Although the opposition to the compulsory transfer was successful, many local governments had already voluntarily taken over primary schools: 345 had done so by 1993 and another 290 authorities did so for 1 January 1994. Together they now account for nearly one-third of primary schools, 35 per cent of primary schoolchildren, and 40 per cent of primary schoolteachers (Jezowki, 1994).

What is particularly interesting is that various official technical examinations and, indeed, a government-sponsored opinion survey have found that there have been significant and noticeable improvements in the management and conditions of schools after transfer to local government supervision.

An Uncertain Future

Aside from the various hostile statements towards the previous *powiaty* proposal, it has remained difficult to define precisely the position of the PSL and its leadership as regards administrative reform. Thus, although the chairman of the URM, Michal Strak, stated at the PSL's National Local Self-government Conference in March 1994 that the creation of *powiaty* in January 1995, as previously envisaged, would be just a pure political and economic adventure, no alternative vision or hint of a proposal was put forward. This opposition to *powiaty* is not shared by the leaders of the SLD, and it is an opposition which, as Michal Kulesza himself has said, is difficult to understand given that it is in the rural areas, where the PSL are strongest, that local power is being most circumscribed. The PSL leadership stated that the issue would have to be solved during preparation of the new Polish constitution. Instead, reorganization of the central administration was identified as the primary target of the new government (*Wspolnota*, 12 March 1994). Eventually when legislative proposals finally emerged they concentrated exclusively on the organization of the Council of Ministers, the local state administration and the state civil service; *powiaty* were not even mentioned. On this evidence the strengthening of local self-government has suffered a long postponement and the tameness of the proposals finally induced the resignation of Michal Kulesza from his post as plenipotentiary for administration reform. He stated that, in his opinion, the decentralization of the state had basically stopped in Poland. He also condemned the re-creation by Strak of a common feature of the communist period in Poland: the politicization of the civil service. His open resignation letter makes it clear that there had been many months of non-cooperation and obstruction of his work by Strak: only one conversation between Strak and Kulesza had been held in over six months (Kulesza 1994).

A survey, in mid-April 1994, by SMG/KRC Poland (*Wspolnota*, 4 June 1994), however, appears to indicate that there is a substantial majority in favour of administrative reform and further decentralization: 72 per cent of respondents regarded further changes in public administration as necessary, whilst only 15 per cent thought that further changes would have negative results. The report does, however, indicate that those with lower education are far more likely to hold the latter negative view than those with higher education. An even greater majority – 80 per cent against 9 per cent – favoured 'as much public money as possible' being spent according to the decisions of local self-governments, rather than according to those of central government.[5]

Appendix

Structure of Polish local government

The legislation did not alter the territorial division of Polish local government introduced in 1975, based on the two-tier structure of 49 voivods and a lower tier of 2,121 *gminy* (rural communes) and 819 *miasta* (towns), which in 572 cases formed joint town-communes. Warsaw was divided into 7 *dzielnica* (districts). This gave 2,375 basic units of lower level administration – the units of local self-government. Table 6A1 shows the average and ranges of population, area and population density for these units.

Table 6A1: Regional and local government units in Poland

	Voivodships	Miasta	Gminy
Population ('000)			
• Average	774	28	6.9
• Maximum	3954	1651	24.7
• Minimum	245	0.8	0.4
Area (sq km)			
• Average	6367	25	138
• Maximum	12327	458	575
• Minimum	1523	1	19
Population density (per sq km)			
• Average	114	1147	50
• Maximum	748	4446	475
• Minimum	45	31	2

Source: Swianiewicz (1992).

Finance of Polish local government

The 1990 legislation has provided local authorities with four principal categories of income:

a) *local taxes*: on property, on motor vehicles, on dogs, on inheritance and donations and on economic activity. Most local authorities also benefit from the proceeds of an agriculture tax and receive revenues from municipal property and from local fees and charges. In Poland many exemptions exist in the case of the payment of local taxes. An example with significant effects is that farmers are exempt from local property taxes on the strength of their payment of agriculture tax. Consequently, some local authorities in rural areas have no significant local tax resources, as the level of agriculture tax can be very low indeed.

b) *assigned shares of national taxation*: in 1990 there were 5 shared taxes:

- 5 per cent share of the revenue from national tax on legal entities;
- 30 per cent share of the revenue from national tax on wages, salaries, and the equalization tax paid by employers (3 taxes);
- 50 per cent share of the revenue from the national personal income tax, paid only by individuals who have 'independent' sources of income (such as people with their own commercial businesses or those in professions such as the law, architecture, etc.).

However, following national tax reforms many of the above were abolished on 31 December 1991 and now local authorities have shares in only two national taxes:

- 5 per cent share of the revenue from national tax on legal entities;[6]
- 15 per cent share of the revenue from the new national personal income tax.

c) *earmarked (specific) grants* from the central government relate to the provision of responsibilities delegated to them by the central government. They are not usually sufficient to enable the local authority to finance a minimum level of provision of the service delegated to it. In respect to delegated responsibilities they are not included in the local government component of public expenditure but are included in that relating to central government.

d) *general grants* are paid by the central government to local authorities. They are based on a formula linked to the population of local authorities and an element intended to achieve some degree of financial equalization between local authorities with varying tax capacities. It is provided to local authorities which have less than 85 per cent of the national average of tax income per capita. The financial equalization grant itself is 90 per cent of the difference between the individual local authority's tax revenue per capita and the national average. Local authorities with a high financial capacity are obliged to pay into the financial equalization fund only if their per capita tax resources are over 150 per cent of the national average. Although in principle the other element of the general grant should be based upon a formula linked to the population of local authorities, in practice wide discretion is exercised in its distribution.

Local authorities may borrow from commercial banks to assist in the financing of local authority activities. In the case of current expenditure, loans are limited to 8 per cent of planned expenditure in the first half of a year and to 4 per cent in the second half. In the case of capital expenditure, the annual credit costs may not exceed 5 per cent of planned expenditure.

There is, in fact, a high emphasis in Poland on central government-oriented financial policy and a relatively low emphasis placed on the financial autonomy of local authorities and on equalization of resources between local authorities.[7] Thus, most of the local taxes are subject to tax rate ceilings set by central government. In addition, there are many exemption provisions in, as well as complicated schedules in a number of, local taxes. This, as well as the fact that with tax diversity tax yields are small, means that tax administration costs are inordinately high.

Table 6A2: Poland – *Gminy* budgets: outturn 1991, estimated outturn 1992, Plan 1993 (mn. old zloties)

	1991	1992	1993
'Own' Local Taxes and Charges	**22784.1**	**29960.5**	**43501.9**
Property Tax	7658.2	11737.0	16431.8
Agricultural Tax	1959.7	1500.0	3322.7
Vehicles Tax	555.1	1991.2	2027.5
Karta Podatkowa (Local Business Taxes)	1180.7	1903.9	2703.6
Administrative charges and Stamp Duties	2307.3	3761.9	5341.9
Other Incomes	9123.1	9066.6	12874.6

Shared National Revenues	14490.2	13622.5	20858.1
Interpersonal Income			
Equalization Tax	339.2		
Personal Income Tax	1676.9	12264.7	18476.4
Wages/Payroll Tax	6861.1		
Enterprise Income Tax	5613.0	1357.8	2381.6
Incomes before central grants	37274.3	43583.0	64360.0
General Grants-in-aid	6771.1	7571.2	10700.0
Subsidies and Specific Grants	6007.8	N/A	N/A
Total Incomes	50053.2		
Total Expenditures	44788.2	53011.5	74494.8

Source: Ministerstwo Finansów (1992); Wieczorkowska, (1992).

Notes

1. Delegated powers include the registration of births, deaths and marriages and the provision of identity cards.
2. Thus Balcerowicz stated in his inaugural lecture at the Main School of Commerce, Warsaw, given in September 1992, that 'In this transition process it is crucial ... to build up a system of genuine local self-government ... it is very important because it lies on the crossroads between politics and the economy. [Local self-government] is an important school of democracy as well as a school of sound management and daring initiative' (Balcerowicz, 1994).
3. Thus according to the instruction from September 1994, only 31 institutions of this kind, with all-Polish and regional character (financed by voivods), were not going to be transferred to *gminy*. The new government, introducing correction into the programme, reduced its extent by excluding voivodships' libraries and the majority of theatres and museums. Finally the list of exclusions covered 154 institutions.
4. Such demand for languages is being met extensively in the free market.
5. The respondents also generally valued the *wojt*, *burmistrz* or president of their own town more highly than the prime minister. Trust in the representatives of local government was declared by 45 per cent of respondents, whereas trust in the prime minister was declared by 35 per cent of respondents. Still less credibility appeared to be given to voivods and members of parliament for respondents' own constituencies: voivods were trusted by only 27 per cent of respondents, and members of parliament from their own constituency by only 24 per cent of inhabitants.
6. The tax share was set at 2 per cent for the period April to December 1992.
7. There is some degree of equalization among *gminy* within voivods owing to the operation of the shared national personal income tax where the proceeds are distributed to *gminy*, within each voivod, on the basis of population rather than on the basis of actual tax raised in each individual *gmina*. This tends to assist rural *gminy*.

References

Balcerowicz, Leszek (1994), 'Democracy is no Substitute for Capitalism', *Eastern European Economics*, 32:2, pp. 39–49.
Cielecka, Anna and John Gibson (1994), 'Local Government in Poland', in Andrew Coulson (ed.), *Local Government in Eastern Europe*, Aldershot: Edward Elgar.
GUS (Annual), *Rocznik Statystyczny Wojewodztw*, Glowny Urzad Statystyczny, Warsaw. (GUS, 1993).
Gorzelak, Grzegorz and Krzysztof Mularczyk (1991), *Polish Local Government Reform*, Foundation in Support of Local Democracy, International Union of Local Authorities, Warszawa and The Hague.
Jezowski, Antoni (1994), 'Gminy zatrudniaja 40 proc. nauczycieli', *Wspolnota*, 20/218, 14 May.
Kulesza, Michal (1994), 'Dlaczego Rezygnuje', *Wspolnota*, 22/220, 28 May.
Ministerstwo Finansów (1992), *Ustawa o finansach gmin*, Ministerstwo Finansow, Departament Budzetu Panstwa, Warszawa, 27 July.
Sabbat-Swidlicka, Anna (1994a), 'Education Reform in Poland', *RFE/RL Research Report*, 3:3 pp. 43–7.
— (1994b), 'Local elections Redress Political Imbalance in Poland', *RFE/RL Research Report*, 3:27 pp. 1–8.
Swianiewicz, Pawel (1992), 'The Polish Experience of Local Democracy: Is Progress being Made?', *Policy and Politics*, 20:2, pp. 87–98.
Taras, Wojciech (1993), 'Changes in Polish Public Administration 1989–1992, *Public Administration*, 71, pp. 13–32.
Vinton, Louisa (1993), 'Poland's New Government: Continuity or Reversal', *RFE/RL Research Report*, 2:46, pp. 1–7.
Wieczorkowska, Anna (1992), 'Utrwalanie Prowizorium', *Zycie Gospardarcze*, 6 December.

7. Citizens' Committees in the Process of Formation of Local Power: A Polish Case Study

Andrzej Bukowski

The round table talks initiated at the beginning of 1989 by representatives of the Communist Party and opposition resulted in the political compact which opened the way to evolution of the communist system. Partly democratic parliamentary elections, held in June, rendered it possible to form a government with the first prime minister in the post-war history of Poland who enjoyed social support and was not nominated by the communists. A reform of the most important institutions of social life was begun, with a view to building a democratic system.

The general philosophy of the systemic and civil reforms that were started in Poland then can be described with the help of concepts which characterize the planned course of changes in four basic domains of the social life. I employ here a typology proposed by Jan Kubiak (1991). His grouping of change is:

1. pluralization (politics);
2. decentralization (administration);
3. privatization (economy);
4. diversification (culture).

At the local level these tendencies would find their expression in the following processes:

a) autonomization of local power structures;
b) creation of local administration and empowering it with a separate range of powers;
c) communalization of property;
d) restoration of local and regional diversities and differences.

The self-government reform begun at the beginning of 1990 constituted

one of the most important legal and political methods of implementing
the plans presented above. There were three objectives that the
originators of the self-government reform had in mind. First, they
aimed to reconstruct an administration which had grown weak in
communist times and was fitted only to implement the policies of the
totalitarian state. Under the new law, the power of the central state
administration was considerably reduced, and simultaneously some of
the centre's past prerogatives were transferred to local government.
Moreover, implementation of the law which introduced the changes in
the organization of administration provided a pretext for evaluation and
selection of members of the bureaucratic apparatus, who were
sometimes accused of boycotting decisions of the non-communist
government.

Second, at the same time, there were numerous struggles and
manoeuvres over the control of local communities. Before the local
elections, local administration was dominated by old political
connections from the communist epoch. Councillors and Heads of
Communes (mayors) were either members of the Communist Party or
at least enjoyed the party's support. A widely shared conviction that
nothing had changed sprang from the fact that the old *nomenklatura*,
which had not been legitimized by democratic elections, was still in
power. Hence, for the Solidarity elite, local elections were the
continuation of the political struggle with communism, and public
approval for 'Solidarity' at that time gave them a good chance of
winning. The new power elite tried to ensure that the old political class
disappeared from the scene – local, as well as national.

Third, perhaps the most important objective was to involve citizens
in the process of democratization by granting full rights of self-
government to local communities. The reform of self-government was
to provide an antidote to the passivity of people by making it possible
for them to participate directly or indirectly in the process of making
decisions about local, everyday problems. According to this conception,
efficient self-government would demonstrate to the people the essence
and value of the democratic system, while their active participation in
the work of self-government was to become a school of civic
responsibility. The natural consequence of the Local Government Act
coming into effect was the local elections held two months later – the
first fully democratic local elections in Poland.

The present chapter provides analysis of a conflict in a Silesian town
almost immediately after the local elections. It brought about the final

split of two victorious Solidarity groupings which had entered the elections as a coalition. This event, apart from its local specifics, has also a wider supra-local aspect, which is twofold. First, it sheds light on similar phenomena that occurred in other towns and communes all over the country. On the other hand, it cannot be explained without referring to factors of a global nature, characteristic of the society as a whole.

Conflict in Racibórz: The Course of Events

The first legal, independent structures began to be created in Racibórz in 1989. Factory organizations of Solidarity were being founded at that time. On 24 April 1989, eight of them created the Local Coordinating Commission (TKK) of the independent self-governing trades union Solidarity. On 8 May, in the face of approaching parliamentary elections, the TKK together with opposition activists connected mainly with the church Ministry of Working People, and with some political newcomers, brought into being a Citizens' Committee in the town of Racibórz. The functions of a Citizens' Committee included all kinds of pre-election activities within the Solidarity coalition. A formal note stated that the Citizens' Committee was created by the TKK in order to underline the trade-union roots of this form of civil activity. Already, at this stage, there arose a personal conflict between the chairman of the Citizens' Committee and the leader of the TKK. The former – a man with a background in the humanities and interested in art – is spontaneous, dynamic and uncompromising. The latter – an engineer and a pragmatist – is flexible in his actions, self-possessed and resolute. Both are known in the town as splendid organizers, although each of them in his own field. The controversy concerned the way in which the Citizens' Committee was to operate in a town still dominated by representatives of the communist *nomenklatura*. The chairman of the Citizens' Committee opted for radical solutions that antagonized supporters of both the old and the new order. The leader of the TKK was for limited cooperation with the Communist Party for the sake of the town and its inhabitants' welfare.

After the June 1989 elections the coalition fell apart. Some activists of the Citizens' Committee together with its chairman decided, contrary to suggestions from the National Executive Committee of Solidarity to create a new organization, independent of the TKK, named Citizens'

Committee Solidarity. This provided a new motive for conflict. The TKK was against the use of the trade-union symbol in independent bodies (especially activity that was independent of Solidarity's structures). However, the registration decision of the court was irreversible.

Before the local elections, the problem of a possible coalition of groupings originating from Solidarity arose again. Once more they decided to join forces in such a way that both the TKK and the Citizens' Committee Solidarity were to conduct internal elections and to form a joint list. In this way all seats in the future Town Council were filled by Solidarity candidates. Moreover, it was decided that the 'team' constituted by the Citizens' Committee Solidarity and the TKK should also include representatives of the Association of People of German Origin, which was one of the most powerful social organizations in the region.

Election results confirmed the correctness of the pre-election coalition tactic. Reformist groupings were successful, obtaining 27 of the 34 Council seats. The rest of the seats were gained by the PSL (Polish Peasants' Party), by KPN (Confederation for an Independent Poland) – each getting two seats – and by independent candidates. Organizations of communist provenance suffered total defeat, as they did not manage to secure a seat in the Council for any of their candidates. It should be noted that the three candidates representing the population of German origin won on average three times more votes than other members of the coalition. Obviously, their supporters were the most active and disciplined.

In the atmosphere created by the coalition's victory and the defeat of the outgoing political elite, a session was held during which the town mayor was to be chosen. Neither of the leaders of the two main coalition groupings ran for the post. However, they proposed and actively supported different candidates – well-known local politicians. It proved impossible to elect a mayor in either the first or the second round of voting. During the third round, the candidate of the TKK resigned claiming that he was 'not Jaruzelski, to be chosen by a majority of one vote'. The candidate proposed by the Citizens' Committee Solidarity thus became the mayor.

Leaving aside what happened behind the scenes of the meeting (i.e. various and changing alliances), I will concentrate on the most interesting aspect, the political consequences of the mayor's election. After the election, the TKK and factory commissions of Solidarity in the town went into open opposition to the mayor and the Commune Board. Almost every step taken by the local authorities was criticized by the TKK. In the light of this situation it seems interesting to present interpretations of the origins of the conflict provided by the two main adversaries. With each of them I conducted a three-hour interview. I did not ask openly about the reasons for the split so as not to arouse suspicions, or provoke a disinclination to talk or any evasion on their part. Thus, I asked indirect questions and, on the basis of those fragments of conversations that concerned the conflict, I have summarized them as follows.

Arguments of the chairman of the Citizens' Committee Solidarity against the TKK:

- the TKK consists of representatives of large factories which want to dominate the town;
- the TKK is very conservative in action, we are go-ahead. We are the trail-blazers;
- there is nobody to defend culture. The Council is dominated by technicians.

Arguments of the leader of the TKK against the Citizens' Committee Solidarity:

- experts are needed, and not just activists behaving in a dilettante fashion;
- there are no activists of the old school any more. The mayor, instead of starting to work immediately after he had been chosen, went on holiday;
- I do not like the style of work of the chairman of the Citizens' Committee. He has a background in humanities, I am a technocrat – perhaps that is the reason.

As anyone can see, there is hardly a reference to differences of substance dividing the two sides. In fact, both adversaries have a similar vision of the town and commune and even have the same concrete ideas on how to solve local problems. However, those fragments of their utterances which refer to their opponents are dominated by personal and ideological contentions that obscure the real reasons why activists from the same political tradition decided to split.

So we must pose a question: do the arguments presented above justify such antagonism? It is also curious that the conflict flared up anew after the clear victory of the coalition, when it seemed that the only thing to be done was to seal the alliance by sharing out the key posts in the town. Is it possible that the identity of the elected mayor and the withdrawal of his opponent made nonsense of their shared past in Solidarity? In order to settle these questions we must refer to the wider social context, examining the history of opposition activities in the commune, and look beneath the surface of the conflict, thus freeing ourselves from official interpretations.

Conflict in Racibórz – Social and Political Background

Racibórz is a middle-sized town, inhabited by 65,000 people. It is opulent and well looked after, which distinguishes it from most other Polish towns of similar size. Its geographical situation and relative isolation from other centres are conducive to the creation of local bonds. Racibórz is an industrial centre; there are two factories belonging to the main industry and many middle-sized enterprises. Agriculture is limited mostly to market gardening and fruit-farming, which is the reason why the region is considered to be the garden of Silesia. Before privatization was started, the trade network was not well developed. Handicrafts, apart from cooperatives, were weak owing to the loss of an old tradition which had been severed by the war.

It is worthwhile to underline a cultural division between long-established inhabitants, biased towards their contacts with families in Germany (for a long time Racibórz was affected by emigration) and people who settled there, mostly after the war. The latter outnumber the former, but the former are socially and culturally dominant. The social structure in Racibórz is determined by socio-occupational factors. People in farming, handicrafts, trade or private entrepreneurship still constitute a small percentage of the working population of the town. The main influence on the social and political life of the local community is exerted by state employees working either in state enterprises or in the social services sector. They constitute a group of 22–25,000 people out of 30,000 in employment. The occupational structure in the town reflects the fact that, alongside many industrial enterprises, mentioned above, Racibórz possesses many state institutions, rather a lot, indeed, for such a small centre. Suffice it to say that there are 16 primary schools in the town, eight secondary schools, a university's subsidiary campus, a big hospital and several health service centres, and many cultural, sport and recreation centres.

The general division into the social services sector and the industrial sector is reflected in the specifics of political representation in the commune. The Solidarity camp was made up of representatives of both those groups. On the one hand, there are teachers, physicians, people employed in cultural centres, and on the other hand, technical and managerial staff (not workers) in the large enterprises. From their speech, one might assume that what really differentiates them is the kind of social circle they belong to, rather than their educational background. Both groups have created networks of a professional, personal or social nature, constituting as a whole an intellectual and opinion-making counter-elite for the former decision-making centres in the town. The complementary qualifications of the people constituting the new elite enabled them to curb effectively the activities of the former authorities of the town and commune and to familiarize themselves with the complicated problems of the local environment. Nevertheless, while specifying problem areas which are potential bones of contention between 'public servants' and 'technocrats' – as I will call them briefly – we must consider:

1) animosities connected with the economic situation of the two groups;
2) attitudes towards the past;
3) kinds and areas of public activity;
4) attitudes towards current reforms.

Economic Situation of the Two Groups

It was extremely difficult to obtain from my interlocutors information from which one might compare their financial situation with that of other socio-occupational groups. However, the problem hung in the air. And as it soon turned out, there had been an affair which caused a serious stir in Racibórz and which concerned precisely these economic inequalities.

The management and staff of one of the two biggest factories decided to try to privatize. The good financial condition of the enterprise, and buoyant foreign orders, encouraged the Board of Directors to take steps leading to privatization. A substantial part of its shares was to be allocated to the management and employees. Although attempts to get the Ministries of Industry and Privatization to give permission were unsuccessful, the very fact of the enterprise trying to privatize irritated other social groups, especially the teachers and physicians. Wages in the enterprises were already above local rural, and most urban, incomes.

During my interviews with representatives of these circles, I heard many bitter remarks about differences in earnings between highly educated groups of teachers or doctors, on the one hand, and workers whose pay was two or three times higher on the other hand – and who were additionally given enormous bonuses to get round the POPIWEK (an acronym which stands for the 'tax on excess income', a tax-based incomes policy instrument imposing penal taxes on employers who increase wages by more than a prescribed percentage). These attacks were directed not so much towards engineers or managers, but rather towards the discrepancy between one's education and one's financial standing. I think, however, that the hidden resentment could be transferred to the 'technocrats', who were also a financially privileged group.

Attitudes towards the Past

My respondents generally agreed that the communist system had to collapse. They were not so unanimous, however, in their evaluations of it. 'Public servants' claimed in unison that the system was disastrous for the nation and the state. In contrast, 'technocrats' varied on that subject. Many of them believe that the previous period should not be condemned out of hand. Many valuable initiatives and investments were, they would say, realized at that time. Channels of promotion, limited as they were, still enabled many specialists to pursue their professional careers. Though, of course, contemporary reality was full of absurdities, there were ways of neutralizing or avoiding them.

Generally, the two attitudes may be defined as fundamental and pragmatic. The former refers to such intrinsic values as freedom, justice and truth, and from that point of view pronounces a severe judgement on the past. The latter analyses the previous epoch in the light of pragmatic values, concentrating on everyday life, with all its ambiguity and complexity. Criticism is directed at the system's inefficiency, with an emphasis on unwise decisions or defective structural and organizational arrangements.

Kinds and Areas of Public Activity

In the course of their opposition activity, the activists of both factions worked out different, though complementary, methods of work. For teachers' circles it was, of course, educational activity: various forms of lectures, seminars, meetings with people of science or culture, organized mainly under the auspices of the Church, either by Clubs of the Catholic Intelligentsia (KIK) or by Ministries of Working People. The main stress was put upon development of civil self-consciousness and immunization against the influence of communist ideology. On the other hand, representatives of the industrial sector focused their attention on increasing the economic independence of state enterprises and on creating enclaves of private entrepreneurship. They also dealt with workers' problems in factories.

Different kinds of activity were reflected in the two approaches to concrete problems and in rules according to which the hierarchy of these problems was addressed. Representatives of the social services sector gave priority to culture, education of the younger generation and protection of the people by ensuring an adequate level of health care. As far as the last point is concerned, their objectives were close to those of the 'technocrats', who concentrate, however upon protection of the natural environment and technological changes in those factories which are the most harmful to their neighbourhood. Nevertheless, the 'technocrats' attach much greater importance to economic, financial and property transformations.

Attitudes to Reform

According to the 'public servants', Balcerowicz's fiscal policy was the only effective way to overcome the crisis. Let inefficient Polish producers go bankrupt and foreign goods and capital enter our market, rather than allow domestic monopolies to operate unhindered, which would manifest itself in price rises and a drop in production. 'Technocrats' have different views. Polish enterprises need the state's assistance, they argue. They cannot be blamed for their outdated technologies, the lack of markets and the low quality of their products. Closing down factories will be of no avail, as unemployment will only perpetuate recession.

Issues concerning national politics do not in general arouse distinct controversies. But the two interlocutors have different opinions, especially as far as Mazowiecki's 'thick dividing line' is concerned. The chairman of the Citizens' Committee Solidarity is against going easy on communists; the leader of the TKK supports this political strategy.

The divergences of opinion described above are a generalized model. I became acquainted with them on the basis of conversations, interviews, documents and press publications relating to both sides of the conflict. As with every model, the one presented here also runs the risk of over-simplification or ambiguity. Its function is not to explain the phenomenon, but rather to describe it more clearly, which in this case means identifying the basic dividing lines that exist somewhere in the whole spectrum of arguments and conflicts conducted on various levels and many fronts.

The division seems in fact to stem from different political styles. The Citizens' Committee in Racibórz proved too narrow an organizational form to accommodate the two approaches. Thus it was that the 'public servants' freed themselves from the tutelage of the TKK and created their own organizational structure, called the Citizens' Committee Solidarity. The pre-election coalition had been felt by both sides to be necessary in face of what were still seen as the dangerous political forces of the old system. After the elections, when the danger had passed, nothing stood in the way of direct confrontation. The opportunity arose soon enough. Candidates for the office of town mayor put up by Citizens' Committee Solidarity and by the TKK Solidarity were the embodiment of the differences between the two organizations. The candidate of the former was a psychologist, an employee of the Educational Centre for socially maladjusted youths, a local self-government campaigner, a socially-minded humanist (he had also studied theology and philosophy), and an activist of the Labour Party (*Stronnictwo Pracy*). His opponent was a food-industry engineer who had received some training in the USA and Holland. He had been working in industry for a long time, in posts of authority. He had received both professional and state awards. He was an excellent organizer. In addition he had a track record of standing up against the old regime. In October 1981, as a Solidarity candidate, he had been chosen by the People's Town Council as mayor. He had not, however, taken up the office because of the imposition of martial law.

It seemed at the outset that the TKK candidate had a good chance of success. However, during the session a question arose which galvanized the debate. The candidate of the Citizens' Committee Solidarity declared that, if elected, he would remove from the local administration representatives of the old *nomenklatura*, and he would sever all relations with them. The candidate of the TKK, faced with this challenge, began to be suspected of sympathizing with the communists, especially as he had become the president of a company generally supposed to have been founded by members of the communist *nomenklatura*. During the session this matter came to the fore.

It had been known for a long time that in the commune and its surroundings, especially in the farming and food sector, in the last few years many '*nomenklatura* companies' had been formed by functionaries of the Communist Party apparatus and the managerial staff of some enterprises. Their cooperation, which had lasted for a long time, assumed the form of private economic activity. Without directly threatening state enterprises (except to the extent that the latter's assets had already been made use of), '*nomenklatura* companies' created a network of semi-formal economic and personal links. The managers of these companies, with their established connections with the old elite, joined state enterprise managers in lobbying the government. The state enterprises wanted subsidies and protection, while the managers of '*nomenklatura* companies' wanted to gain politically with their help.

On the local level, strong organizational and personal connections with this lobby encouraged representatives of the outgoing power to go onto the counter-offensive after losing the elections. They decided to take advantage of cleavages in the victorious coalition, focusing on the TKK candidate, who had a strong position in the new structure of power and who, as a so-called pragmatist, could guarantee their maintaining a certain control in the town (for example, by leaving some appointments in the local administration unchanged). At the session these intrigues were disclosed. Thereafter, despite the pre-session predominance of the TKK candidate, the voting was evenly balanced. The further course of the debate has already been related.

Conflict in Racibórz: The Wider Context

The local socio-political background presented above cannot by itself answer all questions about the sources of the conflict. In particular:

does this conflict reflect cleavages between the most important local groups and interests, or is it merely a squabble amongst narrow groupings and circles interested mainly in getting and keeping power?

Actually these are two slightly different although closely connected questions. The first one concerns the nature of divergences which occurred on the local political scene. The second one refers to the problem of political representation, and thus to the process of creating the local power elite.

Ideological and Economic sources of the Conflict

On the basis of the material presented above we may conclude that the main dividing line between the hostile groups was not so much to do with everyday life and the problems connected with it, as with norms and beliefs. This may be seen both in the different perceptions of economic and political reforms and, above all, in the evaluation of the previous system and in attitudes towards its functionaries. The opinions presented here reflect a certain community of beliefs within each of the groups. This, on the other hand, refers us to the sense of community which resulted from the different social standing of representatives of the two sides of the conflict in communist-ruled Poland. To reconstruct it we must mention the planning and distributive roles of the political-administrative centre, which in so-called 'real socialism' took the place of the market mechanism. According to its ideological and, often also tactical premises, the governing elite formulated rules and criteria governing distribution among various bargaining groups (Kolarska-Babinska and Rychard, 1990). Because of this feature of the system the positions of 'public servants' and 'technocrats' in relation to the distributing centre were quite different.

The former were not favoured in the old system. Relative pauperization of teachers, physicians or people working at lower levels of the state administration had become more and more severe. The lack of bargaining power *vis-à-vis* the governing elite doomed this group to frustration and to a hostile attitude towards the centre. In the case of managerial staff of enterprises the situation was quite different. Their bargaining position in relation to the central or local authorities was much stronger. Many members of this group belonged to the 'external elite' described by Antoni Kamiński (1988). They had opportunities to go abroad for contract work or to receive further training. Although they did not belong to the Party or were only rank and file members, they often constituted pressure groups at local level, and as employees of powerful industrial organizations they exerted an influence upon the centre.

The differences described above do not, as might be supposed, belong to the past. As a legacy of the previous system these are still in Poland a category of so-called 'state employees' who dominate the socio-professional structure in the country. They are wage-earners employed directly by the state. Generally, and simplifying a little, we may divide them into two groups: employees of the social sector and of the industrial sector.

What is characteristic of the first group is the constant dependence of their earnings on the condition of the state budget; but at the same time they enjoy relative stability of employment and social security. On the other hand, employees in the industrial sector have begun to be governed by the harsh laws of the market. This has both negative and positive consequences. On the one hand, they increasingly feel the pressure of competition; they have to improve or sometimes even change their qualifications; they also risk losing their jobs. On the other hand, the effects of their efforts are beginning to influence their earnings. The state has not cut itself off from this group and has not as yet declined to take responsibility for it. This is manifested on the one hand by various legal and financial guarantees given by appropriate ministries and, on the other hand, by a tax system exacting payments for the state treasury.

Within the system, at the time referred to above, the so-called POPIWEK was in operation. The tax was for a time imposed only on state employers and was aimed at preventing pay rises out of proportion with the economic condition of a company and, as a tool of macro-economic policy, at curbing inflation. Towards the end of 1990 the management of many state enterprises, taking advantage of loopholes in the law, paid out large sums of money, thereby circumventing the POPIWEK. Although, according to the Act, the average level of remuneration of public servants was supposed to be slightly higher than the average pay in the socialized economy, the operation described above impoverished the state budget, with adverse results for public servants, whose pay was reduced from 104 to 101 per cent of the average pay in five basic economic sectors.

The above was a source of tension arising from the workings of national economic policy. Negotiations over it could not be carried on at the local level since it was a nationwide phenomenon. The question therefore arises – with respect to political representation – why the local community, whose problems are quite different, and unrelated to this particular cleavage, became the arena of conflict.

Responsibility for this state of affairs could perhaps be ascribed to the socio-occupational structure in Racibórz. Diverse aspects of social differentiation and conflicting interests based on it found, the argument might go, their political articulation in the forum of local government displacing – at least in the initial phase of development – other problems. In other words, this was a distributional conflict that involved many people in the community. However, there are serious doubts about this explanation. An average state employee, no matter if he works in an office, factory, or school, believes that it is the state, the government, which is the power that bears responsibility for his personal economic condition. Few are aware of the rules under which the state budget functions and of the bargaining methods which are used against the central administration.

Everything indicates that the socio-occupational structure in Racibórz cannot be seen as the source of the conflict in the town. The conflict seems to have been limited to a small circle of people coming from the Citizens' Committee (before the split) and playing major part in the political life of the town, who transferred a conflict over a nationwide issue on to the local scene. To answer the question how this could happen, we must refer to the role played by Citizens' Committees in the creation of a new political configuration for Poland's municipalities.

Emergence of Local Power Elites

Citizens' Committees were major participants in the formation of local power elites after the local elections. They won 40 per cent of mandates in commune councils. In the initial phase of their existence, that is, before the parliamentary elections in June 1989, Citizens' Committees constituted a form of 'general rebellion'. This had two characteristics, each of which enhanced the quality of the other: organizational effectiveness and dynamism (see Dunin and Rykowski, 1990). The first one was obtained through the pre-existing structures of Solidarity, various Church organizations and independent regional initiatives. On the other hand, the capacity for dynamic action was the effect of the spontaneous reaction of many people in Poland, including those who had not been involved in opposition activity up to that time, to the historical chance of participating in the first free parliamentary elections in the post-war history of Poland.

At that time nobody thought of constructing on the basis of Citizens' Committees a political counterbalance to the communist power elites on the local level. It was only after the parliamentary elections that the next stage of democratization of public life – local elections – created the possibility of building local political forces other than those that had existed so far.

This process began a few months before elections with the reconstruction of the personal base of the then inactive Citizens' Committees. Active members from the June 1989 election campaign constituted the core to which new members were added. Admission to a Citizens' Committee was usually decided by a simple declaration that the person concerned was interested in joining or by a personal guarantee by an existing active member. The method of cooption, characteristic of this period of the Committees' existence, did not mean that they were closed organizations. On the contrary, activists of many Citizens' Committees complained that their activity met with indifference from local circles and that there were no people willing to work in the social movement (Borkowski *et al.*, 1990). Leaving aside any investigation of reasons for this phenomenon – it would require a thorough analysis – we must state that such external 'isolation' of Committees was often, for their activists, the source of temptation to close ranks or to limit political consultation to selected groups. In consequence, it often happened that the organizers of the most important public events were simply those people who had been willing to participate in the public and political life of the local community. Thus the initial phase of recruitment and crystallization of new opinion-making circles – which in my opinion was decisive for the shape of the later local power system – met with rather limited public interest. What is more, this phase was characterized by a certain randomness in the selection of people, which sometimes resulted in friction and personal conflicts.

The lack of a wide social base for the Committees became evident when they came to choose their own political representatives to local government bodies. In many towns and communes, Citizens' Committees had serious problems with appointing any candidates at all. Sometimes they resorted simply to appointing candidates for councillors from among acquaintances, friends or persons connected with members of Committees by professional links (see Kurczewski, 1990). It often happened that activists of Citizens' Committees themselves competed for councillors' mandates. In spite of the extreme scarcity of appropriate candidates, in many cases Committees applied a so called 'internal sieve'. Although extensive systems for public approval of Citizens' Committees' candidates for council seats were created (meetings, conventions and so on), it was precisely the stage of appointing candidates for consideration at these meetings that usually remained the preserve of the activists (Jałowiecki, 1990).

Summing up the role of Citizens' Committees in the creation of new local political elites, we can assume, of course with certain qualifications, that: first, they monopolized the local political scene; and second, their vague institutional situation made it possible to manipulate the selection procedures and thus limit the recruitment base of the Committees. We should also take into account the fact that the formation of new subjects of local power was something in which the wider community showed little interest. All of this undoubtedly weighed on the character of local events, and the friction and conflicts. Local politics came to be seen as dominated by personal bias, individual ambitions and conflicts of narrow interests irrelevant to the community at large. They rarely assumed the form of serious disputes about programmes affecting the most important problems of the local community.

All of this is exemplified in the case discussed here. The conflict which initially flared up within the small group of Citizens' Committee's activists in Racibórz was a result of an organizational split between warring fractions. The key role that both Citizens' Committee Solidarity and the TKK played on the local political scene caused the conflict to acquire an undeservedly high visibility. The monopolization of public life in Racibórz by activists of both sides made it impossible to ease the tension or reduce its importance. Just the opposite: the electoral victory of adversaries united in a tactical coalition institutionalized the differences that divided them. In this way, an antagonism that was unimportant from the point of view of the local community acquired the status of a basic factor differentiating local political and social forces.

Notes

1. The public sector employs persons working in education, the health service, culture, police, army, judiciary and state administration. They are paid from the state budget. In this article we call this category 'public servants'.
2. 'The thick dividing line' was a political conception of the Mazowiecki government according to which the new elite should refrain from political revenge on representatives of the *ancien régime*.
3. Its importance to the budget is shown by the fact that the POPIWEK constituted, on average, approximately 40–45 per cent of state enterprises' obligations towards the State Treasury (beside such taxes as turnover tax, income tax, levy on fixed assets etc.).

References

Borkowski, T., A. Bukowski and A. Marcinkowski (1990) 'Raport o Komitetach Obywatelskich' (Report on Citizens' Committees), Cracow: Department of Sociology of Work and Organization, Institute of Sociology, Jagiellonian University, April.
Dunin, K. and Z.W. Rykowski (1990), 'Komitety Obywatelskie: organizacja czy reprezentacja', (Citizens' Committees: organization or representation) in S. Kowalski (ed.), *Pierwszy krok do Europy*, (*First step to Europe*), Warsaw.
Jałowiecki, B. (1990), *Narodziny demokracji w Polsce lokalnej, Seria Rozwój regionalny – rozwój lokalny – samorząd terytorialny*, (Birth of democracy in the Local Poland, Series: Regional development – local development – local government), Warsaw: Warsaw University.
Kamiński, A. (1988), 'Reforma czy rewolucja (granice reformowalności)', (Reform or Revolution: and Limits of Reformability), *Res Publica*, no. 7.
Kolarska-Babińska, L. and A. Rychard (1990), *Polityka i gospodarka w świadomości społecznej*, 1980–1990, (Politics and Economy in Social Consciousness, 1980–1990), Warsaw.
Kubiak, A., I. Przybyłowska and A. Wojciechowska-Miszalska (1990) 'Mechanizmy wyłaniania kandydatów w wyborach samorządowych. Przypadek Łodzi', (Mechanisms of selecting candidates in local elections. The case of Łódź', in *Pierwszy krok do Europy, op. cit.*
Kubiak, J. (1991), 'Culture, Administrative Reform and Local Politics: Overlooked Dimensions of the Post-Communist Transformation', *The Anthropology of East Europe Review*, no. 2.
Kurczewski, J. (1990), 'Dziennik wyborczy', (Electoral diary) in *Pierwszy krok do Europy, op. cit.*

8. Českij Krumlov: Housing Policy, Privatization and Local Development

Daniel Hanšpach and Zdenka Vajdová

Introduction

We begin with a brief description of the Czech Republic's housing policy in the 1980s and at the present time, as background information on the continuously changing environment for local government management. The case of Českij Krumlov's local government is a case of a complex approach to community management, characterized by strong emphasis on strategic policy-making, setting priorities and focusing on key issues, where local leaders not only respond to the scale and complexity of change in the society but are also innovative. Their policies and approaches serve as examples for other municipalities in the Czech Republic. The local developments examined in this case study are from the period 1990–93.

Housing Policy in the Czech Republic

An overview

Socialist housing policy and housing systems were simple and similar in all Eastern and Central European countries, with only some small differences.[1]

(a) In the Czech Republic, there were three main forms of housing economy and housing provision, all under the political control of the state (Michalovic, 1990):

- state housing (this also includes enterprises' housing);
- cooperative housing ;
- individual family-owned houses.

(b) The emphasis given to extensive industrial development reduced housing provision simply to meeting the target number of flats planned. Forecasting and long-term planning of housing construction demand proceeded from the expected development of census households. The right to ask the state for help in solving one's housing problems was given to every citizen regardless of his or her socio-economic status. Social policy in this area aimed to provide every household with a separate flat, with 12 square metres of living area per person.

This policy, within the framework of the centrally planned economy, led to a housing situation by the end of the 1980s which had the following characteristics.

Forms of housing: housing estates with multi-storey blocks constructed using pre-fabricated panels and a highly uniform character (average living area per flat 73 square metres); family houses (average living area 120 square metres); older blocks of rented apartments usually forming the core of towns and cities (these buildings were mostly neglected, having been constructed in the inter-war period or earlier, and nationalized in the 1950s).

Rent: this was determined solely by the physical characteristics of the apartment, regardless of its position and surrounding environment. As a consequence, rents for flats in housing estates on the outskirts of a town were much higher than for those in older buildings located in the centre.

Access to housing: rental housing was accessible through a 'waiting list' which every allocating institution had to maintain and regulate according to specified criteria.[2] Whatever the explicit criteria, political interventions into the rank order of the 'waiting list' often occurred; political control even extended to individual housing, if only indirectly. For most property a market did not exist – officially it was possible to buy or sell only family houses.

Municipal housing was in the domain of state administration at the local level, which in the 1980s meant the National Committees. The role of local government in the system was that of an allocator of rented state housing within the municipality for tenants and of housing plots for individual housing. Municipalities themselves had no property, only the role of managing state property.

The systemic changes in the society after 1989, among them

restitution, privatization and the creation of local self-government bodies with their newly independent sphere of responsibilities, along with the transfer of some state property assets to municipalities, created new conditions for housing policy.

Nevertheless, only amendments to pre-existing laws on state housing policy had been adopted in the period studied here. New laws on rent liberalization, private ownership and a housing allowance scheme were still under discussion in early 1994. Taking part in the discussion have been not only national and local self-government bodies, but also other interest groups such as the Association of Tenants and the Association of Private Owners of Rental Houses. It was expected that the new legislation would define the main features of housing policy and help to introduce a housing market.

It was also expected that the fundamental laws would create a framework for all participants in the area of housing policy and reflect wider considerations relevant to housing: 'Housing cannot be treated in isolation: it is inextricably inter-related with broader issues of inflation, incomes policy and income maintenance, inner city decline and a perplexing range of difficult social and economic trends, (Cullingworth, 1979, p. xix).

Local Government as an owner of housing stock

By the end of 1991, local governments had already become the owners of the blocks of rented apartments and housing plots in each local government area. These had been transferred from the property of the Czech Republic to become the property of municipalities.[3] Thus the municipalities own, amongst other buildings, older rental property that had not been restored to the original owners; often historical town centres (which were usually very neglected); panel-construction apartment blocks of various ages; apartment blocks under construction; and housing plots.

It is, of course, possible to treat this property in different ways.[4] Two possible extremes are on the one hand to sell everything and on the other to keep, manage and rent everything. There is, however, no universally agreed formula to determine how municipalities should deal with their housing stocks.

The initial circumstances in which local government had to operate could be described as follows.

(a) The contemporary legislation enabled municipalities to sell property, including apartment blocks, but the fundamental laws regarding housing were still missing.

(b) Municipalities suffered from a significant lack of financial resources and, at the same time, face a number of very basic problems. According to their order of importance as perceived by local councillors these can be listed as follows: local security, sewerage and water cleaning, environmental protection, water supply, refuse collection and its disposal, and renovation and maintenance of housing.

(c) New people, very often inexperienced, started to work in local government organs after the local elections of 1990 (71 per cent of councillors were elected for the first time).[5]

Under these circumstances municipalities have often tried to sell rental houses or privatize them in other ways. The leading philosophy has usually been the simple, short-cut idea that 'municipalities should not own housing stock at any cost'. Nevertheless many local governments have evaluated the value of their property and its possible role in municipal development within a broader framework.

The evaluation of housing stock in its mutual interdependence with other municipal resources – financial, informational and human – could enable local government to evaluate community capacity (Clarke and Stewart, 1990, p. 30) to satisfy needs and resolve problems within its community. The case of the town of Českij Krumlov is an example of this more multi-faceted approach to housing policy.

Českij Krumlov

Geography, history and inhabitants

Českij Krumlov is a South Bohemian town of medieval origin with 16,000 inhabitants. It is situated 170 km south of Prague, near the Austrian and German borders, at the foot of the Čumava mountains. The river Vltava meanders through the town. A National Nature Reserve was established in 1991, covering the border area to the south-west of Českij Krumlov with the objective of preserving the flora and fauna of the area (to enter the border area had been forbidden from 1948 until 1989). Access to Českij Krumlov is possible by train (via Prague or from České Budêjovice, a regional trade and business centre with about 100,000 inhabitants) or by car (some short sections of the Prague–České Budêjovice–Linz motorway are complete). The main structure of the town was completed around the middle of the fourteenth century. Under the rule of the Rozenberg family, Krumlov developed into the leading political and cultural centre of the Czech Kingdom, capable of competing with Prague. However, with the sale of the Krumlov estate to the Habsburg Emperor Rudolf II in 1602, the decline of the town started.

The extensive industrialization of the Czech lands at the end of the nineteenth century, and particularly the construction of a railroad, promoted the growth and industrialization of the more centrally located České Budějovice and confirmed the peripheral position of Krumlov. This is the main reason why there has been little significant redevelopment in Českij Krumlov for nearly four centuries, thereby ensuring that the town has kept its Gothic–Renaissance appearance almost intact.

After the Second World War the town lost 70 per cent of its population because of the movement out of citizens of German nationality from Czechoslovakia to Germany. Newcomers from other parts of Czechoslovakia, both close and distant, only slowly populated the town, amongst them Slovaks and Roma and other ethnic groups. The turnover of inhabitants was high for a time but, nevertheless, most of these newcomers have now become established residents, in spite of their ethnicity.

At present, almost 90 per cent of inhabitants wish to remain in Českij Krumlov for the rest of their lives. The social contacts of three-quarters of people are local, within the town and its surrounding area; they both earn their living and have their friends within the area; 95 per cent of the people 'feel at home' in Českij Krumlov and its locality.

According to the 1991 Census, 91.2 per cent of the inhabitants of Českij Krumlov declare themselves to be of Czech nationality, 4.7 per cent Slovak, 1.5 per cent German, 0.7 per cent Roma; 41 per cent of the inhabitants described themselves as of no religion, 37 per cent as Roman Catholics. Sixty-two per cent of the population were economically active; 23 per cent of the population were aged 14 or younger.

In the 1980s, after 40 years of neglect, the communist government decided to repair part of the inner town. But a decisive improvement in the town's prospects emerged only after 1989. The newly opened borders to the West permitted a flow of foreign tourists and, with them, much-needed flows of money. The uniqueness of the town was internationally recognized when UNESCO included Českij Krumlov on the list of cultural and natural heritage sites of mankind in December 1992.

Housing – one issue among others

According to the 1991 Census there were 5,720 flats in Českij Krumlov, 1,347 (23 per cent) of them within privately-owned buildings. The average number of persons per flat was 2.8, exactly the same as the average in the Czech Republic as a whole; the average residential area per person was 15.8 square metres, with an average of 2.5 rooms; both of these last two averages were a little lower than the national figure.

If we exclude flats in privately-owned buildings, then 57 per cent of flats are the State Housing Cooperative's property, 36 per cent municipal property (some flats in old houses, but the great majority in blocks of flats in housing estates on the outskirts of town) and 7 per cent the property of local enterprises.[6] Our survey allows us to estimate that 55 per cent of inhabitants live in housing estates of panel construction, 20 per cent in private housing and 20 per cent in older apartment blocks.

In 1993 the town council was considering 549 applications for flats. The council had, in fact, suspended allocation of flats until the new system of measuring social need was set out and it became clear who was in real need of the town's help. To complete the whole process of privatization of the housing stock, or part of it, was the second consideration before recommencing the allocation of flats.

Sixty per cent of the inhabitants of Českij Krumlov, according to opinion surveys (see note 5), believe that the town council should have responsibility for ensuring that there are enough municipal flats.

> The town has a duty to take care of its citizens and therefore cannot be indifferent to the housing situation. But this does not mean that the town alone has to be responsible for investment in housing. It does not mean that the town must itself have a significant number of flats of its own. And nobody can force the town to allocate a flat if the difficult situation of an applicant is caused by his own irresponsibility.

Thus spoke the mayor of Českij Krumlov in the first of a series of public information addresses about privatization of the town's housing stock. In fact, even before the above series was launched, a number of relevant actions and initiatives had been undertaken, as we shall describe below.

Understanding community capacity:[7] the strategy of property privatization and local development

The process of decentralization gives more scope for local initiatives and more autonomous local policies implemented by freely elected local governments. The case of Českij Krumlov could serve as one of the more successful examples of how to make effective use of the opportunities offered, with its approach to the privatization of municipal property and its local development strategy. Both issues are very much interconnected in the case of Českij Krumlov, which as a municipality possesses a huge portfolio of real estate, historical monuments, land and forests. As in other municipalities in the former Sudetenland, the share of private restitutions has been rather small and most property has been transferred directly to the municipalities.

Three years ago, Českij Krumlov was facing the problem of how to deal with a large amount of deteriorated property that needed a great deal of investment. Local leaders did not want to sell the municipal property and allow any money received to be devalued by inflation. They wished to foster private initiative and at the same time to safeguard the controlling function of the municipality for the sake of the strategic development of the town. The prevailing attitude was, though, that the municipality should not possess too much property.

The starting-point of the freely elected local council has been the definition of a general development strategy based on the main potential of the town: Českij Krumlov should become a tourist and cultural centre profiting from its unique architectural heritage and its proximity to Austria and Germany.

Ninety-six per cent of the inhabitants of Českij Krumlov think, according to opinion surveys, that 'historical monuments have to be preserved' and 50 per cent think that 'monuments should be the town's property' (rather more than in the Czech Republic as a whole, where 85 per cent of the population shares the former view and 40 per cent the latter). For one-third of Českij Krumlov's inhabitants the greatest importance of historical monuments is that they are a source of income for the town; half of the population consider the preservation of historical monuments a top priority and think the town would lose its character without them.

The attitudes of the citizens of Českij Krumlov to the development of tourism could be distinguished as positive, negative, or positive with some reservations. The frequency of strongly negative attitudes could be estimated as only 1 per cent, with positive and qualified-positive attitudes being split in the ratio 3:2. About 60 per cent of Českij Krumlov's inhabitants are willing to change their job and work in services oriented to tourism: 10 per cent already work in such services.

An important part of the municipal activities has been the development of methods of privatizing municipal property and of principles for local development financing. The basic guideline adopted for this is that the municipality is regarded as largely unable to manage and reconstruct its property, and private activity is considered the best solution for the municipality's problems and its local development.

However, amongst the general population, positive attitudes to privatization were not so frequent in Českij Krumlov as they were in the Czech Republic as a whole and attitudes to privatization are more polarized – to privatize nothing or to privatize everything are both attitudes found more frequently in Českij Krumlov than in the Czech Republic as a whole (from the 1992 surveys – see note 5); 28 per cent of the inhabitants of Českij Krumlov and 25 per cent of the inhabitants of the Czech Republic think 'all houses and flats should be privatized'; 14 per cent of the inhabitants of Českij Krumlov and 5 per cent of the inhabitants of the Czech Republic think 'none of these should be privatized'. Nevertheless 56 per cent of the inhabitants of Českij Krumlov are willing to buy the flat where they are living now; half of them could pay the price of 60,000 Czech Kronas (just over $2,000 in 1993).

The preferred strategy of the council was that the municipality should perform entrepreneurial activities only indirectly, for example, as a partner in joint ventures or development programmes. Joint ventures with private capital were seen as the ideal way of stimulating local development, both in areas where some municipal control was seen as necessary and in clearly commercial projects. Foreign investment is considered necessary, but preferably with careful preparation of tendering procedures. It was certainly felt that much effort should be taken to avoid a monopoly source of foreign investments, by achieving diversified sources of international capital.

About 60 per cent of the town's inhabitants are in favour of permitting the inflow of German capital into Českij Krumlov (close to the average level for citizens of the Czech Republic in relation to their own towns). But about 88 per cent of the town's inhabitants were opposed to the sale (or transfer) of houses, flats, land, historical and cultural monuments, to German individuals or entrepreneurs. In the case of historical and cultural monuments, this attitude of Českij Krumlov's citizens was significantly more negative than the average for the Czech Republic as a whole: 70 per cent had strongly negative attitudes in Českij Krumlov compared to 50 per cent in the Czech Republic; for strongly positive attitudes the figures were 13 per cent in Českij Krumlov and 23 per cent in the Czech Republic.

Most of the year 1991 was devoted to preparation of criteria and guidelines on how to deal with the municipality's property. In spite of severe and continuous problems in the municipality's finances, the local council postponed all property transfers until the new strategy was prepared and approved. Part of the property (70 per cent in terms of quantity, not value) is being privatized under a municipal decree that stipulates the rules and procedures concerning the sale of municipal property to natural and juridical persons. The list of municipal real estate for sale is to be approved by the local council. The property is to be sold by the particular procedure set out in this decree. This method of privatization is specific to the Czech context because the prevailing practice in small-scale privatization in other former communist countries is public auction.

The objective of the municipal decree is to support local individuals and tenants. There are specified 'advantaged persons' who have a preferential position in the selection procedure, in the following order:

- a bidder occupying business premises;
- a native person carrying on business in the privatized unit;
- a Czech or foreign financial institution if it is going to provide pertinent services;
- a tenant living in the privatized unit if no other tenant has submitted an application;
- two or more tenants living in the privatized unit if they apply jointly;
- a tenant living in the privatized unit if another tenant has also submitted an independent application.

Having a preferential position does not necessarily entitle the applicant to buy the privatized unit: the municipal board evaluates applications. Regardless of the preferential position of the applicant, the board can rank first someone whose business activities are considered of major importance for the town. The privatized units are sold for contractual prices negotiated with the selected bidder. The starting price is usually double the official price settled by a specialist. The sale to a particular buyer has then to be approved by the municipal council.

Enhancing community capacity – Českij Krumlov's Development Fund

An important vehicle for attempting to achieve effective treatment of municipal property has been the setting up of the Českij Krumlov Development Fund Limited. The founder of this company was the local council. The fund is fully owned by the municipality and its highest body is the general meeting that consists of local councillors. The town has put into this company its 50 most important and commercially attractive buildings. A feasibility study concerning these buildings has been prepared and also an architectural and building study, because most of the buildings are valuable cultural monuments. This preparatory investment framework is complemented by the tourist development plan that advises what should be done, and in what sequence, in the area of tourism in order to make Českij Krumlov a cultural and tourist centre.

The Českij Krumlov Development Fund Limited was established in the autumn of 1991, under the joint recommendation of the town's main advisors – Barclays de Zoete Wedd of Prague and Commercial Bank of Prague. The studies were carried out by the tourism consultation firm Horvath Consulting London. American Appraisal of Prague estimated the value of the buildings. The international character of the companies involved in the preparation of the whole project should also help to create the image of Českij Krumlov as an attractive place for foreign investors and offer them the sense of safety, reliability and predictability.

The main entrepreneurial tasks of the Fund are: to prepare and execute a strategy for using the Fund's property in a manner in correspondence with the overall development strategy of the town and in a way which will result in balanced growth; to carry out transactions in the Fund's property; to provide information to potential investors; to provide consultation services on a commercial basis, and to prepare and carry out additional investment in tourism and local development. In order to fulfil these goals, the statutory bodies of the Fund, appointed and dismissable by the general meeting, should have sufficient room for manoeuvre to perform their functions. Thus the ongoing activities of the Fund are to buy, sell and rent real estate, to run the tourist facilities and provide corresponding services, to run a travel agency, to invest in reconstruction, to build up new tourist facilities and to manage its own property. The Fund might also perform some complementary activities such as publishing, organizing cultural and educational events, running small businesses and managing some property of third parties.

This large-scale project was not accepted unreservedly by the general public. Some people felt they had been misled about it, and complained that the project disregarded specific local conditions and traditions. There were major disputes about educational and social facilities that were designated for conversion and rebuilding into luxurious tourist centres for foreign visitors. The public was also disappointed because the Fund had originally been conceived as an open public investment fund where the citizens of Českij Krumlov could also have been shareholders, but this idea was abandoned after consultations with the banks. One argument used in favour of the project has been that some new public facilities sponsored by the Fund are also planned.

The mayor rationalizes the existence of the Fund from four different perspectives: strategic local development, long-term economic effect, short term economic effect and the security situation (see below) in the town. The argument that is particularly emphasized concerns the necessity of harmonizing private activity with the town's development plan. The Fund, it is argued, will be able to group more premises into one unit, which will provide better prospects for attracting investors. In the long term the town would like to find the highest quality investors, which is why so much emphasis has been devoted to the careful preparation of the project. The aim is to increase the value of the business environment. In the short run some immediately available financial resources are also necessary in order to solve some urgent problems inherited from the past. The security situation argument is that the existence of the Fund should eliminate the flow of 'dirty money' into the town and protect it from possible problems of law and order that might go hand in hand with such money.

The town has also set up a number of foundations: the Social Foundation, the Cultural Foundation, the Sports Foundation and the School Foundation. The mayor has put the advantage of this structure as follows:

> The budgets of the town and of the Fund and the Foundations form a comprehensive system which covers all areas of municipal life. Using this system of financing, it is possible to support those areas which are in need of such support, and activities which correspond with the town's interest.

Conclusions

Is the town of Českij Krumlov an example of the complex approach to housing and more generally to town management? The best answer is the following quotation from a speech of the mayor of Českij Krumlov at the beginning of 1993:

> Two years ago, when we were elected town representatives in the first free municipal elections, we set out our first general strategy as follows:
>
> •   to define the major potential of the town, which would be developed, and towards which the majority of our activities would be focused;
> •   to undertake an audit of our main problems and set the priorities;
> •   to assess carefully our ability to solve the problems and to define the areas where we would seek help from outside;
>
> The strategy is now being focused on the individual issues which are to be solved; and a reasonable time-schedule is being drawn up.
>
> We have decided to choose a more focused approach in the following areas:
>
> •   a general approach to the town planning system;
> •   privatization of municipal flats;
> •   development of tourism;
> •   a general review of the town's economy;
> •   a study of the future operation of the current energy network and selection of the most suitable heating systems; and
> •   continuous monitoring of social and demographic development.
>
> The town has paid special attention to the development of a property privatization scheme and the principles of financing development.

From today's perspective, it seems that Českij Krumlov has been going through a rather successful period of its development, following the main strategic guidelines that were agreed in late 1990. A strategic approach, an ability to set priorities and the provision of civic and political leadership for their community, are all factors which have helped local leaders in their effort to revitalize and develop the town. They have proved their ability to use one of the town's weaknesses (a huge amount of deteriorated housing stock) as a catalyst of local development. They were helped, of course, by the fact that the town centre has enormous historical and cultural value. Cooperation between local council, local entrepreneurs and major right-wing political parties has resulted in a sound local development policy, even though that policy has sometimes tested the limits of public acceptance. Despite some tension, most of the population seem to share the local politicians' vision of a rich town with rich citizens, and to believe that such a situation is achievable within a generation.

Notes

1. The contributions of participants from Bulgaria, Hungary, Poland, Romania and Czechoslovakia at the 7th Meeting of the CIB Working Commission W69 (Siksio, 1990) are illustrative.
2. Average waiting time is not known, but to wait ten years was nothing out of the ordinary for citizens without good contacts.
3. The Act of the National Council of 23 April 1991 dealt with the transfer of some assets from the property of the Czech Republic to the property of municipalities, and The Act of the National Council of 11 November 1991 changed and amended the Act regarding municipalities of 4 September 1990, and the Act regarding the transfer of 23 April 1991.
4. Municipal responsibilities related to citizens' housing are not directly listed in the Act regarding municipalities. But some items on the list (paragraph 14) create the framework in which local government will develop and perform its own housing plan. They are: the municipality manages its property, establishes organizations and facilities, has duties in education, health care, social care and culture, and maintains and administers facilities in its property serving its citizens' needs.
5. Here and later in the text the results of the research project 'Sociological Aspects of Local Government' and an international comparative research project 'Local Democracy and Innovation', related to each other and carried out by the Institute of Sociology of the Academy of Sciences of the Czech Republic, are utilized. Financial support for the former project has been provided by grants from the Academy of Sciences and Ministry of Interior of the Czech Republic. Financial support for the latter has been provided by the Norwegian Ministry for Foreign Affairs and the Norwegian Research Council for Applied Social Science. The survey covered samples of mayors, councillors, chief administrative officers (data collected from November 1991 to January 1992 – one year after the local elections), a sample of citizens in two Czech towns, one of them Českij Krumlov (data collected in spring 1992) and a representative sample of Czech citizens (data collected in autumn 1992).
6. This and other information related to Českij Krumlov came from interviews with local officials and written material supplied by the Town Hall.
7. The first part of the subtitle is borrowed from Clarke and Stewart, 1990.

References

Clarke, M. and J. Stewart (1990), *General Management in Local Government: Getting the Balance Right*, London: Longman.

Cullingworth, J.B. (1979), *Essays on Housing Policy. The British Scene*, London: George Allen & Unwin.

Michalovic, P. (1990), 'Harmony versus Uniformity' in O. Siksio (ed.): *Housing Sociology in times of Change. Proceedings from 7th Meeting*, CIB Working Commission W69 Housing Sociology, pp. 125–34.

Siksio, O. (ed.), (1990), *Housing Sociology in times of Change. Proceedings from 7th Meeting*, CIB Working Commission W69 Housing Sociology.

Part III. Local Power and Economic Change

9. Economic Change and the Russian Provinces

Philip Hanson*

Introduction

The attempt to turn Russia into a decently-functioning capitalist economy has been under way since the end of 1991. At the end of 1994 it still has a long way to go. In comparison with Poland, Hungary and the Czech Republic, Russia's transformation attempt has been extremely problematic.[1] Macro-economic stabilization – not yet achieved – has already taken longer than it did in the leading reform countries. Russian output has, correspondingly, been falling for a longer period than was the case in East–Central Europe. One of the reasons for this – though only one – is the turbulence in relations between the central government and the provinces. There have even been suggestions that the Russian state could break up.

The main purpose of this chapter is to consider why centre–periphery relations are so especially troublesome in Russia's economic transformation. Something will also be said about policy options and future prospects. Spotting winners and losers amongst the Russian provinces is not the aim, though some thoughts about particular regions' prospects are provided in passing.

The chapter deals only with the 89 'federal subjects' of Russia – 21 republics, 57 oblasts and krais and 11 lesser autonomies (okrugs and an autonomous oblast). The second tier of sub-national government – the truly local level of towns and districts – is so far, it appears, less of a problem. Resource allocation issues seem to be more tightly and cooperatively managed between first and second tiers than they are between the federal government and the regions (see, for example, Freinkman and Titov, 1994).

The political economy of the Russian regions since the fall of communism has been influenced by factors that could be put under the following broad headings: institutional, political and structural. What I mean by these cryptic labels is, as a first approximation:

the influence of the state institutions inherited from the Soviet period, and of the constitutional modifications made since 1991;

the agendas and organizational support of those who hold or seek political office at both regional and national level in Russia;

the economic structure with which each region initially faced the post-communist future.

The chapter is organized into three main sections, dealing with each of these in turn; there is then a review of the economic policy issues in centre–periphery dealings; and finally, some brief conclusions.

What economic transformation entails is something that is more or less taken for granted in what follows. Briefly, the view taken here is a conventional one: that an ex-communist country, if it is to develop into a reasonably effective capitalist state, has to undergo the de-control of prices and of most internal and external transactions; has to get or keep inflation down to low levels and create confidence in the value of its currency (allowing at least resident and non-resident current-account convertibility without rapid depreciation of the currency); has to have property rights clarified and most capital come under private owner-ship; has to permit and legislate for the development of appropriate institutions (from commercial law to stock exchanges); and should become reasonably open to imports and foreign investment.

Progress on all these fronts in Russia in 1992–4 is best summed up as patchy.

Institutions

The Soviet Union was *de jure* federal, and *de facto* a unitary state. Russia in late 1994 might best be described as *de jure* unitary and *de facto* federal. At the same time, the administrative territories of which Russia is composed are roughly those of which the old RSFSR, within the USSR, was made up. Aside from the break-up of the USSR, the change in the *de facto* situation is the result of the collapse of the

Communist Party, which provided top-down control of the regions from Moscow. That control, from Brezhnev's time, was often lax, but power of appointment, and patronage generally, was clearly housed in Moscow.

The disappearance of the CP chain of command left the new leadership of an independent Russia rightly apprehensive about its ability to control events in the provinces. Elizabeth Teague's chapter analyses the subsequent debate over constitutional issues, and the outcomes so far. The most important consequences, so far as economic change is concerned, are twofold: the retention of an administrative–territorial structure derived from the old order leaves, in present circumstances, an undesirable fuzziness about the distribution of powers, and it preserves an anomalous mix of territories with different statuses, where the differences can be traced back to Stalin's nationality policies.

As Elizabeth Teague points out, the ambiguity of Russia's centre–periphery arrangements is their clearest characteristic. In particular, a great many powers and functions are supposed to be jointly exercised by the federal government and federal subjects, with little indication of what this means. And the nationality ingredient in the structure carries with it a great many built-in sources of conflict amongst regions and between regions and centre. It is true that other countries (Italy and Finland, for example) have some regions with a special status related to their being ethnic-minority enclaves, and this arrangement is not a source of any great difficulties for the country as a whole. But the Russian structure is full of anomalies that no sober legislature, engaged in building a state from scratch, would have dreamt of creating. Elizabeth Teague's chapter sets them out.

The principal difficulty for economic policy that these anomalies create (over and above the lack of clarity about powers) is that leaders in standard provinces can argue that the republics are being given preferential resource allocation at their (the standard provinces') expense. This only intensifies the conflict over budget allocations and hinders the acceptance of a given set of rules of the game in fiscal–federal matters. It is true that many of the republics are relatively poor and might be expected anyway to be net recipients in inter-regional re-allocations of public money. But others that are not relatively poor (Sakha, Tatarstan, Bashkortostan) have also been able to get special tax deals. Indeed, treaties signed between the Russian and Tatarstan presidents on 15 February 1994, and the Russian and

Bashkortostan presidents on 3 August 1994, and the 1 July 1994 presidential edict (making Ingushetia a special 'offshore zone' for tax purposes) are simultaneously indications of the centre's weakness and, arguably, provocations to the standard provinces (*Financial Times,* 17 February 1994, p. 2; Oxford Analytica, *East European Daily Briefing,* 10 August 1994; *Financial Times,* 24 August 1994, p. 2).

The weakness of the centre is in part the result of its own internal divisions: presidential apparatus v. government v. legislature, compounded by sharp and public divisions within the government. In this situation regional leaders can play off one part of 'the centre' against another. Perhaps even more fundamental is the strength of the old elite networks within each region: the centre cannot operate through regional federal officials who cannot work with the regional elite. Whatever the formal powers of appointment and veto on appointments, the regional elite seems in 1994 to be largely self-appointing (McAuley, 1994).

Other institutions have not so far developed in ways that would clarify and order centre–province relationships. The courts in different regions are more likely to be controlled by local elites than to be independent. They do not, so far, seem to play the role they might, as channels through which local deviations from centrally-prescribed legal rules can be halted. Thus, in the course of a backlash in the Kuban against private farming, reportedly prompted by the old local *nomenklatura* of collective farm chairmen, it appears that the courts of the Krasnodar region acted under instruction from that local elite (*Argumenty i fakty,* 1994:16, p. 5).

Similarly, President Yeltsin's attempt to impose prefectural rule in Russia's regions has been at best a partial success. It is not being assumed here that top-down executive control of regional public administration, through a system of prefects, is necessarily good for economic efficiency. There is, on the contrary, an abundant literature that supports the idea that efficient allocation of resources through the public sector will in general be promoted by a high degree of local fiscal autonomy, operated by elected local government (see Oates, 1992). But, for reasons to be described in the next section, economic change in Russia since 1991 has been pushed by a mostly liberalizing central government in the face of mostly traditionalist local governments. For the sake of economic transformation, therefore, there is at least a *prima-facie* and short-run case for prefectural government.

In fact, Yeltsin got parliamentary agreement in 1991 to his appointing and dismissing regional heads of administration (or 'governors') in the oblasts and krais, at least until late 1992 (legislation in *Vedomosti Verkhovnogo Soveta RSFSR 1991*, no. 41, pp. 1718–66 and no. 51, pp. 2045–6; the directly-elected mayors of Moscow and St. Petersburg, both initially reformist strongholds, were an exception). But the prefectural system did not extend to republics, and proved by no means immune to governors – who were often from the local *nomenklatura* elite to begin with – going native. In 1993 several regions insisted on holding elections for governor and thus replacing Yeltsin appointees unpopular with the regional establishment. The pendulum swung back in late 1993 when Yeltsin dissolved the federal parliament and then in effect dissolved most regional elected councils. In a 7 October 1993 edict, Yeltsin again empowered himself to appoint and dismiss regional governors for a time (for details see Elizabeth Teague's chapter; also Wishnevsky, 1994).

The regions once more, in 1994, began to elect representative bodies in which traditionalists from the old *nomenklatura* predominated, as they had after the March 1990 elections (Teague, 1994). The power and status of those elected bodies may have declined in the face of the renewal of the prefectural system, but they still seem able to fudge and thwart, in many cases, the regional implementation of nationally-decreed reform legislation.

Meanwhile, as the Russian press has pointed out, oblast and krai governors can draft measures for the regional representative body (often now called a Duma), in which they themselves can also be members. That representative body then monitors their implementation of the approved local legislation (*Izvestiya*, 2 February 1994). Not surprisingly, a 6 September 1994 conference of the Union of Russian Governors called for their appointed status to continue until at least 1996 (*RFE/RL DR*, 7 September 1994).

These authoritarian elements in centre–province dealings might be defensible if they were proving effective in the regional development of economic transformation. What seems to be the case, however, is that only a minority of regional leaderships have been promoting liberalization and institutional reform on their turf. The reasons for this are to be found in the interplay of local economic circumstances and the political agendas of local politicians.

Parties and Political Agendas

In the March 1990 elections at the RSFSR, Russian regional and local levels, there were no well-established democratic parties. Moreover, there was a general suspicion of the word 'party' itself. At the regional level the elected councils seemed to be made up predominantly of members of the old CP *nomenklatura*. That does not mean that former party secretaries and the like necessarily stayed in power at the regional level – though in quite a few cases they did. The *nomenklatura* consisted of officials and managers approved for responsible posts by the party. From Rutland's (1993) estimates of the size of the *nomenklatura* in the USSR as a whole, it can be guesstimated that Russia inherited *nomenklaturshchiki* numbering about 0.7 per cent of the population. Typically, they were managers of large enterprises, chairmen of collective farms, and the like, as well as party apparatchiks.

The cities of Moscow and St. Petersburg, which have oblast status in their own right, seem to have been the only clear exceptions to this legitimation of the old elite at the regional level. This circumstance, together with a handful of Western studies of elections in particular regions, supports the view that the retention of local power by the old elite may not have been achieved primarily by gerrymandering and electoral fraud but rather through the incoherent organization of the embryonic 'democratic' groupings outside the two biggest cities (McAuley, 1992; Helf and Hahn, 1992). The role of electoral skulduggery remains unclear, but the results in those regional elections already held in 1994 have been broadly similar. Nikolai Petrov, from a detailed study of all the regional elections from late 1993 to mid-1994, concludes that the upheaval in Russian politics has passed the regional assemblies by, leaving the old elites unaffected. In the March 1990 elections, interest centred on the Russian national level. By the time of the 1994 regional elections, fatigue had set in. Turnouts were low; gerrymandering and abuse of electoral procedures were rife; the especially low urban turnout, combined with a gerrymandering of constituency boundaries to create an under-representation of urban voters, had produced what Petrov describes as a ruralization of Russian regional politics (Petrov, 1994a, 1994b.)

The cohesion of management and party elites – the old establishment – within a region in the old days was convincingly described by Andrle (1976). Lacking a chain of command from Moscow after the collapse of the Communist Party, the local establishment could reasonably be expected to adhere to a localist agenda, shaped by their personal interests and their new circumstances. Members of the local establishment are likely still to have useful contacts in the central administration in Moscow (which is one reason for local citizens to vote for them), and to see the state enterprises they have been managing as both a local support and power base and a resource from which they can hope to extract rents.

The agendas of particular members of local establishments no doubt vary considerably. But certain characteristic items of these agendas can be suggested *a priori*. The protection and subsidization of state enterprises, continuing after their formal (typically insider) privatization, is one. This would be partly a matter of individuals protecting their own power bases, and partly a general preference for the redundancies and bankruptcies flowing from stabilization to occur anywhere but on their turf – NIMBY (not in my back yard) stabilization. Another is the ability to maintain price controls locally, as a way of courting popularity, and therefore the ability to control the 'export' of consumer goods from their region with its local shortage economy. Another, not of course specific to present-day Russia, is a larger slice of public money for their region.

The overlapping of roles in Russia's local elites and the lack of development of national political parties give these hypothesized agenda items unusual force. The overlap between representative and executive bodies at local level has already been mentioned. It should have the effect that the attempts at a top-down prefectural system may have done less to tilt local agendas towards liberalization than might have been expected. The overlapping of business and political roles is also likely to be exceptionally large. Not only are many elected regional politicians senior state-sector managers when elected, but few opt to become full-time politicians; the norm is to continue to run a (probably now privatized) business. Even if that were not the norm, the entanglement of government in the economy remains great at regional level: licences to operate, to export, to act on behalf of the region, all give opportunities for corruption.

A notorious example is provided by the rise of Evgenii Nazdratenko, the governor of Primorskii krai, on the Pacific coast. According to Savvateeva (1994), Nazdratenko effectively came to power, replacing a reformist Yeltsin appointee, as the nominee of the PAKT group, formed by the leaders of 213 state enterprises of the region, who used

PAKT as a vehicle for enriching themselves by siphoning output from 'their' state enterprises through it, at transfer prices well below the re-sale price. When the previous governor, Vladimir Kuznetsov, would not give them the export licence, quota and budget deals they wanted, they manoeuvred to get him replaced by Nazdratenko. Nazdratenko was subsequently able to remove the heads of the regional intelligence service (SFK), internal affairs department (MVD) and tax police, who were not helping PAKT, and also the mayor of Vladivostok. Savvateeva asks whether the pattern of local power acquisition represented by Nazdratenko is really much different from what has been going on elsewhere in the country (see also Kirkow 1994, and the chapter by Peter Kirkow in this book.)

Even when there may be no corruption involved, it is still regarded as normal that regional political figures should act as though they were directly managing the region's economy. In first-half 1994 58 per cent of GDP was officially reckoned to be generated by the non-state sector, but that does not appear to have destroyed this relationship. The governor of Sverdlovsk oblast, for example, was reported in September 1994 to have proposed arms sales from his region's factories to China, at a meeting with the Chinese head of state, and to have made similar proposals even for a non-military branch (steel-making equipment), as well (Interfax, 6 September 1994, cited in *RFE/RL DR*, 7 September 1994).

In general, the traditionalist local elites could be expected to be well-disposed to privatization (on their own terms, in other words, with control by the established management continuing, and with subsidies and protection also available), but hostile to stabilization, in so far as it produces local redundancies and bankruptcies, and hostile to liberalization in so far as it entails a loss of their ability to court voters with low prices attributable to their own actions. Exceptions could (and do) exist, but one would expect to find them chiefly where reformers without a local elite background have obtained a strong position in the representative body or where the appointed head of administration is a determined reformer who has somehow been able to co-opt local elite interests.

The attitudes to economic policy on the part of Russian regional politicians I suggest are likely to prevail are in part to be expected in any representative of regional interests anywhere. What is likely to be distinctive in the Russian case is, first, the deep entanglement of local politicians with local producers (indeed, the fact that in Russia they can quite often be the same people); second, the strength of the tradition of relying on government support; third, the absence of a structure of nationwide political parties that would give local politicians a career interest in following a national party line when it conflicts with the wishes of local elites.

Regional Economic Differences

One obvious reason for policy differences between regions and possible conflicts between some regions and the centre is the variety of economic starting-points amongst Russia's regions. Russian economic geographers considering the prospects of regional fragmentation have suggested groupings of regions into categories determined by certain key features of their economic profile, such as: agricultural, manufacturing, raw-material, 'gateway', etc. (for example, Petrov and Treivish, 1994). Some of the elements of regional differentiation will be briefly reviewed here under several headings: income levels, urbanization, industrial structure, links with the outside world, and, arising from the initial differences, chances of successful adaptation.

The 89 Russian provinces probably differ more widely in development level than the member states of the European Union. Certainly, differences in per capita real income, in urbanization and in the extent of industrial development are very large. In many respects, moreover, Russia is not yet a single economic space. One illustration of this is the fact that prices and real wages differ widely. The differences in money wages and per capita money incomes, however, are quite misleading, because the price differences are so huge.

One estimate shows levels of per capita real personal income amongst the eleven former planning regions, with adjustments for price differences. It is shown in Table 9.1. This estimate, by Nemova, is very close to that of Illarionov, Layard and Orszag (1994) for March 1993. The latter is average per capita nominal rouble household income, adjusted by a measure of regional food prices. Since regional data on non-food prices seem not to be systematically collected, the meaning of Nemova's estimates is probably the same.

If comparable estimates could be made for the 89 federal subjects, the range from poorest to least poor would presumably be even greater than the 1:2.5 range between the North-West and West Siberia shown in Table 9.1. Regional convergence through the movement of labour and capital, which has been observed as a long-run phenomenon in most capitalist countries, is hardly likely to be managed quickly in Russia. The sheer size of the country is only part of the problem. So long as most housing is socially owned, geographical labour mobility is inhibited.

Table 9.1:   **Russia: real household income per capita, 1993 I+II, by economic regions**
(Russian Federation average = 100; local price differences reportedly allowed for)

North	126.9	North Caucasus	86.6
North-West	60.4	Urals	109.8
Central	74.0	West Siberia	154.1
Volga-Vyatka	83.3	East Siberia	113.4
Central Black Earth	100.4	Far East	112.5
Volga	126.4		

Source: L. Nemova, 'Rynok truda', *Eko*, 1993:10:39.

This could, it is true, be a dwindling impediment: figures given by Struyk and Daniell (1994) imply that private ownership of the urban housing stock had risen from 21 per cent of dwelling units in summer 1991 to 42 per cent at the end of 1993. But Struyk and Daniell give reasons for supposing that the housing privatization process will slow down; in any case, the development of a housing market will probably lag behind privatization by sitting tenants. Meanwhile the actions of provincial authorities in maintaining local price controls, and therefore barring some deliveries of goods across provincial borders, further impede the creation of a single market. More will be said about this in the next section.

Illarionov, Layard and Orszag give figures of the Table 9.1 kind for six dates between January 1992 and March 1993, inclusive. They also give the rouble-income and food price levels (all relative to the Russian average) from which these food-purchasing-power measures are derived. An increase of regional differentiation during the first 15 months of the transformation attempt emerges clearly. Between January 1992 and March 1993 the coefficient of variation among the 11 planning regions increased as follows: nominal rouble incomes 0.18 to

0.30; food prices 0.12 to 0.20; food purchasing power of rouble incomes 0.16 to 0.25. As these figures imply, the correlation across these 11 regions between food-price and rouble-income changes, though positive, was well below 1; it was in fact 0.5.

These numbers should not be over-interpreted. The raw data on both rouble incomes and food prices are of only modest quality. Private-sector incomes are known to be poorly counted; the food prices are collected only in cities and may have little bearing on food consumption in many rural areas. The exclusion of hard-currency income data probably makes for underestimation of nominal incomes in some regions relative to others. Food prices do not tell the whole story.[2]

Nonetheless, these estimates do at least suggest increasing inter-regional income differentiation during transformation. They also suggest that real incomes have fallen sharply in the North-West and Central planning regions, which include St. Petersburg and Moscow, respectively; indeed, they tell us that these are the only planning regions where real income has fallen; elsewhere it has apparently risen.

Price liberalization and economic adjustment could perhaps explain such a shift (if the figures are really telling an approximately true story about regional differences in real income). The supply allocation privileges of the two biggest cities should have been ended. The steep decline in activity in the defence sector may have been particularly detrimental to these regions, and so on. But, in so far as the reality matches the statistical appearance, increased differentiation might also come about in part because of an increased regional divergence in the extent of price control and a growth in inter-regional trade barriers. Evidence of both these tendencies will be considered in the next section.

In any event, if there has really been an increased divergence of regional average real incomes, it would appear that neither government resource re-allocation nor labour and capital movement was sufficient to offset this tendency in 1992 and early 1993.

Another measure of regional change during transformation has been devised by Michael Bradshaw: official unemployment plus recorded short-time working as a proportion of the employed population. His compilation of figures for end-1993, taken from Goskomstat data, is given in Hanson, 1994b. In principle, these numbers should reflect the situation in all sectors of the economy, and not just in industry. And adding reported short-time working to officially-registered unemployment avoids undue reliance on the official unemployment figures. The latter are still quaintly low for a country whose officially-recorded GDP has fallen by almost a half since 1989. At the same time, it must be assumed that effective stabilization would produce a much larger shake-out of labour than even this combined figure shows. Whether that shake-out would follow the regional pattern existing now is not clear.

At present, anyway, this indicator shows a plausible regional pattern. There is relatively high unemployment plus short-time working in three regional clusters – Volga-Vyatka, the ethnic republics of the North Caucasus, and the southern Urals – and in two regions of the Central area – Ivanovo and Vladimir. In the case of Ivanovo, a region with a heavy concentration of textile production, the break in cotton supplies from former Soviet Central Asia may be part of the story. The Volga-Vyatka and Urals areas could both be seen as rust-belts. They have a high concentration of heavy engineering and the less research-intensive parts of the VPK (Horrigan, 1992, and communication on work in progress from Julian Cooper). The North Caucasus republics are relatively backward in general, had a record of labour surpluses even in the Soviet era, and have been convulsed by conflicts in the recent past. Ivanovo is a textile region with less of the research-intensive defence industry than is characteristic of the Central area. It is also noticeable that the poorer republics generally – not only those in the North Caucasus – have relatively high unemployment and short-time working.

To return to the degree of regional divergence at any one time: differences in the extent of urbanization are also striking. In the 1989 census, the average percentage share of urban in total population for Russia as a whole was 73.7. Amongst the 89 federal subjects (excluding the cities of Moscow and St. Petersburg and the region of Murmansk, where anything but urban habitation is perilous) the urban percentage ranged from 37.4 in the Republic of Kalmykia to 87.3 in Kemerovo. Of 77 main regions (not counting the autonomies separately, and with Chechnya and Ingushetia taken together) six were less than 50 per cent urban (five of the six were republics).

Natural resource endowments and industrial structure also vary widely. Tyumen oblast is the obvious example of a region rich in oil and gas. Areas with at least potential strengths in agriculture include the Central Black Earth (former planning) region, containing Belgorod,

Voronezh, Kursk, Lipetsk and Tambov, and also parts of the North Caucasus – Rostov, Krasnodar and Stavropol.

Some industries are highly concentrated regionally. Horrigan's calculations of regional dependence on military industry (VPK) employment in 1985 can serve as an example (Horrigan, 1992). There are some acknowledged deficiencies in the Goskomstat data Horrigan used: they do not cover all VPK employment (in particular, they exclude military R & D institutions), and they probably include some non-VPK employment (for example, in gold-mining); but for our present purposes they can be treated as a proxy. Her estimated percentages of 1985 population who were members of households containing at least one VPK employee range from zero in Tuva to 36.4 per cent in the republic of Udmurtiya, against a Russian average of 12.1 per cent.

Finally, there are border, or gateway, regions and hinterland regions. The former include St. Petersburg and, on the Pacific coast, Primorskii Krai. With its new borders with other ex-Soviet republics, Russia now has more border regions than before. For the time being, however, the gravitational pull of the economically-small non-Russian FSU states is weak. The lack of effective payments mechanisms so far between the new CIS currencies is another, probably more temporary, impediment. For some time to come, the most significant gateways are likely to remain those that open on the capitalist world.

The pull of foreign trade already has strong regional effects. In the case of the Russian Far East, the combination of its Pacific Rim location and its relatively weak input–output links with the rest of Russia has prompted speculation about its drifting economically away from the rest of the country. The Russian government was sufficiently worried about its own Far East becoming a speck on Moscow's horizon to arrange a meeting of the government's Commission for Operational Problems on the subject on 25 May 1994 (*Kommersant-daily*, 26 May 1994, p. 3).

In the measure that Russia's economy adapts towards a functioning market system, this pull of trade with established capitalist countries will strengthen. Gravity-model projections of the future patterns of trade of the former Soviet republics predict a massive re-orientation towards Western partners, as and when the post-Soviet economies come to behave like normal market economies (Williamson, 1992). That is not surprising, because the logic of these projections is that the trade-partner composition of trade flows between market economies is strongly determined by the economic size of each country and the distance between each pair of trade partners. The relatively large economic size of not-too-distant Western countries, compared with that of East European and Soviet-successor states, will tend to produce predictions of just such a re-orientation. Other circumstances might affect the outcome, but the predicted tendency is plausible.

It is tempting, but unprofitable, to seek guidance to local economic policies in the economic prospects of particular regions. It might be thought that the prospect of a particular region being a loser or a winner from economic change would tend to influence regional leaders' policies towards market reforms. One attempt to find such a link with 1992 data, with the rate of small-scale privatization in 77 regions as the variable to be explained, did not produce a statistically significant result (Bradshaw and Hanson, 1994). More generally, it is hard to detect a systematic variation in approach to economic change that corresponds to variations in what might be thought to be the prospects of different regions.

One plausible reason for this has been suggested by a Russian economic geographer, Andrei Treivish (interview, 4 May 1994). It is that there is so little confidence about the nature and direction of future economic developments in Russia that local political leaders, in general, have no clear idea about the prospects for their particular regions. In other words, the chances of each region seem to be too uncertain to be a guide to a region's policies.

One qualification should however be made to this judgement. It is that resource-rich regions at present show a disinclination to reform, since they are making plenty of hard currency without changing their ways. That is how, for example, the Russian politician and economist Grigorii Yavlinsky justifies his concentration on Nizhny Novgorod as a pilot region for attempting his own bottom-up reform policies. When asked why he did not start in Tyumen, with a strong hard-currency base, he points to the complacency of local elites there; in contrast, Nizhny Novgorod, with its heavy defence-industry dependence, had leaders who saw no way ahead except through radical reform (discussion with Yavlinsky at Ebenhausen, 13 April 1994). It should be added, though, that by no means all VPK-dependent regions have local leaders who share the Nizhny Novgorod governor's enthusiasm for reform.

It seems safest to argue that certain features of the economic geography of a region may be a deterrent to reform policies at the local level. For example, confidence in a region's ability to generate hard currency may tend to deter local leaders from reform. And experience of a particularly steep fall in economic activity in a region may tend to intensify, in that region, the antipathy that all local leaders have to macro-economic stabilization. On the other hand, the reasons why a few local leaderships have been more reformist than most have less to do with economic geography, and more to do with the social circumstances that allow a reformist counter-culture to be formed, and perhaps also with the role of a few individuals.

Economic Policy and the Regions

The relationships between regional and national policy-makers, in the setting and implementation of reform policies, are reviewed here under the headings of the conventional building-blocks of economic transformation: stabilization (including fiscal policy and therefore, in this context, the issues associated with fiscal federalism); liberalization; privatization; and internationalization.

Stabilization

Macro-economic stabilization is an effort to provide a national public good – a stable currency; but no elected regional government within a single currency area has an interest in the observance of financial discipline in its own backyard. The gain that is hoped for is a national one, in which, with luck, all will eventually share. The regional political leaders, however, will not gain any credit from that. Meanwhile, the pain is felt locally in restricted public services, bankrupt enterprises and redundant workers. If one region can avoid the pain, its elected political leaders, or any local political elite that feels vulnerable to local public discontent, will seek to do so. It is only the reformers at the national level who will regard stabilization as their responsibility.

The options for local politicians faced with a national regime of financial stringency are to seek special favours for producers in trouble in their region or to attempt an exit from the single currency area by developing a local surrogate currency. Numerous local ration coupons schemes in Russian territories exemplify the latter; the former is endemic, though the mechanics of favour-seeking depend on the structure of political institutions.

One variant might be an attempt to establish a regional central bank of one's own that could determine local money supply. That would amount to setting up a separate currency. Boris Fedorov, the former Russian Finance Minister and the most consistent and determined exponent, when in office, of monetary control, says that some of the republics have tried to move in this direction by seeking greater autonomy for the regional branches of the Russian Central Bank located on their territory. For that reason he advocates a smaller network of regional branches of the central bank, with each branch spanning several administrative territories (*Izvestiya*, 26 April 1994, p. 2).

The national policy issues surrounding the Russian state budget are well known. The main issue with respect to stabilization is simple: there is a need to curtail the overall government financial deficit. The aim of reducing the budget deficit is hard to implement. The machinery for raising government revenue from taxation is primitive and faulty, and the pressures on the government to spend are high. Much of the spending consists of subsidies or subsidy equivalents in the form of soft credits initiated by the government. To complicate matters, controversy over the meaning and reliability of official budget numbers is intense.

The inherited system of tax collection involves the initial collection of most tax revenue by regional organizations, and the 'sharing upwards' of the revenues according to supposedly standardized region-to-centre percentage divisions of revenues from particular taxes. This is then followed by various kinds of redistribution of funds from the centre 'back' to the regions. The redistribution has not been based so far on a standardized formula that would compensate for differences in requirements for local public services, relative to the local tax revenue base.

The organization and operating rules for government revenue and expenditure are under repair – or perhaps one should say, are being established properly for the first time. One of the most difficult parts of that process is sorting out the budgetary relations between the federal and lower levels of government.

In a country of Russia's size and regional diversity such problems are far more important than they are in smaller and more homogeneous nations. The present difficulties of regional development are compounded by a lack of order and transparency in the regional distribution of public money. The regions have sometimes held back substantial funds due to the federal budget. The total outstanding was equivalent to 1 per cent of GDP in November 1993 (Freinkman and Titov, 1994). The regions have at all times been engaged in *ad hoc* bargaining with the centre over the division of revenue; and they have in most respects rather limited fiscal autonomy.

In reviewing the issues, it is simpler to start with the revenue side. The Federal Tax Service (with its own armed Tax Police) is now an agency separate from the Ministry of Finance and strictly federal in subordination. Its local branches are descended from units that had dual subordination (local and national) in Soviet times, and are often still responsive to local pressures; but in the ordinary Russian regions, as distinct from the republics, tax revenues are paid into regional branches of the Central Bank of Russia (CBR), and are then not readily diverted from their Moscow destination. In the 20 nominally non-ethnic-Russian republics (21 if Chechnya is included) the bank connections are less strict, and there is more scope for regional sequestration of funds.

The most significant tax rates and bases are set by the federal government. Under 1993 legislation, there are 15 taxes whose rates and bases are set by the federal government (though one of them, the profits tax, now includes a portion that can be set between 0 and 25 per cent at the regional level, on top of a basic federal rate of 13 per cent); four taxes whose rates are set or partly set at the regional level; and a further 23 whose rates can be set at local or regional level: for details see Freinkman and Titov (1994) and Wallich (1994).

The first group of taxes includes the major revenue sources: profits tax, value-added tax (VAT), excises, and household income tax, and the quasi-taxes on exports and imports. Together these accounted for 76 per cent of the consolidated budget (federal plus regional) revenue in the first half of 1994 (*Russian Economic Trends*, vol. 3, no. 2: Table A15). In addition, non-tax revenue sources such as proceeds from the sale of hard currency and CBR profits accrue largely or entirely to the federal government. There are 'sharing' ratios set each year for splitting some of the main tax revenues between centre and regions: for example, VAT is at present split 75:25 in favour of the centre but 22 of the 75 percentage points are supposed to be ear-marked for redistribution across regions by the centre.

The taxes over which there is formal regional discretion are so far, conversely, of minor importance. They include business registration fees, a levy of up to 1 per cent of enterprise wage bills to support spending on education, property taxes, land tax, taxes on second-hand car and computer sales, and a hotch-potch of other levies, fees and charges.

Regional fiscal discretion would therefore seem to be tightly constrained. In practice, this is less the case than it appears. Regions have gained considerable freedom to switch spending between budget heads. They have also been developing their own extra-budgetary funds, which are partly hidden from the centre. Freinkman and Titov (1994) estimate these in total as equivalent to a 7.7 per cent addition to the Russian consolidated budget in 1992. They are likely to have been increasing in 1993–4. These have by tradition been outside the control of elected councils, and have been built up in some secrecy between local administrations and their local allies in the management *nomenklatura*. In Moscow in early 1994 the city Duma's new budget and finance committee was trying to find out what was in these funds, and who controlled them (Moscow edition of *Ekonomika i zhizn': Vash partner*, 1994, no. 9).

The regions also get to keep portions of the federal government's extra-budgetary funds. This is a mixed blessing. Reportedly, some 80 per cent of the employment fund (designed to finance unemployment and related benefits) is retained at regional level, presumably in proportion to the each region's employment-fund 'base' (the wage bills of enterprises). The centre's ability to direct unemployment benefit to especially needy regions is correspondingly impaired.

Finally, the regions have been able to put pressure on Moscow to transfer funds to them in steadily increasing real amounts. Identifying the true scale of inter-budget transfers is impossible, but the official data show transfers of the order of almost 3 per cent of GDP in the first half of 1994 (see below and Table 9.2).

On the expenditure side, social spending responsibilities, especially for health, primary education and 'culture', have been formally devolved to the regions. Spending under the old Soviet budget heading 'On the national economy', which in fact includes much social spending in the form of housing investment and maintenance, and subsidies to agriculture and consumer-goods production, is in practice partly devolved to regional and local levels.

The greatest single source of disarray and conflict in the Russian fiscal system is the lack of orderly and transparent rules of the game for allocating funds from the centre among regions so as to provide a minimum provision in all regions of particular forms of expenditure (such as on health and education). Poor information on the real revenues and requirements of most regions, compounded by large inter-regional differences in price level, hinder the development of such rules.

Table 9.2:   Russian government budget balances and transfers, 1994-I+II (% 1994-I+II GDP)

	federal	regional	consolidated
Initial revenue split	12.0	12.3	24.3
Spending at own level	-14.7	-14.5	-29.2
Balance before inter- level transfers	-2.7	-2.2	
Transfers (from -, to +)	-2.8	2.8	
Revenue after transfers and credits received	12.0	15.1	
Budget advances	-3.7	-0.2	
Total spending, excluding transfers	-18.4	-14.7	-30.4*
Overall balance	-6.4	0.4	-6.0

Notes: Accounting balances do not always equal zero because of rounding.
             Credits extended are treated here as expenditure.
             * Net of inter-level transfers.
Source: Derived and adapted from *Russian Economic Trends* vol. 3, no. 1 (1994):
             Table A15.

Meanwhile, in the best Soviet traditions, each region tries to under-assess its revenues and exaggerate its spending needs, in order to get more from Moscow. The process is made more antagonistic by the perceived privileges of the nominally 'ethnic' republics, and the extreme disparities across regions.

The extreme unevenness of development levels makes a working fiscal federal system especially hard to achieve. According to specialists at the President's Analytical Centre, a dozen regions, containing a third of Russia's population, provide three-fifths of the

federal tax revenue. These regions include Moscow and St. Petersburg
cities, Samara (the home of Lada cars), Nizhny Novgorod, Sverdlovsk,
Krasnoyarsk and the oil-and-gas rich Khanty-Mansi and Yamal-Nenets
regions. At the other end of the scale are poor regions like the various
republics in the North Caucasus, the Marii-El, Altai, Tuva and Kalmyk
republics and ordinary Russian provinces of Magadan, Kamchatka and
Altai (there is both an Altai republic and an Altai province) where
revenues cover less than half of actual regional expenditure (Lavrov,
1994).

In an environment of poor information and lack of trust, orderly fiscal
federal arrangements are still a long way off. Meanwhile, the
government, afraid of losing a semblance of control over those regions
that are either remote or particularly assertive, or both, has tended to
concede revenue and spending *de facto* to the regions. In the first half
of 1994 regional budget revenue was 12.3 per cent of first-half GDP,
against 12.0 per cent for the federal budget, and expenditures (again as
percentages of GDP) were 14.7 and 14.5, respectively. By transferring
an amount equivalent to 2.8 per cent of first-half GDP to sub-national
levels, the government maintained the usual appearance of regional
budgets being in overall surplus (*Russian Economic Trends*, vol. 3, no.
2, and Table 9.2). This is almost unavoidable, since the regions cannot
print money and, though they have formal powers to issue bonds,
rarely do so. St. Petersburg, with a 2.1 trillion rouble bond issue,
accounts for almost all municipal or regional borrowing so far
(*Finansovye Izvestiya*, 24 November 1994: III).

The state budget for 1995 that is being debated in the Duma at the
time of writing is the federal, not the consolidated (federal plus local),
budget. The rationale for this focus, constitutional niceties apart, is that
the regional budgets will have to be in balance or surplus, so the size
of the deficit in the consolidated budget will be determined at the
federal level. But part of the deficit in the federal budget will continue
to be created by pressure from 'below' on a weak centre.

At the same time, when federal spending commitments to a particular
region are not met, as often happens, that region will continue to be
tempted to withhold revenue from Moscow. The problem of regional
withholding of tax revenues, however, has been reduced since President
Yeltsin dismissed parliament and the elected local governments in
autumn 1993, and cut yet another round of special deals with some of
the more powerful republics.

The centre has developed the habit of striking *ad hoc* budget deals with regions. This generates a leap-frogging of claims by various regions against the centre. According to the Ministry of Finance, in 1993 every federal subject had by the end of the year secured a budget deal that differed from the allocation originally set by the centre (*MinFinVE, 94*). A common complaint is that regions that make the most fuss or have the most political leverage get the most, to the detriment of equitable treatment across regions.

To sum up: the regions' budgets remain an intractable problem and a source of constant, though probably containable, tension between Moscow and the provinces. Meanwhile, the lack of coherent rules of the game for regional budgets impedes both the development of a real federation and the attempt at macro-economic stabilization.

Liberalization

The picture is not much different in the case of liberalization. The initial Russian price liberalization of 2 January 1992 was in several respects less thorough-going than that in Poland two years earlier. One difference was that the Russian central government left open to lower-level authorities in the regions the option of maintaining some price controls at their own discretion. The variation in the exercise of this power across the administrative territories has been enormous and persistent. Ulyanovsk, for example, has the reputation of maintaining as much of the old order as possible. That includes price controls and (therefore) rationing of price-controlled goods and border controls on shipments from the region. Nizhny Novgorod, St. Petersburg and some others have been at the other end of the spectrum.

The resulting price differences (at least for rationed goods) show up in the regular Goskomstat price surveys in 132 cities. On 1 September 1993, bread prices were controlled in 40 per cent of those cities, sugar in 11 per cent and milk in 26 per cent (*Delovoi mir,* 18 September 1993, p. 7). Correspondingly, the total rouble cost of a consumer basket of 19 basic food items varies greatly among cities. For this as well as other reasons, regional differences in money incomes can be misleading.

Table 9.3 illustrates the extent of this distortion in the case of the two usual suspects for high and low food prices: Magadan and Ulyanovsk, respectively.

Table 9.3: **Money incomes, food prices and food purchasing power of average incomes, Magadan and Ulyanovsk, 1993–4**
(roubles/month and % of Russian Federation average)

	food basket mid-Sept. 1993 (% RF av.)	food basket Jan. 1994 (% RF av.)	average income Jan. 1994 (r/month)	average 'real' income Jan. 1994 (r/month av. RF prices)
Magadan	268.8	241.3	165364	68530
Ulyanovsk	52.3	51.9	54584	105170

Sources: Izvestiya, 22 September 93: 4; *GKStat Jan 94*: 107, 217; last column derived.

Are food prices a good guide to the overall cost of living in different regions? They probably are, since traditionalist local leaders who have kept extensive food-price controls are likely also to have kept low levels for controlled rents and other basic items. If that assumption is correct, real incomes in Ulyanovsk were on average higher than in Magadan, despite the fact that average money incomes were three times higher in the latter than in the former. In general, the money income data by themselves tell us nothing about welfare. They are however of relevance to investors, including foreign investors, provided that hidden social protection costs for employers (subsidized workplace food supplies, subsidized enterprise housing, and the like) are not systematically higher where money wages are lower.

Local price controls impede the development of a single economic space across Russia. Their deployment in particular regions is a traditionalist gambit on the part of the local leadership. It may at first help to maintain local support for the region's political leaders, but it will tend to be undermined by the growth of the private retail sector, which is less amenable to control. So long as the private sector is relatively small, the price-controlled official distribution system may force all prices to be kept relatively low; but once the price-controlled sector begins to account for a smaller share of local sales, the political dividends from maintaining controls tend to fall (Berkowitz, 1993).

Meanwhile, however, price controls tend to be supported by local controls on deliveries across the region's border, and by rationing.

Regional leaders practising this sort of control are probably buying short-term local support at the expense of longer-term structural change and the development of local private enterprise. This certainly seems to be the case in Ulyanovsk, where subsidies to basic food items are funded by local taxation on other items, and by the regional administration stepping in and appropriating regional output (for example of lorries) at cost and re-selling at market prices (*Izvestiya*, 3 December 1994, p. 5).

Ulyanovsk may be an extreme case, but it is not an outlier. A study by the government's Working Centre of Economic Reforms between early 1992 and mid-1993 found that, of 75 regions, 9 or more items in the 19-item 'food basket' used to calculate living costs were price-controlled in 17 regions, and 3–8 items in a further 20 (Expert Institute, 1994). The study concluded that the level of prices of food-basket items was indeed kept relatively low in the more price-controlling regions, but that the rate of inflation was not greatly different (see note 1).

Whether these regional price controls are maintained or not will depend in part on the buoyancy of local finances. A toughening of the fiscal stance in Moscow, and therefore fewer hand-outs to the regions, would in this respect help liberalization. Meanwhile, the impediments to a single market for goods in Russia remain considerable.

Privatization

The centre–region issues with respect to privatization are different in nature from those with respect to stabilization and liberalization: less a confrontation characterized in most areas by regional resistance, and more a matter of varied regional policies, with the problems lying more in local distortion of the process than (typically) in direct resistance to privatization in any shape or form.

In 1991–2 the Russian government divided responsibilities for privatization between small-scale (trade, catering, small-scale building and transport, etc.) and large, with the former being devolved to municipal level. Larger-scale units were divided into four categories: those subject to mandatory privatization, those for which privatization was forbidden, and, between those categories, two intermediate categories: enterprises whose privatization required the approval of the

State Property Committee (GKI) and those whose privatization required the approval of the government as a whole.

During 1992–4 a number of government decisions and legislative acts reduced the scope of the no-privatization category, in part by extending privatization to a large segment of the designated military-production (VPK) sector. In the revised version of the 1993 privatization plan, local governments were given a free hand to privatize enterprises with a 1992 book value of assets below 1 million roubles, and the percentage breakdown of privatization routes by 1992 book values was: excluded from privatization 30, requiring government approval 31, requiring GKI approval 20, at the discretion of regional authorities 17 (Dmitrii Vasil'ev of GKI in *Izvestiya*, 20 May 1993, p. 4; the missing 2 per cent may or may not be due to rounding).

The role of regional initiative has in practice been substantial in all forms and channels of privatization. Local committees of the GKI have been closely linked with the local administration and council, and the latter, particularly the elected councils, have in turn been closely linked with the local state-management elite. Well-informed analysts say that in practice the privatization process has largely been pursued 'from below' – in the sense that the initiative to move ahead with corporatizing and then privatizing an enterprise tends to come from its management, who are not always tightly constrained in practice by the framework of rules and procedures set by the government and the GKI (Boycko *et al.*, 1994; Vacroux, 1994).

It should follow from this that variations in the rate of privatization across regions will be a good guide to the general orientation of the local elite within a region. However, there are difficulties in applying this criterion:

Data on cumulative numbers of enterprises or initial book value of assets privatized are not published for end-1993 or end-March 1994 by region (though regional data for privatization *during* first quarter 1994 are available).

The development of small-scale and large-scale privatization is not necessarily positively correlated across regions (see Table 9.4 for evidence that they are not). This leaves the observer in a quandary as to how to characterize particular regions:

The role of environmental influences, as against that of local policy orientation, can be hard to disentangle. The best information available in a number of regions will no doubt indicate that the scope for any particular kind of privatization is in varying degrees limited by legal prohibitions and poor economic prospects for the privatized concerns. Ideally, policy orientation should be judged against the limits of the possible and the attractive. Those limits, however, are hard to judge without more information than is available to observers from outside a region.

Table 9.4: Industrial and farm privatization for selected regions

Region	No. of ind. ents priv'd/mandatory no. (ratio) Feb. 1994	pte. farms/'000 rural population Jan. 1994
Stavropol	4.6	16.2
Altai krai	3.72	5.2
Ryazan	2.72	4.4
Voronezh	2.6	3.2
Vologda	2.58	4.3
Tambov	2.32	8.3
Krasnodar	1.62	8.2
Rostov	1.52	8.8
Arkhangel'sk	1.51	2.7
Lipetsk	1.32	3.7
Nizhny Novgorod	1.14	4.2
Kemerovo	0.97	7.9
Omsk	0.95	10.5
Saratov	0.5	18.3
Moscow oblast	0.48	4.1
Perm'	0.46	7.2
Sverdlovsk	0.46	5.2
Kaliningrad	0.38	12.7
Irkutsk	0.32	5.9
St. Petersburg	1.05	
Moscow city	0.33	
RF Average	0.79	6.9

Sources: *CEER* vol. 2, no. 2, p. 13; *RazvReg93:* 90–2.

Table 9.4 gives some information for 21 regions. They are the 20 regions that had the highest absolute numbers of privatized (medium and large) enterprises by 1 February 1994, plus Kaliningrad. The 'performance' of each region in industrial privatization has been assessed (column 1) by the ratio of that number to the reported target number of required privatizations (mandatory privatization targets) for the region. Thus Moscow city, for example, had a high absolute number of privatized enterprises at this date, but a performance, in this sense, that is below the national average.

The second column of figures is a measure of performance, for these 21 regions, in the creation of private farms. The measure used here is the number of private farms per thousand rural population at 1 January 1994. This might sometimes give a different picture from a measure of performance by the share of farmland privatized. (For example, the Altai krai, with very large average-sized private farms, might look more impressive on the hectare basis.)

A correlation between the two variables of +0.02 indicates that the relationship between the two performance indicators is almost non-existent. This could be because farm privatization is determined by rural district elites, and not by the leadership of the region as a whole or the leaderships of the main towns in the region – which will influence the rate of industrial privatization.

In general, the use of indicators such as those set out in Table 9.4 as measures of a region's 'reform orientation' is tricky. Privatization outcomes by region may have more to do with the prospects facing the two sectors in each region than with regional policy-making.

Thus, farm privatization has apparently gone faster in the more fertile regions within this group of territories, than in the poorer, more northerly, ones. (The full set of data on farm privatization is shown in Table A2 of Hanson, 1994b.) So far as industrial privatization is concerned, it could well be that Moscow's original setting of targets for numbers of enterprises for mandatory privatization, by region, bore little relationship to the extent of feasible and attractive industrial privatization by region, so that performance measures based on comparison with those targets are misleading.

At all events, it is interesting to see which regions emerge – for whatever reason – as leaders on these measures. They should, on the face of it, be regions where the institutional setting for enterprise behaviour is changing most. The regions within this group that score well on both performance measures are Stavropol, Tambov, Krasnodar, Rostov, Kemerovo and Omsk. These six regions all have scores above the national average on both indicators.

St. Petersburg is excluded from the reckoning because it has no farm land to begin with. On any general assessment it would need to be added. Moscow city, excluded from the reckoning for the same reason, can still not be added to the list of fast privatizers. Its low score on privatization reflects, amongst other things, a long-running battle over privatization between the mayor of Moscow, Luzhkov, and the GKI under Chubais.

The Moscow city administration has, in effect, been seeking to exclude itself from the national privatization programme. The conflict came to a head in May 1994. At the beginning of April Mayor Luzhkov suspended the privatization process in Moscow. Chubais fought this behind the scenes for some time. According to *Kommersant* (1994, no. 20, 7 June, pp. 28–32) he argued that the mayor of Moscow was breaking the law by refusing to implement national legislation. On 25 May Prime Minister Chernomyrdin, probably at Chubais's insistence, issued an order to Luzhkov, giving him three days to resume the registration of joint-stock companies in Moscow. At this time, GKI information was that there were 8 million Moscow-issued vouchers that had not yet been used to purchase assets, though the period of validity of vouchers was due to end on 30 June, and across the country as a whole the overwhelming majority of vouchers had been used.

Luzhkov told journalists on 30 May that he was not obeying the prime minister's order. Chubais said publicly on 2 June that he would seek to have Luzhkov removed from office. Luzhkov persisted, saying that he wanted the usage of vouchers in privatization to be specially extended in Moscow beyond mid-1994. In the event – and with little regard for the damage to the government's authority – President Yeltsin intervened to allow a special extension of voucher use in Moscow.

The reasons for this conflict in the capital city are unlikely to bear much resemblance to those in Udmurtiya (with its exceptionally high VPK dependence) and Ulyanovsk (with its notoriously unreconstructed Brezhnevite leadership). Why should this problem be so acute in the open, sophisticated capital city? One strong possibility is that this is to do with Western capital. Until 1991 almost all Western joint ventures were in Moscow (see below, especially Table 9.5). The city administration probably developed a cosy relationship with Western investors or with their Russian state-enterprise partners, or both. Privatization of assets in Moscow would tend to exclude them from the making of such deals and the collection of kick-backs. Nowhere else in Russia had this kind of relationship loomed large when privatization was launched.

Nizhny Novgorod is another special case. Its farm privatization performance measure may be misleading. The region scores low on farm privatization in Table 9.4, yet its particular approach to farm privatization was endorsed by the government as a model for other regions, in a decree of 16 April 1994 (Russian TV, 18 April 1994). These two observations could be reconciled in various ways. For example, there may in fact be little enthusiasm for farm privatization in the rural areas of the province, and a locally-devised scheme that looks impressive but has not in fact been applied may have been endorsed for the sake of appearance rather than reality. A less cynical interpretation, however, is also possible. Special attention, and Western technical assistance, have been focused on privatization in this province, and that applies to farm as well as non-farm privatization. The particular approach adopted in Nizhny Novgorod has been to link the privatization of farm land with opportunities for the new private farmers to purchase lorries and to acquire a stake in the wholesale and retail distribution of farm produce in the region – in other words, to develop vertically integrated private firms that extend forward to transport, processing and distribution (Grigory Yavlinsky in discussion at Ebenhausen, 13 April 1994). This approach presumably takes longer to put into practice than the usual selling-off of land as an isolated exercise. In so far as it is carried through, however, it should put the new farmers in a stronger position than the 'vertically disintegrated farm privatization' approach: less at the mercy of transport and distribution networks with monopoly power.

With these *ad hoc* amendments, then, the short list of regions with particularly promising starts in privatization across sectors of the economy becomes the following: Stavropol, Tambov, Krasnodar, Rostov, Kemerovo, Omsk, St. Petersburg and Nizhny Novgorod.

At first sight, the southerly location of most of these regions might seem surprising. Isn't the South anti-reform? That is an over-simplification, in two respects.

First, the observation of particularly weak support for Yeltsin during 1991–3 refers to 29 regions. Of the 29, 23 are indeed below the 55th parallel. Not all southerly regions, however, come into this category (Teague, 1993).

Second, the measures by which the 29 regions were identified were measures of political support. There is no necessary connection between the popularity of democratic politicians in a region and the alacrity with which people in that region embrace private enterprise. Two of the eight regions to whom we have given good marks for privatization, Tambov and Nizhny Novgorod (yes, Nizhny Novgorod, so often described as the front-runner in economic change), are amongst the 29 regions showing relatively traditionalist voting behaviour. In the December 1993 parliamentary elections (not included in Teague's account of regional political patterns earlier in 1993), voting in the city of Nizhny Novgorod favoured the democratic groups (particularly Yavlinsky's Yabloko), but voting in the rest of the region favoured the communists (Yavlinsky at Ebenhausen, 13 April 1994).

There is, after all, no reason why a Russian citizen should not be unhappy about the rise of crime and insecurity and continue to feel more trust in the old *nomenklatura* of a region than in the smart young democrats, while simultaneously making the most of the new opportunities for enrichment. The *nomenklaturshchiki* themselves are doing just that. At the same time, regions with relatively strong farm sectors may exhibit the political traditionalism that seems to go with tilling the soil anywhere; yet they may come to flourish in the future, while more urbanized regions with larger contingents of democratic voters find that modernization is, for them, the route to the rust-belt.

Internationalization

Any account of the role of regional leaders in influencing the opening of the economy is impeded by the poverty of relevant statistical data on trade-dependence and foreign investment by region. The available published data on foreign trade by region, the Russian State Statistical Office, from Goskomstat (*Vneshneekonomicheskie*, 1993) are subject to crippling limitations.

First, they report exports and imports by place of shipment for export and, in the case of imports, by location of importer. The importance of foreign trade to regions, and of particular regions to foreign trade, depends on where the value is added to the export (perhaps successively in different regions at different stages of processing), and where the final user of an imported consumer or investment good is located. Only the use of detailed and reliable regional input–output tables could provide this information. The resulting distortions can be considerable. For example, Samara looks in the official statistics to be a leading exporting region. This is mainly because it contains the VAZ (Lada) car plant. But part of the value of the cars exported from Samara derives from coal, steel, rubber and plastic inputs into the final product, a substantial part of the value of which was added by labour, capital and natural resources in regions other than Samara.

Examples on the import side are provided by Moscow and St. Petersburg. They seem in the statistics to be dominant 'importing' regions for consumer goods, when much of the inflow of consumer goods into those cities is subsequently re-distributed to retail outlets in other regions: it is true that in the case of raw material exports like timber and crude oil, the region of shipment generally is the region where all or almost all the value of the export will have been created.

However, this is not too much help, because of the next problem with the numbers: the regional trade data are in domestic rouble prices.[3] These, unfortunately, still bear little relationship to world market prices. In particular, the rouble trade data by region cannot tell us about the weight of regions in the dollar value of Russia's trade, even if the first problem with the numbers could be disregarded. If the rouble totals for 1992 are compared with the dollar totals for Russia's non-CIS trade (the latter from *Russian Economic Trends*, vol. 2, no. 4), they imply exchange rates of R38 to the dollar for exports and R26 to the dollar for imports. The actual exchange rate, determined on the Moscow Inter-Bank Currency Exchange (MICEX), rose from R180 = $1 at the start of the year to R418 at the end of the year.

This might not matter too much if the dollar values by region could be derived just by scaling up the conversion rate. They cannot, however, because the structure of Russian domestic prices of tradeable goods, though adapting towards the structure of world market prices, was still far from it in 1992, and even up to mid-1994 (*Russian Economic Trends* vol. 3, no. 2, Table 27). In particular, domestic pricing grossly understates the relative dollar value of oil and gas, and therefore understates the importance in exports of regions like Tyumen. The Goskomstat numbers showing, for instance, that Samara was the leading export region in 1992 are extremely misleading, both because of the value-added problem and especially because of the domestic price problem.

It is true that the regional trade values in domestic prices could be of interest as a measure of the perceived importance of foreign trade within a region, provided that we had GDP or net material product (NMP) data by administrative region. Unfortunately, we have not.

The third and last problem with the regional trade data is a mundane one. It applies to all Russian trade data, whether in dollars or roubles, regional or national. It is not therefore necessarily trivial, however. It is that there is, quite simply, a great deal of unreported trade – perhaps particularly in consumer imports. So far as regional patterns are concerned, allowance for unrecorded trade, if it could be made, would very likely show border regions looming larger than they otherwise would.

In mid-1994 the publication for the first time of customs-based trade data (for first-quarter 1994) indicated the extent of the problem. The import total for the quarter was 65 per cent higher than the Goskomstat total. The export totals were closely similar, but the two sources gave widely different figures for individual products. And these are not differences between figures for goods deliveries and figures for payments, where one would expect divergence. Both series are for deliveries. The Goskomstat data are based on enterprise reporting to the statistical authorities; the customs data are based on customs forms from ports and other transit locations (*Finansovye Izvestiya*, 23 June 1994, p. II.)

For all these reasons, the regional pattern of foreign trade will be discussed here only in a broad and qualitative way.

In 1992 and 1993 together, when total Russian non-CIS merchandise exports were running at about \$42 billion a year, oil, natural gas and petroleum products accounted for 45.8 per cent of the total. Machinery, equipment and vehicles, presumably including the Ladas, were 5.5 per cent (derived from *Russian Economic Trends*, vol. 2, no. 4). As the major oil and gas producer region, Tyumen looms large as a source of exports.

Notoriously, the gains to the region itself from this circumstance have been restricted. One reason is that the internal price of energy has remained under control, and relatively low. Also, partly to offset this and impede diversion to exports, the centre has continued to control quantities exported and to impose an export tax. In 1993 the export tax rates were (per cent): crude oil 30, natural gas 18, petrol 40, diesel fuel 30, residual fuel oil 8 (*Russian Economic Trends*, vol. 2, no. 4).

In the past, the grievances of major exporting regions like Tyumen were exacerbated by the central control of all trade, under which export earnings were used to buy imports that were concentrated on final users in European Russia. Of course, there is no reason why the most economically efficient regional allocation of a given set of imports should correspond to the regional pattern of production of the exports that 'paid for' those imports. In the case of Russia, the concentration of population and industry west of the Urals made some such redistribution entirely sensible. The sense of grievance in most fuel and raw material exporting regions was not alleviated, however, by considerations of that sort. As information about the outside world became more readily available during the 1970s, people in Surgut and Nizhnevartovsk noted that, during a boom in the world oil market, Saudi Arabia, Houston and Aberdeen were flourishing places. West Siberia was not, even by Soviet standards.

Moscow continues to commandeer hard currency for centralized imports. The scale of centralized importing, however, is being reduced. In 1992 centralized imports (mainly of machinery and food) were 59 per cent of all non-CIS imports; in 1993 they were only 41 per cent of a much-reduced total (*Russian Economic Trends*, vol. 2, no. 4).

Two factors seem likely to produce a certain regional re-allocation of trading patterns.

First, the adaptation of Russia's product-mix away from value-subtracting manufacture and towards fuel and raw material extraction and primary processing is already evident, despite the lack of substantial new investment (see Hanson, 1994a, for evidence, and McKinnon, 1991, for an exposition of the idea of value-subtracting activity in communist economies). It is likely to continue. Many Russian policy-makers claim to be horrified at the loss of high-tech jewels in Russia's industrial crown, and the tendency to become a hole-in-the-ground economy. The jewels are probably far fewer than they think, however, and several hole-in-the-ground economies are a great deal more prosperous than Russia. Thus economic activity in general may tend to become more concentrated on natural resource regions.

This tendency might also apply to agricultural regions, but with quite different implications for trade. The development of the farm sector is likely to be a matter of import-substitution behind protectionist defences. The tariffs and quotas would be keeping out products dumped by West European and American producers over-producing behind their own protectionist defences – a sad, wasteful business, but not Russia's fault.

The second tendency is likely to be towards trade liberalization and therefore the reduction of centralized imports. Import subsidies were abolished with effect from January 1994. Export taxes and quotas are supposed to be abolished by January 1996. Some important quota controls were dismantled in early 1994. Import tariffs remain, and some have recently been raised, but that is chiefly to do with the move away from direct central control of importing.

Both these tendencies, if they continue, are likely to lead in the near term to some greater linking of regional imports to regional exports. In so far as the weight of raw-material regions in the whole economy increases, that will mean simply that the weight of their import demand will increase. To the extent, however, that internal barriers within the economy are broken down, and Russia really becomes a single market, there should not be administrative tying of imports to exports, region by region.

Regional approaches to foreign investment are also part of the picture. Foreign investment going into Russia is extremely small, with a wide variance amongst estimates of its size. What there is is chiefly direct investment, though portfolio investment is becoming possible as privatization proceeds, and foreigners' access (often through proxies) to voucher auctions also increases. But this flow, whatever its real dimensions, is far smaller than the outflow of capital from Russia over the past three years. In general, it would be hard to underestimate its importance.

Table 9.5: Distribution of operational JVs in the top 10 regions for JV operation, 1989 and mid-1993 (%)

	1989 (n = 322)	mid-1993 (n = 4138)
Moscow	82.6	31.8
St. Petersburg	7.1	14.0
Krasnodar	0.3	3.0
Karelia	0.9	2.8
Murmansk	0.6	2.2
Novosibirsk	0.3	1.5
Samara	0.3	1.4
Komi	0.0	1.4
Moscow obl.	0.9	1.3
Bashkortostan	0.0	1.3

Source: data-base developed by M.J. Bradshaw.

Potentially, however, foreign investment could be of the greatest value, partly as a source of capital funds from abroad that do not bring future balance of payments burdens with them in the way that loans do, but above all as a vehicle for technology transfer. So far as their regional impact is concerned, data on numbers of joint ventures registered, though problematic, give some indication of the pattern. One thing that is clear is that liberalization has brought a rapid diffusion of joint venture registrations away from Moscow.

Table 9.5 shows this. The geographical diffusion of joint venture activity clearly reflects the opening up and regional devolution that has occurred in the Russian economy since the end of communist rule. But it is noticeable that there is only one region in common between this list and the short list of eight regions with high all-round privatization indicators. That is the city of St. Petersburg. It looks as though the factors determining joint venture location so far have little to do with those affecting the rate of privatization.

Moscow city exemplifies this: a conspicuous laggard in privatization remains the leading location for joint ventures. It was suggested earlier that in Moscow there is even a trade-off between the two: that the lure of access to hard currency suggests alternatives to privatization, for those who control state assets in the capital city.

Conclusions

This survey of the Russian regions as players in the Russian economic reform game has, I hope, brought out three things.

First, relations between regional and national government are both chaotic and close to the centre of the whole process of policy-making in Russia. This is not true in the smaller East–Central European countries, where the re-creation of genuine local government now looks more like a return to a humdrum working arrangement.

Second, the prospects of any one region in Russia are especially hard to forecast, since so much depends on the particular path that national policy takes, and that in turn is highly uncertain.

Finally, and perhaps less obviously, what has been said in the previous sections of this paper suggests that in Russia at present the aspirations of political liberals may be at odds with the aspirations of economic liberals. In my concluding remarks, I shall focus on this last point.

On the one hand, most democratically-elected Russian regional legislatures tend in some (not all) ways to resist policies designed to create an effective market economy.

On the other hand, some of the localities where there has been electoral support for democrats, rather than traditionalists – chiefly in large cities – may prove to be areas that will suffer most from further de-control and tighter money. Cities and regions with concentrations of better-educated people have tended to support modernizers against traditionalists. These better-educated people also tend to be employed (or, nowadays, to have been employed) in research and development and science-based manufacturing; yet the sad truth is that much of Russia's 'advanced' industry faces sharply decreased demand (especially for military hardware) or is value-subtracting, or both.

The national policy-makers in any case face a real dilemma in their dealings with the regional politicians. If the tightening of monetary policy is adhered to, plant closures and redundancies will sharpen the resistance of many regional leaders to the centre and its stabilization efforts. Resistance from local elites will be more seriously supported than before by their electorates. This will probably come about even in areas where support for the modernizers has hitherto been strong.

Negotiating these hazards without either resorting to authoritarian rule or abandoning macro-economic stabilization probably requires a more systematic regional policy. So far, government subsidies and soft credits have been handed out on a first-come-first-served basis, modified by the principle that he who shouts loudest shall receive. The alternatives are not so much between a regional policy and an austere abstention from government hand-outs as between a regional policy and wasteful and indiscriminate hand-outs.

Part of this policy would be regional in effect rather than in design. The provision of an effective social safety net and employment service (already an area in which Western assistance is being received) would yield regionally-differentiated flows of unemployment benefits as unemployment developed at different rates in different places. The calculation of nominal benefits that would give the same real 'floor' income in different regions is extremely difficult because of the large differences in price levels across the country. But a continuation of the tendency to devolve such social spending responsibilities to the regions would be a recipe for trouble, as the divergences in their public revenue bases increased. In short, a consideration of the regional issue gives added strength to the case for the development of a proper national social safety net, and for the World Bank and other Western assistance with that development.

Another element in such a policy would be the establishment of the national taxation service and the regional grant equalization process discussed earlier. In other words, regional re-allocation of public money needs to be primarily an outcome of general, nationwide rules of the game, not an exercise in picking branch or regional winners. Such an exercise remains exceptionally difficult in the circumstances of incomplete liberalization and a fragmented economic space.

Notes

* The penultimate section of this chapter includes a modification and up-dating of material published in Hanson, 1994b.

1.   True, the rest of the former Soviet Union, Baltic states apart, seems to be in an even worse mess; but in considering the reasons for Russia's difficulties it is helpful to compare it with the paragons, not the laggards. For a brief review of the whole range of reasons for Russia's lag behind the reform leaders, see Hanson, 1994a.
2.   Russian official data on the consumer price index (CPI) by the eleven regions plus the cities of Moscow and St. Petersburg have also been published. They, too, show an increasing variance in *rates of change*, at any rate from June 1993 to June 1994: the coefficient of variation increases from 0.06 to 0.12. That the relative dispersion of rates of change has been less than that of levels of food prices may, depending on the precise patterns of change, indicate some tendency of price levels to converge. The matter is taken up again below.
3.   A recent Goskomstat source gives 'inflow' (*postuplenie*) of foreign currency arising from merchandise exports by region for 1993. For all 89 territories, these figures sum to $17 bn out of the national total of $43 bn. These figures are telling us something interesting, but what it is is unclear.

References

Andrle, V. (1976), *Managerial Power in the Soviet Union*, Farnborough: Saxon House.
Berkowitz, D. (1993), *Price Liberalization and Local Resistance*, Washington, DC: National Council for Soviet and East European Research.
Boycko *et al.* (1994), 'Mass Privatization in Russia', paper presented at the 2–4 March 1994 meeting of the OECD Advisory Group on Privatization.
Bradshaw, M.J. and P. Hanson, (1994), 'Regions, Local Power and Reform in Russia', in R.W. Campbell (ed.), *Issues in the Transformation of Centrally Planned Economies: Essays in Honor of Gregory Grossman*, Boulder, CO: Westview.

CEER (1994), 'Russia's Regions', *Central European Economic Review* (of the *Wall Street Journal Europe*), 2:2 (Spring), 12–15

Expert Institute (1994), Expert Institute of Russian Union of Industrialists and Entrepreneurs, *Russia's Regions in Transition*, Moscow: RUIE.

Freinkman, L. and S. Titov (1994), 'The Transformation of the Regional Fiscal System in Russia: the Case of Yaroslavl', World Bank Internal Discussion Paper, report IDP-143 (August).

GKStat 93, Goskomstat Rossii, *Osnovnye pokazateli sotsial'no-ekonomicheskogo razvitiya i khoda ekonomicheskoi reformy v Rossiiskoi Federatsii za 1993 god*, Moscow: Goskomstat, 1994.

GKStat Jan 94, Goskomstat Rossii, *Sotsial'no-ekonomicheskoe polozhenie Rossii. Yanvar' 1994*, Moscow: Goskomstat, 1994.

Gorod Sankt P (1994), *Gorod Sankt-Peterburg 1993*, St. Petersburg: Mayor's office.

Hanson, P. (1994a), 'The Future of Russian Economic Reform', *Survival*, vol. 36, no. 3 (autumn), pp. 28–46.

— (1994b), *Regions, Local power and Economic Reform in Russia*, London: Royal Institute of International Affairs, Post-Soviet Business Forum paper.

Helf, G. (1994), *All the Russias: Center, Core and Periphery in Soviet and Post-Soviet Russia*, PhD dissertation in Politicial Science, University of California at Berkeley.

— and J.W. Hahn (1992), 'Old Dogs and New Tricks: Party Elites in the Russian Regional Elections of 1990', National Council for Soviet and East European Research, mimeo.

Illarionov, A., R. Layard and P. Orszag (1994), 'The Conditions of Life', in A. Åslund (ed.), *Economic Transformation in Russia*, London: Pinter, pp. 127–57.

Kirkow, P. (1994), 'The Rise of Autocratic Rule in the Primorskii krai', CREES, University of Birmingham, mimeo.

Lavrov, A.M. (1994), 'Byudzhetnyi federalizm obraztsa 1994 g.: shag vpered, dva shaga nazad', *Rossiya regionov. Byulleten'* no. 1, Moscow: Analiticheskii tsentr pri Prezidente RF, Rabochaya gruppa po regional'nym problemam Prezidentskogo soveta (October).

McAuley, M. (1992), 'Politics, Economics and Elite Realignment in Russia: A Regional Perspective', *Soviet Economy*, January–March, pp. 46–89.

— (1994), 'Regional Politics in Russia: St. Petersburg v. Krasnodar', paper given at the CREES General Seminar, University of Birmingham (December).

McKinnon, R. (1991), *The Order of Economic Liberalization: Financial Control in the Transition to a Market Economy*, Baltimore: Johns Hopkins University Press.

MinFinVE 94, Ministerstvo Finansov Rossiiskoi Federatsii, 'Rossiiskie finansy v 1993 godu', *Voprosy ekonomiki*, 1994, no. 1, pp. 3–86.

Nemova, L. (1993), 'Rynok truda', *Ekonomika i organizatsiya promyshlennogo proizvodstva*, 1993, no. 10, p. 39.

Oates, W.E. (1992), 'Fiscal Decentralization and Economic Development', *National Tax Journal*, XLVI, vol. 2, pp. 237–44.

Petrov, N.V. (1994a), 'Chto predstavlyaet sebya novaya predstavitel'naya vlast'?', *Rossiya regionov. Byulleten'* no. 1.

— (1994b), 'Regional'nye vybory-94: itogi i uroki', *Rossiya regionov. Byulleten'* no. 2.

— and A. Treivish (1994), 'Riski regional'noi dezintegratsii Rossii', Moscow: mimeo.

RazvReg 93, Goskomstat Rossii, *Razvitie ekonomicheskikh reform v regionakh Rossiiskoi Federatsii v 1993 godu*, Moscow: Goskomstat, 1994.

Rutland, P. (1993), *The Politics of Economic Stagnation in the Soviet Union: The Role of Local Party Organs in Economic Management*, Cambridge: Cambridge University Press.

Savvateeva, I. (1994), 'Evgenii Nazdratenko kak zerkalo rossiiskikh reform', *Izvestiya*, 1 December, p. 5.

Struyk, Raymond J. and Jennifer Daniell (1994), 'Housing Privatisation in Urban Russia', Moscow: the Urban Institute, mimeo.

Teague, E. (1993), 'North-South Divide: Yeltsin and Russia's Provincial Leaders', *RFE/RL Research Report*, vol. 2, no. 47 (26 November), pp. 7–24.

— (1994), 'Russia's Local Elections Begin', *RFE/RL Research Report*, vol. 3, no. 7 (18 February), pp. 1–5.

Vacroux, A., (1994), 'Privatization in the Regions: Primorskii krai', in Ira W. Lieberman and John Nellis (eds), *Russia: Creating Private Enterprises and Efficient Markets*, Washington, DC: World Bank, pp. 35–45.

Vneshneekonomicheskie (1993): Vneshneekonomicheskie svyazi Rossiiskoi Federatsii, Moscow: Goskomstat.

Wallich, C.I. (1992), *Fiscal Decentralization. Intergovernmental Relations in Russia*, Washington, DC: World Bank, Studies of Economies in Transition, no. 6.

— (ed.) (1994), *Fiscal Federalism in Russia*, Washington, DC: World Bank.

Williamson, J. (1992), *Trade and Payments after Soviet Disintegration*, Washington, DC: Institute for International Economics.

Wishnevsky, J. (1994), 'Problems of Russian Regional Leadership', *RFE/RL Research Report*, vol. 3, no. 19 (13 May), pp. 6–14.

10. The Siberian and Far Eastern Challenge to Centre–Periphery Relations in Russia: A Comparison between Altaiskii and Primorskii Kraya

Peter Kirkow

A characteristic feature of the economic geography of the former Soviet Union was the excessive metropolitan dominance over peripheral regions,[1] with the centre developing remote territories as monocultures, i.e., with these territories specializing heavily on particular extractive industries (oil, gas, coal) or agriculture. There was also, as was outlined in Chapter 1 on Russia, a highly concentrated form of urbanization, typically with one big capital city in each region controlling rural areas and, in fact, mirroring national centre–periphery relations in miniature. Both metropolitan dominance and concentrated urbanization were particularly striking features for Siberia and the Soviet Far East, which have a huge diversity in resource and labour endowment but were traditionally treated by the centre as both a raw materials appendage and a military fortress.

The collapse of the central planning system raised the issue of institutional restructuring in terms of ownership, materials supply and sales networks as well as the setting up of new, 'horizontal' economic links between regions. However, the lack of investment funds and technical expertise, and also open resistance to market reform outside Moscow and St. Petersburg, raise the question whether an authoritarian top-down reform approach is desirable or whether there is any scope for 'reform from below' or, in the worst case, leeway for local discretion in retarding economic reform. The latter phenomenon was discussed by Philip Hanson on the wider national scale and will here be scrutinized in two case studies.

This chapter looks at two regions which have distinctive geographical features and are peripheral in rather different ways. While the Primorskii krai (PK) is a gateway to Asian and Pacific countries, being located in proximity to international financial and trade centres, the Altaiskii krai (AK) embraces a remote territory with limited access to modern transport and communication networks. However, both are comparable in terms of administrative status, size of territory and population, as well as in their degree of industrial specialization, particularly their specialization on natural-resource extraction. Moreover, both had, at the beginning of radical economic liberalization in early 1992, a reform-oriented executive administration embarking enthusiastically on market reform, although the balance of political power swung back in the opposite direction in late 1993. While the PK now has an absolutist executive power suppressing oppositional forces, the AK is largely controlled by traditionalists of an orthodox communist–agrarian alliance in the new regional parliament.

The analysis in this chapter will focus on the interaction of politics and economics at the regional level, and will examine the conflict between the national policy agenda and regional interests. It will draw particular attention to the regional scope for autonomous development towards market reform and ask whether the existing institutional structure, balance of power and incentive system are conducive to radical changes. In addition, the character of the new regional leaderships and their interaction with the centre will be scrutinized, with the aim of reaching some preliminary conclusions on which region is likely to prosper or reform (which may not necessarily be the same thing).

This chapter will start by introducing the major geographical and socio-economic features of the two regions. There will then follow a discussion of the institutional structure and balance of political power for each region separately. Finally, a comparison of the two regions' potential for autonomous restructuring will be carried out, by means of a review of privatization, fiscal arrangements, foreign trade and the financial sector. The analysis draws on earlier papers on each region; and this chapter will be the first comparison of results from these regional studies.[2]

General Outline of Specific Socio-Economic Features

Both regions have not only a location peripheral to the centre in Moscow, but are also peripheral within their macro-region: the southern part of Western Siberia and the Russian Far East, respectively. The AK has a state border with Kazakhstan and a customs frontier with the recently established autonomous Republic of Altai (former Gorno-Altaiskaya autonomous oblast). The creation of the new republic was a unilateral decision by the new authorities of the republic and represents a further fragmentation of the economic space of Russia. The PK has a state border with China and North Korea as well as an open exit to the Sea of Japan. While both are, in administrative status, kraya, the AK contains a higher territorial subdivision into 77 (60 rural) raiony, compared with only 25 (14 rural) in the PK. Both regions are characterized by a high concentration of urban settlements, the PK having an industrial agglomeration of more than one million people in the south (Vladivostok–Nakhodka) and the AK one of 600,000 in the north (Barnaul–Novoaltaisk).

Table 10.1 (see below) indicates a considerably higher density of population in both the AK and PK than the Russian average. Moreover, both peripheral regions are major junctions for migrants and refugees. The AK had an in-migration of 27,200 people in 1993 (down from 34,760 the year before). These were mainly refugees from Central Asia. In contrast, out-migration was continuously increasing: 4,421 people in 1991, 9,600 in 1992 and 10,100 in 1993.[3] Besides the dominant Russian population, there is a considerable national minority of 127,000 Russian Germans in the AK.

The 1,162-km border of the PK with China has become a very sensitive issue. About 74 million people are living in the two Chinese provinces opposite to the PK alone, and these mountainous areas have a relatively high rate of unemployment. It has been claimed that, after the Russian government introduced visa-free entry in late 1992, there was a mass influx of Chinese people. Estimates range up to 200,000 Chinese citizens who have crossed one of the five checkpoints of the PK alone in 1993 and a lot of them are said to have remained in Russia after the expiry of the permitted term of their visits (UR, 16 November 1993, p. 1). A report in *Kommersant-daily* (26 May 1994, p. 3) claimed that there were 150,000 Chinese citizens resident in the PK at that time. Alarms about the alleged influx led the PK administration to restrict visa-free entry for citizens of neighbouring countries in September 1993,[4] a decision which violated the prerogative of the Russian government in international matters (UR, 24 November 1993, p. 1). They also gave 14,300 hectares of land to 200 Cossack families in the Khasanskii raion, who would, in return, defend Russian interests in this border district (RFEU, December 1993, p. 5). Another example of ethnic tensions, though on a smaller scale, was the expansion of the logging business by the Russian–South Korean joint venture *Svetlaya* into the traditional habitat of the Udeghe indigenous people (RFEU, December 1992, p. 7).

Apart from timber and, in the case of the PK, fish and precious metals, both regions have no other particular raw materials which could be traded on a mass scale on the world market, as is possible with products like oil, gas or coal. Traditionally, the PK accounted for 17 per cent of all-Union food production by value (as a result of the dominance in fishing – most of the home ports of the Pacific fishing fleet are here – with 80 per cent of the catch exported from the region); the PK also produced 80 per cent of all fluoride concentrates and 90 per cent of boron in the former USSR (Osipov, 1992, p. 13). It also has substantial deposits of ferrous and precious metals (tin, lead and silver); timber, copper and furs were exported; and the territory delivered 9 per cent of the rice and 15 per cent of the soybean production in the Russian Federation (Savalei, 1991, p. 73). The AK has some resources for the construction industry (building materials, sandstone) and a few deposits of mineral salts. The main natural asset for the AK remains the 7.3 million hectares of arable land, which includes the considerable extension of arable land at the end of the 1950s as a result of Khrushchev's virgin soil campaign (Kurakin, 1960, p. 41).

The economic structure inherited from the former Soviet system of industrial branch planning was strongly influenced by the specialization policies of all-union branch ministries, with their perception of Siberia and the Far East as an enormous treasure trove and supplier of raw materials, whose exploitation was conditioned by the drastic under-pricing of transport services. Table 10.2 compares the structure of the industrial sector of the two regions and Russia as a whole. Unfortunately, comparable data for the same year or years are not available, and substantial relative price and output changes between the 1980s and 1993 blur the comparison. For example, the weight of the machine-building and metalworking sector has been falling in Russia as a whole. However, some comparative features of the branch structures are clear.

Table 10.1: Physical and demographic features of the Altaiskii and Primorskii kraya in comparison with Russia, 1 January 1994

Indicators	Russia	AK	% of Russia	PK	% of Russia
Territory (thousand sq. km)	17,075.4	169.1	1.0	165.9	0.9
Population (thousands)	148,400.0	2,684.3	1.8	2,287.0	1.5
Density (people per sq.km)	8.7	15.8	–	13.8	–
Natural increase (compared with 1992, thousands)	-300.0	2.3	–	7.8	–

Sources: Compiled from Goskomstat RSFSR, *Narodnoe khozyaistvo RSFSR v 1990g.*, Moscow, 1991; *EkiZh*, no. 6, February 1994, p. 9; Mel'nik and Rodionova, 1994, p. 27; AP, 10 February 1994, p. 2, and UR, 3 February 1994, p. 2.

The substantial difference between the two regions, on the one hand, and Russia, in the fuel and energy sector, is due to the fact that it includes, by definition, oil, gas, coal and electricity production, while only the last of them is relevant for the AK and PK, apart from some coal production in the PK. While metallurgical industries had a relatively lower share than the Russian average, that of machine building and metalworking was considerably higher, reflecting both the small energy-sector shares and the presence of huge production complexes for the defence industry in both regions, although the AK's share has been falling substantially, to 32.3 per cent in 1992 (Loginov, 1993, p. 14). The relatively heavy weight of non-fuel primary industries is indicated by higher percentage figures for the food industry. This applies still more strongly to the PK, where fisheries and fish-processing alone amounted to more than 30 per cent of the gross value of industrial output in 1985–90 (Goskomstat RSFSR, 1991, p. 131). Finally, the chemical and timber, paper and pulp industries had a higher relative importance than the Russian average in both regions.

Table 10.2:   Branch structure of industry by volume of production in the
               Altaiskii and Primorskii Kraya in 1985 and 1990 in comparison
               with Russia in 1993 (percentage share of sector in gross value of
               industrial output; AK and PK in constant 1982 prices, Russia in
               current 1993 prices)

Sector	AK		PK		Russia
	1985	1990	1985	1990	1993
Total	100.0	100.0	100.0	100.0	100.0
Fuel and Energy Sector	2.7	3.0	7.7	6.6	26.7
Metallurgical Industry	2.4	3.2	3.6	3.8	17.2
Machine building and Metalworking	40.9	37.8	24.3	23.7	20.3
Chemical and Timber Industries	21.2	20.9	8.2	8.1	11.4
Construction Materials Industry	2.4	3.0	6.7	6.3	3.3
Light Industry	13.2	13.0	4.4	4.3	5.2
Food Industry	15.9	18.4	41.6	42.9	12.4
Other	1.3	0.7	3.5	4.3	3.5

Note: The appropriate figures for Russia in 1985 and 1990 were not available
         from Goskomstat RSFSR statistical yearbooks. The percentage figures for
         1993 were calculated by the author from a recent source which indicated
         industrial output in current prices.

Sources: Compiled from Loginov, 1993, p. 14; Goskomstat RSFSR, Vladivostok,
            1991, p. 131, and Goskomstat Rossii, Moscow, 1994, p. 63.

This distinctive industrial structure, which traditionally restricted the
AK and PK to the extraction of natural resources and the supply of raw
materials and military hardware to the centre, is today, under conditions
of high inflation, the reduction of transport subsidies and the decline
of the system of centrally allocated material supply, limiting
opportunities for autonomous development. Moreover, both regions lost
a substantial amount of state subsidies as a previously closed military
district in the case of the PK and state compensations for the difference

between wholesale and retail prices of agricultural products in the case of the AK. Table 10.3 analyses the economic performance in both regions in comparison with Russia in 1993.

Table 10.3:   **Economic indicators for the Altaiskii and Primorskii kraya in comparison with Russia, 1993 (current prices of late 1993)**

Indicator	Russia	AK	% of Russia	PK	% of Russia
Population (thousands)	148,400	2,684.3	1.8	2,287.0	1.5
Industrial output (bn R)	109,400	1,258.9	1.1	1,165.1	1.0
Production of consumer goods (bn R)	36,500	488.1	1.3	705.3	1.9
Capital investment (bn R)	25,200	254.6	1.0	354.8	1.4
Retail Trade (bn R)	58,800	48.3	0.1	603.6	1.0
Services (bn R)	6,400	54.8	0.8	102.6	1.6

Sources: Compiled from EkiZh, no. 6, February 1994, p. 7; Sidorov *et al.*, 1994a, p. 4; AP, 9 February 1994, pp. 1–2, and UR, 3 February 1994, p. 2

Apart from higher consumer goods production and more investment activities in the PK, the difference in retail trade and services between both regions is striking. However, one has to bear in mind that there are substantial price differences between the two regions, which make comparisons difficult. The fact that the AK with 1.8 per cent of Russia's population had less than 0.1 per cent of Russia's retail turnover suggests a considerably lower per capita consumption in comparison with the Russian average. There could be three reasons for this: (a) people in the AK are really poorer; (b) retail prices in the AK are lower; and (c) people in the AK rely much more than the Russian average on subsistence farming or informal, unreported trade or both for their consumption. Probably some combination of the three explains this bizarre figure. Moreover, the relatively low figure of 1.0 per cent of Russia's retail turnover in the PK, which has a population of 1.5 per cent of the Russian total, has clearly not taken into consideration informal, cross-border trade with China. The 1.6 per cent of Russian total services in the PK could also be an understatement.

This becomes particularly clear if one compares figures for average monthly income, as indicated in Table 10.4.

Table 10.4:   **Social indicators for the Altaiskii and Primorskii kraya in comparison with Russia, December 1993**

Indicator	Russia	%	AK	%	PK	%
Average income (thousand roubles, % of Russia)	141,200.0	100.0	118,000.0	83.6	244,400.0	173.1
Personal savings as end-year stock (cash and deposits in billions of roubles and percentage of total income)	19,300.0	24.3	317.9	29.7	303.3	25.3
Official unemployment (thousand people and % of total workforce)	800.0	1.1	15.8	1.1	6.9	0.5

Sources: Compiled from EkiZh, no. 6, February 1994, p. 9; AP, 10 February 1994, pp. 1–2; UR, 3 February 1994, p. 2.

There was a striking difference in monthly money income in December 1993 between the AK and PK at a rate of 1:2.1, while cumulative savings as an end-year stock of cash and deposits was quite high and similar in absolute figures in both regions, which is due to the fact that money income growth in 1993 exceeded the increase of prices. However, while the PK had apparently higher prices, higher money incomes, but also a probably more important non-farm informal economy, the AK population faced lower prices in the formal economy and relied probably much more on unreported subsistence agriculture. Moreover, official unemployment in the PK was less than half that in the AK in December 1993, which is probably due to there being more job opportunities in new commercial structures of the PK.

The results of this comparative analysis could be summarized as follows. Although the AK had a higher total industrial output than the PK in 1993, its retail turnover was less than one-tenth and its services were less than half those in the latter. This, combined with the fact that the PK workforce earned officially, on average, twice as much (in nominal terms) as their counterparts in the AK, suggests that PK enterprises had sources of revenue not shared by the AK, probably from trade in consumer goods with neighbouring China and other Asian countries, the money from which was partly used for wage payments and the value of which does not appear in industrial output statistics. Moreover, new commercial structures have probably developed faster than in the AK. One explanation of these differences is that increased exports of fish resources[5] and precious metals have counterbalanced the general decline of production in the PK (Savalei, 1994, p. 2). However, this does not amount to economic prosperity, nor does it constitute success in institutional reform. Apart from stopping inflation, full price liberalization and the implementation of hard budget constraints, a radical restructuring of the Russian economy in terms of ownership, material supply and sales networks has still to take place in both regions, even though some (enforced) alterations of product mix have occurred in the two *kraya*, as they have in Russia generally.

The Revival of Traditionalists in the AK

At the outset of radical economic reform policy in 1992, there was, as at the national level, a classic stalemate between executive and legislative power in the AK, with a new reform-minded governor and his young, enthusiastic team in office versus a predominantly conservative regional soviet, consisting mainly of old *nomenklatura* members, who could rely on a strong agrarian lobby. Three men were competing for the new governorship in autumn 1991: Yu. Zhil'tsov (the former head of the regional executive committee),[6] A. Nazarchuk (the leader of the regionally influential agrarian lobby *Agropromsoyuz)* and V. Raifikesht (a sovkhoz director from Novoaltaisk near Barnaul). In fact, as part of the administrative policies described in Elizabeth Teague's chapter, President Yeltsin had in 1991 installed a new prefect system, in which he appointed personally or confirmed the new head of the regional administration, who was supposed not only to control the process of economic reform at the sub-national level, but also, if necessary, to override decisions democratically adopted by the regional soviet. Yeltsin's approval of the appointment of Raifikesht as governor, who was considered by the regional elite as the most neutral person, reflected the balance of power in the regional soviet at that time.

Additional executive power was given to the new governor to speed up reforms at the local level. Raifikesht used his power in a traditional Soviet way, mainly to find administrative answers to particular shortages, for example, by organizing additional machinery for the harvest and fuel in the winter. Thus, in July 1993 he gave *Altainefteprodukt* instructions to supply kolkhozy and sovkhozy without prepayment with petrol from their reserve stocks. At this time, he also pressed *Altaidizel'* to send an extra 600 diesel engines to Krasnoyarsk in exchange for 800 combine harvesters (AP, 21 July 1993, p. 1). This kind of continuing administrative intervention was in part a consequence of insufficient restructuring of monopoly associations and Moscow's own centralized issuing of state orders and soft credits as well as attempts both central and regional at price controls for basic foodstuffs.

Institutional changes in the AK farm sector remained state-dominated. For example, the agrarian lobby of *Agropromsoyuz*, which has its roots in former state structures of agricultural production and which has influential representatives in legislative power, set up its own commodity exchange, trade and commercial companies. This is currently being duplicated by the agricultural committee of the AK administration with its own channels of wholesale trade, marketing and foreign trade (AP, 21 April 1994, pp. 1–2). In general, successor state organizations and the Altai administration still remain closely linked. *Altaiagropromsnab* dominates the supply of agricultural machinery, spare parts for tractors, tyres and batteries in the region (AP, 17 November 1993, pp. 1–2). *Altaimolprom* managed, from its monopoly position as regional purchaser of dairy products, to force the price for 1 kg of milk down to R 80 (farmers wanted R 100–110), while, at the same time, a stock of 5,000 tonnes of butter and cheese was piling up in their warehouses in late September 1993 (AP, 11 November 1993, p. 2). Moscow did not set a good example in this sector. Thus Yeltsin, after his return from Sakha/Yakutia in 1993, ordered meat to be sent to the Far North without prepayment. This, it is claimed, cost *Altaimyasoprom* R 5bn (AP, 17 February 1994, pp. 1–2). At a time of very high inflation, payment delays have high real costs.

The new governor took over most of the staff of the former regional executive committee, but appointed six new heads for the eight committees, which were organized according to industrial sectors, and one new secretary for his own 'apparatus'. Among the young doctoral candidates appointed to these posts, including the heads of the committees for property administration (S. Potapov) and for health service, culture and education (V. Kulikov), the most interesting figure in the new team was the then 25-year-old new secretary of the gubernatorial apparatus, V. Ryzhkov, who was described as Raifikesht's 'political brain' and the driving force for market reforms.[7]

The new regional administration got additional executive support from the new representative of the President in the AK, N. Shuba, who was sent there to watch the implementation of Yeltsin's decrees closely and to coordinate federal executive institutions (army, police, secret service).[8] As a former soldier in Afghanistan and head of the regional committee of Afghanistan veterans, he could rely on an informal network of colleagues within the armed forces. While originally working in the shadows, away from public scrutiny, he got increasingly involved in public debates after Yeltsin's edict 'On the stage-by-stage Constitutional Reform in the Russian Federation' on 21 September 1993, using the local press to explain not only the content of this edict, but also the main innovations in the new Russian Constitution.[9]

The regional soviet, elected in March 1990 and consisting of 230 deputies, had two opposing fractions, one of which was a core of orthodox communists and agrarian hardliners (about 35–50 persons), resisting privatization, land reform and new tax policies.[10] This group relied on the powerful agricultural lobby of *Agropromsoyuz* with its charismatic leader Nazarchuk. The other grouping was the reform-minded 'Deputies' Club', which consisted mainly of members of the intelligentsia (lawyers, teachers, doctors) and which tried to initiate new legislative acts on local government, land reform and the introduction of a new banking system (Sarichev, 1994, p. 2).

For day-to-day business (under central legislation of 1992, reforming local government) a 'small council' of 36 deputies, who worked on a full-time basis, was set up. It consisted of eight committees which were delineated by economic sectors and which copied the structure of the administration. This is a further illustration of the point made earlier by Adrian Campbell, from his studies of city governments in Ekaterinburg and St. Petersburg, that the division of function between executive and legislative power has remained blurred.

Headed by its new chairman, A. Surikov, who had previously worked for many years as a director of such construction associations as *Altaiavtodor* and *Altaistroi* (AP, 25 November 1993, p. 2), the regional soviet's distinctive administrative approach was to maintain controlling and redistributional functions. Constantly interfering in the sphere of executive power, the 'small council' tried to have the final word in privatization as well as the redistribution of state credits and other budgetary resources (Sarichev, 1994, p. 2). It could also rely on its own channels in its lobbying efforts to get soft credits from the centre. In the second half of August 1993 Surikov met twice with the chairman of the Supreme Soviet, Ruslan Khasbulatov, once with the Russian Prime Minister, Viktor Chernomyrdin, and also with officials in the Ministry of Finance, as a result of which the AK received R 15 bn for their harvest (AP, 31 August 1993, p. 1). It is a remarkable indication of the role of informal channels that the head of the regional soviet and not the governor of the AK got this money. Moreover, in a clear search for popular support, the AK soviet took the decision to spend additionally 2 per cent of the consolidated budget in 1993 (R 4.9bn) on agriculture; this went mainly to the loss-making state sectors of milk and meat production (AP, 7 September 1993, p. 2).

Both the AK administration and the regional soviet tried to use the inter-regional association 'Siberian Agreement' to lobby in Moscow as a joint force for preferential treatment and the issue of new credits. This association first opted for a self-sufficient supply of machinery, foodstuffs and other resources, and the setting up of a common energy, transport and information network. The association's spokesmen made repeated political declarations of their intention to create a Siberian republic (for example, *Sovetskaya Sibir'*, 7 October 1990). In summer 1993, the AK administration involved the association in its approach to the government, the Ministry of Fuel and Energy and the newly created joint-stock company *EES Rossii*, which controls the national grid, to find forms of compensation for low-income groups in connection with the price increase of electric power in August 1993 (AP, 14 September 1993, p. 1). In September 1993, a session of the coordination committee on agriculture of the 'Siberian Agreement' took place in Barnaul, where a decision was taken to request from the centre a tax exemption for all Siberian agricultural producers (AP, 22 September 1993, p. 1). Another example is the agreement on common price regulation for agricultural products among the more than 20 member regions in Krasnoyarsk in February 1994 (AP, 23 February 1994, p. 1).

In the conflict between President Yeltsin and the Russian parliament in 1993 the AK executive and legislature took different sides. At its special session after the announcement of Yeltsin's edict 'On the stage-by-stage Constitutional Reform in the Russian Federation' on 21 September 1993, the regional soviet declared this document to be 'unconstitutional' and said that it would comply, from now onwards, only with Alexander Rutskoi's (i.e. the parliament's) rule (AP, 25 September 1993, p. 1). After Yeltsin forcibly disbanded the Supreme Soviet in October 1993, Surikov diplomatically changed his position, claiming now that both sides were responsible for these tragic events and, most importantly, the regional soviet continued its work despite calls from the President for all regional soviets to disband themselves (AP, 12 October 1993, p. 1). At the same time, in contrast to several other Siberian regional administrations (Novosibirsk, Chita), that in the AK supported Yeltsin's edict, and Raifikesht linked his hopes of the resumption of radical economic reforms with the return of Egor Gaidar into the Russian government (AP, 30 September 1993, p. 1).

The problem of national policy implementation was complicated by the fact that the creation of national party structures at the regional level is only in its infancy. Philip Hanson discussed this issue in his chapter on general regional development in Russia. So far as the AK is concerned, only two national leaders came to visit the region in the run-up to the elections on 12 December 1993. The leader of the 'Party for Russian Unity and Accord' (PRES), Sergei Shakhrai, arrived in Barnaul on 28 November 1993 and announced his intention to unite all Russian regions (AP, 30 November 1993, p. 1). However, his party had no clear social base in the AK and his candidate in the region, V. Tverdokhlebov, did not do very well in these elections.[11] A few days later, the leader of the Agrarian Party, Mikhail Lapshin, visited the Altai and declared in an interview (AP, 9 December 1993, p. 1) that he intended to create, together with the Deputy Prime Minister, Alexander Zaveryukha, regional structures for his party, relying mainly on the peasants.

Lapshin's representative in the AK, A. Nazarchuk, was meanwhile trying to combine commerce and politics. While he was using his direct access to the head of the Russian Central Bank, Viktor Gerashchenko, to get central credits and to set up *Altaisel'khozbank* (AP, 2 December 1993, p. 1), he started, at the same time, to restructure *Agropromsoyuz* into the Altai organization of the Agrarian Party (AP, 16 March 1994, p. 1), the founding congress of which took place in April 1994 (AP, 19 April 1994, p. 1). In an earlier interview, Nazarchuk declared openly his aim of getting control over both legislative and executive power in the AK (AP, 16 March 1994, p. 1).[12]   For these high ambitions, Zaveryukha provided him with political capital, bringing during his visit to the Altai an additional credit of R 17bn to buy petrol for spring tilling (AP, 30 March 1994, p. 1). The Communist Party of the Russian Federation (KPRF) claims to have 12,000 active members in the AK, of which 30 per cent are pensioners, and relies also mainly on support from rural areas.[13]

Finally, in early October 1993, 'Altai's Choice', a regional organization of 'Russia's Choice', was set up, the founding members of which were, apart from democratic groupings, the Union of Afghanistan Veterans, Cossack groupings, a number of entrepreneurs, heads of raion administrations and directors of state enterprises plus members of the intelligentsia (AP, 7 October 1993, p. 1). Its leader, who was also the head of the governor's apparatus, V. Ryzhkov, received about 100,000 votes during the election to the State Duma (AP, 12 January 1994, p. 1). However, 'Altai's Choice' could not rely on a clear social base and did not manage to create a workable party structure. As a result, it was almost marginalized during the elections to the new regional parliament in March 1994[14] (see below).

While Yeltsin's bombardment of the Russian parliament had no immediate effect on the voting patterns of the AK population in the elections to the new federal parliament on 12 December 1993,[15] as a result of which the most radical reformers (Ryzhkov, Sarichev) moved to Moscow, the configuration of political power in the AK changed dramatically, after their departure in early 1994, in favour of traditionalists in the regional soviet. On 13 January 1994, Raifikesht announced his intention to quit as the governor of the region and to return to his former sovkhoz (AP, 15 January 1994, p. 2).[16]

His personal proposal to the President for a successor was his deputy, L. Korshunov, who was appointed by Yeltsin's edict on 20 January 1994. The new governor had previously worked as the head of the construction organizations *Altaipromstroi* and *Altaikoksokhimstroi* as well as the head of the Rubtsovsk city executive committee (AP, 22 January 1994, p. 1) and he considers himself 'radical in economics and a centrist in politics'.[17]   He is clearly in favour of market reforms and, in his opinion, prices for energy and agricultural products should have been freed right at the beginning of the radical reform programme (AP, 12 February 1994, p. 3). However, although he admitted that credits received from the centre had been squandered, since the regional administration tried to give every enterprise an equal share, and that there was a net drain on budgetary resources by the existing social infrastructure, he favoured a further emission of money 'as long as it keeps enterprises going' (interview with L. Korshunov). He also announced a 'reorientation of his team' (AP, 12 February 1994, p. 3), which could only mean a reconciliation with the regional soviet, since the most radical reformers (Raifikesht, Ryzhkov) had already left.

While there was still a fairly even division of voting preferences in favour of either the Agrarian–Communist faction or the democratic platform during the elections to the federal parliament, the former had a clear victory at the elections to the regional parliament on 13 March 1994. This is mainly due to political apathy in the urban centres[18] (most of the nine voting districts, in which the turnout was less than the 25 per cent required for a valid election, were in Barnaul and Rubtsovsk), where most of the supporters of democratic parties are expected (in Russia generally) to be. This pattern of the 'ruralization' of regional elections is one that has been identified by Nikolai Petrov as a Russia-wide phenomenon of the 1994 regional elections (Petrov, 1994, p. 12).

In the AK, however, there is also evidence of increasing disillusionment among the population generally. According to an earlier sociological survey, only 15 per cent of the AK population supported radical economic reforms at the beginning of March 1994 (Grigor'ev and Rastov, 1994, p. 4) compared with 24.8 per cent in August 1992 (Rastov, 1993, p. 22). Moreover, the more efficient organization of the Communist Party and the Agrarian Party in rural areas reinforced this urban–rural cleavage in voting patterns. The importance of workplace background and the marginal role of party affiliation (candidates were identified in the lists of candidates either by party or by workplace, but not by both) becomes clear from Table 10.5. The only party worth mentioning in absolute figures is the Communist Party which won two seats in the new regional parliament.

For the 50 seats in the new parliament, one-mandate voting districts were set up with an average of 38,400 eligible voters (AP, 12 January 1994, p. 1). Candidates had mostly been proposed by working collectives or voting groups which, according to the election regulations, had to contain 30–50 people, and each candidate needed the support of at least 3 per cent of all eligible voters in one of the voting districts (AP, 1 February 1994, p. 2). Table 10.5 shows that officials from the executive were the most effective of all (from a 20.2 per cent share of candidates to a 34.0 per cent share of elected deputies, or, in absolute figures, every third candidate was elected), while the intelligentsia suffered a considerable defeat.

Table 10.5:   **Candidates and elected deputies of the AK regional parliament by workplace background and party affiliation, 13 March 1994 and 24 April 1994**

	Candidates	% of total	Elected deputies after the first round	% of total	Elected deputies after the second round	% of total
Total	233	100.0	41	100.0	50	100.0
Executive power	47	20.2	15	36.6	17	34.0
Regional soviet	10	4.3	2	4.9	2	4.0
Khozyaistvenniki	76	32.6	14	34.1	17	34.0
Intelligentsia	51	21.9	6	14.6	7	14.0
Communist Party	11	4.7	2	4.9	2	4.0
Other	38	16.3	2	4.9	5	10.0

Note: 'Executive power' refers to heads and deputy heads of raion administrations. *Khozyaistvenniki* includes directors and deputy directors of joint-stock companies, kolkhozy, sovkhozy and poultry farms. Intelligentsia refers to teachers, doctors and scientists of research institutes.

Sources: Compiled from AP (22 February 1994, p. 2; 23 February 1994, p. 2; 17 March 1994, p. 1 and 27 April 1994, p. 1).

At its first session on 29 March 1994, the 41 elected deputies (re-elections for the remaining seats took place on 24 April) voted for Surikov as their new (and old) chairman, while the leader of the regional Communist Party, V. Safronov, became his deputy (AP, 31 March 1994, p. 1). A few days later, Surikov announced publicly the regional parliament's intention to stop privatization [19] and to control prices for energy (AP, 5 April 1994, p. 1). Only six of the elected deputies were willing to work as deputies on a full-time basis (AP, 12 April 1994, p. 2), four of whom are heading the new committees (economics, budget and finance, legislation and social policy). In the un-up to the second session at the end of April 1994, a fraction of 25 traditionalists, supporting the communist–agrarian lobby, was set up,[20] which gave them virtual control of parliament.

The most contentious political issue now is that of local self-government. The regional parliament, knowing in advance about its support in the rural areas, wants to hold elections for the heads of the raion administrations, despite Yeltsin's decree stating that these were to be appointed, until 1996, by the regional governor. This is a clear attempt to undermine the executive power and would decisively change the configuration of political power in favour of the new Nazarchuk–Surikov–Safronov alliance (*Vestnik ATN*, no. 12, 26 March 1994, p. 12).

Towards Absolutist Power in the PK

As in the AK, the first governor of the PK, V. Kuznetsov, was devotedly reform-minded. He embarked on various economic experiments in 1991–92, the most prominent of which was the 'Greater Vladivostok' project. This implied the extension of the free economic zone (FEZ) status of Nakhodka over the whole territory of the industrial agglomeration Vladivostok–Nakhodka. The project entailed more devolution of power and control to the region than the Russian Federation was inclined to grant at that time, including the setting up of an economic development fund based on the transfer of assets from the Federation to a regional authority (RFEU, April 1992, pp. 6–7).

As a former student of the prestigious Moscow Institute of International Relations and a research fellow in an academic institute in Vladivostok, V. Kuznetsov was familiar with economic reforms in South-East Asian countries.[21] But both his tough market approach and his liking for extended travel abroad caused strong resentments, in particular from the regional soviet and industrial management. Like his counterpart in the AK, he was considered by the regional elite more as an instrument of Moscow than as a representative of the interests of the PK. However, he could also be criticized for not changing the structure of the former PK executive committee and retaining almost all of the old personnel.

Hence, an open clash between the new governor and the regional elite was only a matter of time. Although he still enjoyed the support of 21 out of 25 heads of raion administrations in the spring of 1993 (UR, 26

March 1993, p. 1), he later came under severe pressure, in particular
from the regional soviet.[22] At the beginning of April 1993, after the
Russian parliament had withdrawn its support of Yeltsin's power to
appoint regional governors (one of the temporary, special powers
granted him in late 1991) the regional soviet adopted a resolution
ruling the appointment of V. Kuznetsov as the governor of the region
to be unlawful (UR, 6 April 1993, p. 2). It proposed to the President
the new candidature of E. Nazdratenko, assuring him in advance of the
support of the majority of the soviet (UR, 19 May 1993, p. 1). Yeltsin
gave in.

The new governor was originally described as having a 'progressive
conservatism' (Gainutdinov, 1993, p. 2). In 1983, he finished a degree
at the Far Eastern Technological Institute and later became the director
of the mining company *Vostok* in Dal'negorsk, and also a deputy of the
Russian parliament (UR, 20 May 1993, p. 1). He provides an excellent
example of how industrial management is currently moving into power
in Russian regions. In a special interview, he referred explicitly to his
friends, who are directors of enterprises of the defence industry and
local entrepreneurs (from *Dal'zavod*, 'Spasskii Cement Company', the
associations *Askol'd* and *Ikar* in Arsen'ev and a mining company in
Yaroslavskii), which he called a 'legal union of industrialists' (UR, 2
June 1993, p. 2). In terms of his perception of reform policy, he stood
naturally closer to the majority of traditionalists in the regional soviet,
who backed his candidature, than Kuznetsov did.[23]

Most of the deputies in the regional soviet resented ambiguities in the
Federation Treaty of March 1992; in particular, as they perceived it, the
treaty gave the *oblasti* and *kraya* fewer powers of taxation and control
over territorial resources than the republics.[24] As a result, the 'small
council' prepared its own draft of a law 'On the Status of the
Primorskii Krai', emphasizing its special geopolitical location for
'long-term Russian interests in the Asian–Pacific region' (UR, 24
March 1993, p. 1). As 'state priorities' in the PK it defined, among
other things, transport facilities to Asian–Pacific countries, the
modernization of extractive and processing industries to increase value
added to local raw materials and maintain military capacity in this
region. This definition of 'state priorities' very much reflects traditional
thinking, in which the state (central or local) is assumed to be
responsible for the development of various industries. The soviet, for
its part, sought special authority in the following main spheres: (a) the
right for use and disposal of land, raw materials and other natural

resources in the PK; (b) the allocation to it of 5 per cent of the amount of VAT going to the federal budget; (c) the licensing of export of regional products; (d) the right to reduce customs duties for export production of the territory; (e) the power to register foreign enterprises and joint ventures; and (f) the right to establish a 'special economic regime'.

In summer 1993, the regional soviet embarked on a bolder political course. At its session on 8 July 1993, it declared its 'intention to establish, on the territory of the Primorskii krai, a state-territorial entity that has the constitutional-legal status of a republic in the Russian Federation' (UR, 16 July 1993, p. 1). The vice-chairman of the regional soviet, V. Butakov, called this a 'political step' and justified it by the desire to obtain equal rights with autonomous republics in the budgetary sphere and in the use of natural resources.[25] However, at the same time, the soviet required even more preferential treatment in foreign trade (tax holidays for joint ventures, customs preferences with the right to keep a portion of those duties within the PK for infrastructural development).

The obvious political intention to press for more soft credits and further state subsidies becomes clear if one returns to the distinctive industrial structure discussed above with its domination by resource extraction and the evidence of subsidized consumption (national income utilized was 1.6 per cent of the Russian total in comparison with 1.3 per cent for produced national income in 1991 [Osipov, 1992, p. 14]). This gives an idea of the high ambitions of the political leadership[26] and provides part of the rationale of its attempts at getting not only greater fiscal and budgetary autonomy, but also absolute power in the region.

However, these actions attracted the attention of the central authorities. The result was a visit by the Russian Prime Minister, Viktor Chernomyrdin, in the second half of August 1993. His Far Eastern trip included stops in Kamchatka, Sakhalin and the Kurile Islands, and finished in the PK. The visit focused on 'key questions' of the fuel and energy complex, transportation and agriculture. Main regional demands included lower import duties and export tariffs, the consignment of all federal taxes to the region for three years, independence in determining annual export quotas and issuance of export licences (in fish and wood products) and the introduction of special local taxes on transit cargoes (RFEU, September 1993, p. 6). As a result, the Prime Minister announced, once again, the preparation

of a new decree on the socio-economic development of the PK an
promised, in the form of an 'experiment', to leave all tax payments i
the region (UR, 21 August 1993, p. 1). These promises eventuall
materialized in the form of decree no. 1,001 of the Russian governmen
on 8 October 1993, 'On Urgent Measures of State Support for th
Primorskii Krai Economy in 1993–95', which included a subsidy of
17 bn for *Dal'energo* to keep prices for electric power at a level of
40 per kWh for industrial enterprises, but the region had not receive
the money by November 1993 (Knapp, 1993, p. 1).

  This exchange of political declarations only fuelled resentments at th
regional level and helped to legitimize a monopolization of power i
the province. In the PK the executive and legislative were now close
allied. In late summer 1993, Nazdratenko's team continued to initiat
'democratically adopted resolutions' in the regional soviet, includin
a refusal to transfer federal taxes to the amount of R 71.8 bn, whic
they claimed the Ministry of Finance owed them (UR, 17 Septembe
1993, p. 3), as well as the rejection of Yeltsin's edict 'On th
stage-by-stage Constitutional Reform in the Russian Federation' of 2
September 1993 as being 'unconstitutional' (UR, 28 September 199:
p. 1). After Yeltsin forcibly disbanded the Russian parliament in earl
October 1993, the PK administration made a complete U-turn, pledgin
allegiance to the President and ordering strong subordination of th
local executive power under its command (UR, 6 October 1993, p. 1

  Whereas the AK governor hoped for the resumption of radic:
economic reforms, however, Nazdratenko tried to use the Octobe
events in Moscow to strengthen his own power in the PK. While h
was accompanying Yeltsin during his visit to Japan, his deputy /
Pavlov decreed the dissolution of the soviets at all levels (althoug
Yeltsin's decrees up to that date had not explicitly referred to th
regional soviets) and the blocking of entry to all administrativ
buildings by police on 11 October 1993 (UR, 13 October 1993, p. 1
Only after the interference of the personal representative of th
President in the PK, V. Butov, could the deputies of the regional sovi(
resume their work (UR, 19 October 1993, p. 1). This was Butov's fir
active public appearance. Like his counterpart in the AK, he wa
former soldier in Afghanistan and later the deputy military procurato
of the Pacific fleet (UR, 26 November 1993, p. 2). Yeltsin wanted
strengthen his executive power after the October events additionall
through his representatives in the provinces. However, th
configuration of political power in the PK was already in favour (

Nazdratenko's team, who decided to disband the regional soviet on 28 October 1993 (UR, 29 October 1993, p. 1) – a move which affected most of those deputies who originally proposed his appointment.

The mingling of regional government with business is apparent in the PK. Over a period of four months, Nazdratenko managed to appoint a new team in his administration in which a number of deputies (A. Pavlov, I. Lebedinets, V. Shkrabov) were, at the same time, leading executive members of the joint-stock company PAKT formed by the heads of large enterprises of the region (Savvateeva, 1994, p. 5). This allowed the combination of tax evasion, embezzlement of public money and control of political power (including the issue of export licences and distribution of regional quota), which became famous as 'Primorskii Watergate' and was even reported in the central press (*Izvestiya*, 1 December 1993, p. 5). The 213 founders (people, not enterprises) of PAKT represented 36 industrial enterprises, including six defence plants (among others, *Varyag, Radiopribor*), four fishing and fish-processing companies, producers of chemicals and electronic circuits (RFEU, March 1994, p. 11). A. Pavlov, the former head of the regional trade administration, who is today the director of the company *Kommersant* and who was Nazdratenko's deputy for finance, initially held the reins as the general director of PAKT (UR, 4 November 1993, p. 1). He seemed originally to be the real key player of the whole business, while Nazdratenko may at first have been only a political puppet.[27]

Pavlov was accused in *Kommersant* of tax evasion of R 2.5bn in 1992 (UR, 19 October 1993, p. 2). On 4 October 1993, Nazdratenko sent a personal letter to Prime Minister Chernomyrdin, asking him to issue a subsidy of R 3.5bn for *Kommersant* to build a thermal power station in Ussuriisk with the help of Chinese labour and, in order to cover payment arrears and to import consumer goods, to remove customs duties on the export of precious metals and mineral fertilizers to China (UR, 5 November 1993, p. 1). This was to be justified by the use made of the export proceeds to finance imports for the benefit of the region as a whole. However, it turned out that, under this contract, exports amounted to 68 million Swiss francs, while imports were only just above SF 5 million (*Izvestiya*, 1 December 1993, p. 5). Later it was also revealed by the representative of the President in the PK, V. Butov, that PAKT embezzled money from the consolidated regional budget to the extent of R 25 bn in 1993 (UR, 12 January 1994, p. 1), compared with a total budgetary income of R 751.9 bn in that year (see below).

Another important member of PAKT is the former deputy head of the regional tax inspection, I. Lebedinets, who is today not only Nazdratenko's chief of staff, but also the deputy director of the Vladivostok-based trawling and refrigerator ship fleet (*Izvestiya*, 1 December 1993, p. 5). The latter set up 14 joint-stock companies from its former structure (UR, 8 February 1994, p. 2), passing on its fishing quotas to them in order to evade taxation. One of these new companies, *Shel'f*, rented four fishing boats from the trawling fleet in 1992 and paid its hard currency revenues on the account of the latter, for which it received, in return, R 337.1 million (UR, 11 February 1994, p. 2).

Finally, the fourth decisive player of PAKT was V. Shkrabov, a former member of the Primorskii CPSU committee and editor-in-chief of the regional newspaper *Krasnoe znamya* (the former party organ), who was appointed as the head of the committee for mass media in the PK administration, becoming, in fact, his own boss (*Izvestiya*, 1 December 1993, p. 5). This fusion of politics and business in the activities of the highest ranking regional leaders, as well as the attempt at complete control of the mass media, marked a decisive step towards absolutist power in the PK.[28]   Nazdratenko also tried to get the structures of federal power under his control. Two attempts were made to suggest in Moscow the former head of the Dal'negorsk police office (where Nazdratenko's company *Vostok* is based), Lieutenant-Colonel Shul'g, as the new head of the regional tax police (UR, 26 November 1993, p. 1). The appointment of the new head of the regional police department, V. Ipatov, was mostly promoted by Nazdratenko's team (UR, 16 November 1993, p. 1).   He, in return, then showed his gratitude by delaying the legal investigation into the case of PAKT's tax evasions and embezzlement of public money, which was originally started by a special commission of 18 people from Moscow, working in Vladivostok over two weeks (UR, 26 November 1993, p. 1).

However, the most blatant exercise of absolutist power was the suspension of the critical mass media and the open showdown with the democratically elected mayor of Vladivostok, V.Cherepkov. The commercial TV channel 'PKTV' was prevented from running its programmes, after compromising Nazdratenko's reputation by showing him publicly embracing putsch leader Rutskoi, and there was said to have been an assassination attempt on the author of this programme, M. Voznesenskii, on 15 November 1993 (*Izvestiya*, 1 December 1993, p. 5). Under the command of I. Lebedinets, fierce attacks were launched against the oppositional newspapers *Bolshoi Vladivostok* and *Utro Rossii*.

Systematic measures were undertaken to undermine the authority of Vladivostok's mayor, Cherepkov, including the switching off of water and electric power, a cut in the city's share of the consolidated regional budget from 16.8 per cent to 8.4 per cent, the sudden off-loading of one-third of the total housing stock of Vladivostok from former sectoral ministries on to the municipal authorities and acts of sabotage on heating systems (Smirnova, 1993, p. 2). Cherepkov had been elected in summer 1993. He embarked on a number of measures that were opposed by the huge administrative apparatus in the city. His main suggestion for administrative reform was to dissolve city districts, which would reduce the number of state employees from 6,500 to 1,000 (UR, 8 October 1993, p. 2). In reply, the regional administration issued a statement that city district councils should not comply with Cherepkov's commands (UR, 11 March 1994, p. 1). The mayor, for his part, sought popular support by providing free public transport and trying to break the bread and fish monopolies through opening new bakeries and fish markets (Smirnova, 1993, p. 2).

As in the AK, the creation of national party structures was only in its infancy. Parties could not provide organized political resistance to the rise of absolutist power in the PK. Nazdratenko wanted first to run for 'Russia's Choice', but he could not get a vote of confidence from the majority of party members in the region (UR, 4 November 1993, p. 1). He later ran as an 'independent' candidate for the Federation Council, using his contacts to collect the necessary number of signatures, for example, through the police station in Yakovlevskii raion (UR, 16 November 1993, p. 3). He was later elected to the upper house with one of the biggest victory results (65.4 per cent) of any Russian governor contesting the parliamentary elections (*Far Eastern Economic Review*, 7 April 1994). The ruthless use of power to intimidate and eliminate people who were a threat to the PK administration was more effective than any form of party political activity.

Although it was claimed that almost all national party leaders visited the PK in the run-up to the elections to the new Russian parliament[29] (23 November 1993, p. 3), this had apparently no significant effect on voting patterns. As in other parts of Russia (*Financial Times*, 13 December 1993, p. 1), the turnout was just above the 50 per cent barrier needed for the vote on the constitution, and people's protest vote appeared in a clear preference for Zhirinovskii's ultra-nationalist

Liberal Democratic Party (UR, 16 December 1993, p. 1).

Table 10.6:   **Results of the Federation-Wide Election to the State Duma in
the PK Compared with Russia as a Whole, 12 December 1993
(in per cent of the total vote)**

Party	Russia	PK
Liberal Democratic Party	22.8	21.9
Russia's Choice	15.4	13.2
Communist Party of RF	12.3	8.1
Women of Russia	8.1	14.3
Agrarian Party	7.9	2.3
Yavlinskii–Boldyrev–Lukin	7.8	7.9
Party of Russian Unity and Accord	6.8	7.5
Democratic Party of Russia	5.5	6.8
Russian Movement for Democratic Reform	4.0	5.2
Other	9.4	12.8

Sources: Compiled from *Kuranty*, 28 December 1993, p. 1 and UR, 16 December
1993, p. 1.

One of the striking differences was that the Communist Party and the
Agrarian Party received a considerably smaller share of the vote in the
PK than they did in Russia as a whole. These parties had, in Russia as
a whole, strong support in rural areas, as was described in the case of
the AK. While Russia's Choice did not do as well in the PK as at the
national level, Women of Russia had much higher support. This is
probably due to their relatively strong organization in the urban
agglomeration of Vladivostok–Nakhodka. Finally, the remaining
democratic parties and movements also received a slightly larger share
of votes in the PK.

However, the support for Yeltsin's policy in the PK decreased from
730,000 votes in June 1990 and 572,000 at the April 1993 referendum
to 244,000 (total vote for the four leading democratic parties) on 12
December 1993, while 130,000 PK citizens voted for Zhirinovskii
(Brodyanskii, 1994, p. 2). However, the last two figures clearly reflect
the lower turnout, although the regional administration tried to combat
mass apathy during the run-up to the elections. It was reported that
'Igor Lebedinets ... sent a circular to factory managers asking them to

take exhaustive measures to guarantee that the referendum succeeds', including handing out grants for clothes, food and heating (*The Guardian*, 13 December 1993, p. 8). This contributed to a 71.7 per cent 'yes' vote for the new constitution (UR, 16 December 1993, p. 1).

As in the AK, the configuration of power in the PK changed dramatically in early 1994, but in the PK the change was towards the absolute power of the executive. On 4 January 1994, Yeltsin acceded to the demands of the regional administration and sacked his representative in the PK, Butov. In a later interview, Butov referred to the personal friendship between Nazdratenko and the head of the President's bureau, V. Ilyushin, who suggested to the President not only the candidature of Nazdratenko as the new governor in May 1993, but also the sacking of Butov (UR, 12 January 1994, p. 1).

The campaign against the mayor of Vladivostok, V. Cherepkov, was also reinforced. On 30 December 1993, Lebedinets sent an emergency call to Moscow, reporting the alleged break-down of the heating system, paralysed public transport and medical aid not working in Vladivostok, for which he blamed Cherepkov (UR, 6 January 1994, p. 1). On 11 February 1994, an apparent attempt was made to frame him. The city procurator and a number of armed policemen investigated his office for evidence that he had accepted bribes. During the inspection, R 1.2 million were reported to have been placed in his safe and another R 1 million to have been left in one of his coats, during an investigation of his flat (UR, 15 February 1994, p. 1). Cherepkov was kept in custody for a day or so and his son was also arrested, apparently to exert additional psychological pressure on him. At this time Vladivostok's mayor had to be released after public protest; he was later evicted from his office on 17 March 1994 by armed police under orders from Nazdratenko (*Far Eastern Economic Review*, 7 April 1994).

On 21 March 1994, all oppositional newspapers were suspended, including *Bolshoi Vladivostok* and *Utro Rossii*, claiming shortages of paper and the switching off of electricity and heating in their offices (*Izvestiya*, 6 April 1994, p. 2). On the same day, Nazdratenko declared that the elections to the regional parliament would be postponed until 23 October, because there was not enough money to pay for them (*RFE/RL Daily Report*, 22 March 1994). Whether the governor did not feel safe enough at that time remains an open question. He also announced his renewed demand for a special economic status for the province as well as the administrative subordination of the Kurile islands to the jurisdiction of the PK (*Izvestiya*, 22 March 1994, p. 1). These two demands remained among the most important regional policy issues challenging the centre for most of 1994.[30]

In summer 1994, Nazdratenko announced still more assertively his proposal to the President to subordinate the Kurile islands to his (Nazdratenko's) control, claiming to have a stronger position than Sakhalin oblast to help the islands' economic problems. This came at the time when his own campaign to become the elected governor started. It was then considered as an additional attempt to get votes from fishermen as a potentially supportive electorate (KD, 3 August 1994, p. 3).

Nazdratenko also reiterated in summer 1994 his intention to get a special economic status granted to the region. He announced that a development programme for his region had been elaborated which included a 'preferential tax and investment policy regime for two to three years' (*Rossiiskie vesti*, 19 July 1994, p. 2). However, this press release could be a big understatement of the scale of the special regime plans. In March 1994, he had already given a hint of a long-term 'Hong Kong solution' during an interview for the American business journal *GQ*. The internal version of his economic programme, which was made available to this author in September 1994, contained demands adding up to a total of 175.3 trillion roubles (in August 1994 prices) to be paid by federal institutions in the period up to 2010.[31] These demands included among others: (1) higher revenues for regional authorities from state-controlled transit cargoes and freight transport which are crossing provincial territory; (2) federal subsidies for fuel and energy; (3) additional payments for regional enterprises in the form of a special federal programme; (4) the consignment of all federal taxes to the region for a period of ten years; (5) the consignment of all state customs duties to the region for a period of four years; and (6) restricted entering to the province for non-residents for a period of ten years.

Nazdratenko justified these requirements later on the grounds that the region faced high transport charges for shipments from the rest of Russia, and that customs duties, export quotas and most taxes were controlled by central authorities (BBC interview on 1 October 1994). Most of the regional authorities agreed that these demands were unrealistic, but they also emphasized that they stood a better chance of getting more by putting higher requirements forward. For example, regionally collected state customs duties were expected to be left in the province at a rate of 35 per cent in 1994 compared with 10 per cent the year before.[32]

The third and politically most serious challenge to the centre was Nazdratenko's announcement of the election of the governor of the PK, which was to take place on 7 October 1994 in the form of an 'experiment' (KD, 30 July 1994, p. 3). After the October 1993 events, Yeltsin had reasserted his right to appoint heads of regional administrations (a special power which he was granted in late 1991 and later deprived of by the old Supreme Soviet), but the new Russian constitution, adopted in December 1993, left open whether governors are to be elected or appointed by the President (Wishnevsky, 1994, p. 9). The date when there would be elections of governors was a matter of dispute, but Yeltsin issued a new decree at the beginning of October 1994 to strengthen his power in appointing governors until 1996 (*Rossiiskaya gazeta*, 7 October 1994, p. 1). It is widely believed that this decree was the result of a report published in late September 1994 by the leaders of the democratic fractions in the State Duma, Egor Gaidar, Boris Fedorov and Grigorii Yavlinskii, following their independent investigation of human rights' abuses, corruption and authoritarian power in the PK (*Segodnya*, 29 September 1994, p. 2). Although Nazdratenko backed down from his election two days before it was scheduled (*Segodnya*, 6 October 1994, p. 3), it is probably only a question of time before his next challenge to the centre.

The results of the elections to the regional parliament in October 1994 were declared invalid because of low turnout. In only 19 of the 39 voting districts was the necessary quorum of 25 per cent achieved (UR, 3 November 1994, p. 1). Nevertheless, the analysis of candidates and elected deputies by workplace background[33] gives a clear indication of the revitalization of power by former *nomenklatura* members as is shown in Table 10.7.

Even if the regional parliament had convened, it is clear that it would have been dominated by representatives of the executive power and industrial management. Both members of the intelligentsia and social organizations lost considerably in this tentative estimate of the configuration of power. Re-elections were delayed again until 1995 (*Financial Times*, 27 October 1994, p. 3). This gave Nazdratenko further leeway to rule without being faced with at least moderate checks by intimidated and partial members of the legislative power.

Table 10.7:   Candidates and elected deputies to the Primorskii krai parliament by workplace background, 23 October 1994

	Candidates	% of total	Elected deputies	% of total
Total	149	100.0	19	100.0
Executive power	41	27.5	8	42.1
Khozyaistvenniki	55	36.9	8	42.1
Military	9	6.0	1	5.3
Intelligentsia	22	14.8	1	5.3
Social organizations	8	5.4	–	–
Other	14	9.4	1	5.3

Note: Percentage figures in the last column do not add to 100.0 per cent because of rounding. 'Executive power' includes heads and deputy heads of regional and local administrations. *Khozyaistvenniki* refers to directors, managing directors and chief engineers of joint-stock companies, state enterprises, banks, kolkhozy and sovkhozy. Intelligentsia includes academics, teachers, doctors and engineers. 'Social organizations' apply to members of independent trade unions, consumer organizations, etc. Thirty-seven of the candidates (24.8 %) were former deputies of the regional soviet (UR, 15 March 1994, p. 1).

Sources: Compiled from *Utro Rossii*, 12 March 1994, p. 2, and 3 November 1994, p. 1.

Regional Differentiation and the Potential for Autonomy

The scope for 'reform from below' can mainly be found in the areas of institutional restructuring, including privatization, budgetary and fiscal arrangements, foreign trade, the development of a new financial sector, and also of party structures. These issues are now discussed in that order in a comparative analysis of the two regions.

The attitude of regional leaders towards market reform was a significant factor in carrying out privatization in both the provinces examined. This supports findings by other Western authors (Bradshaw and Hanson, 1994), in particular, in the sphere of small-scale privatization. In the AK, there was a determined, reform-minded team in the committee for property administration, which was faced with a high concentration of federal property and state monopolies, the lack of a functioning financial market, and also open resistance by a number of local authorities. On 1 April 1994, 1,844 enterprises or 57.7 per cent of a total of 3,196 enterprises had been privatized in the AK. This included 33 per cent of all industrial enterprises and 37 per cent of all agricultural enterprises,[34] which was higher than the corresponding figures of 29 and 2 per cent for Russia as a whole in late 1993 (EkiZh, no. 6, February 1994, p. 8). Moreover, the rate of small-scale privatization was, on average (72.5 per cent of eligible enterprises), also higher than the national average (68.8 per cent) and Western Siberia (63.1 per cent) on 1 March 1994.[35]

It is true that the future competitiveness of these privatized canteens, which might be achieved by means of serious restructuring and new investment, is in doubt, since 59 per cent of the total was acquired by former working collectives, while only 16 per cent came into independent private hands. But this pattern was to be found across Russia. The committee for property administration was also faced with numerous problems of changing the profile, although in some cases the new owners were supposed to maintain the previous one for a few years (bread and milk shops), as well as handing over parts of the assets to other commercial structures, which occurred in 20 cases by April 1994.[36]

There was also a reform-minded team in the Vladivostok city committee for property administration.[37] At the end of 1993, 250 enterprises in retail trade, public catering and services were privatized, which amounted to 75.7 per cent of the total (UR, 11 December 1993, p. 2). However, the comparison with 1990, when Vladivostok had more than 1,000 shops, catering and service outlets, reveals that at least two-thirds of the original premises were restructured, closed or passed on to other commercial structures, without the city authorities getting control of them, which gives reason to doubt any favourable interpretation of the official statistics. Results for the whole region were even less encouraging. According to an internal report by the PK office of Goskomstat Rossii, the state sector was still producing 80.7 per cent of all consumer goods and employed 91.6 per cent of total labour by the end of July 1993, while the private sector accounted for 7 per cent of the total number of enterprises and 8.2 per cent of industrial output (Goskomstat Rossii, 30 August 1993, p. 1). Since then, further statistics have not been available. Nazdratenko stopped privatization in 'vital spheres' of the economy on 3 August 1993 (*Izvestiya*, 1 December 1993, p. 5).

There was also a lot of local resistance against private farmers.[38] Table 10.8 compares the development of private farming in the AK and PK with that in Russia as a whole.

Table 10.8: Private farming in the Altaiskii and Primorskii kraya in comparison with Russia, 1 January 1994

Indicators	Russia	AK	% of Russia	PK	% of Russia
Number of private farms	270,000	6,645	2.5	4,998	1.8
Used arable land (thousand hectare)	11,300	679.3	6.0	77.8	0.7
Average size of land per private farm (ha and % of Russian average)	41.8	102.2	244.5	15.6	37.3
Average percentage of the total arable land in the examined territory	5.0	9.3	–	10.6	–

Sources: Compiled from EkiZh, no. 6, February 1994, p. 8; AP, 9 February 1994, p. 2; and UR, 3 February 1994, p. 2.

The AK, with 1.0 per cent of Russia's territory and 1.8 per cent of its population, has a relatively high number of private farms, which are cultivating 6 per cent of the total privately used arable land in Russia, having more than twice the national average size of land per private farm. Although 10 per cent of the total arable land in the PK is privately owned, the average size of land per private farmer amounts to merely one-third of the national average, which indicates a lower proportional total of arable land in the PK. However, the head of the committee for land reform of the PK administration, V. Shil'nikov, reported in late 1993 that 70 per cent of all private 'farmers' in the region were not engaged in any agricultural work, but in other commercial activities (UR, 16 December 1993, p. 2). This may easily be an exaggeration, bearing in mind the regional leadership's general anti-privatization stance. In any case, part of the process of liberalization should be the acceptance of owners' rights to use their assets as they think best, within the law.

On the fiscal front, the scope for autonomy was in any case limited. With traditionally only a small percentage of enterprises of both provinces under local jurisdiction, as in Russia generally, regional authorities possessed a quite meagre independent income base and depended almost entirely on union and republic subsidies and allocations handed down as a percentage of locally-collected but centrally-determined turnover taxes and personal income taxes. This high budgetary dependence on the centre did not change with the fiscal reform and introduction of new taxes (VAT, profit tax) in 1992. A remnant of traditional Soviet regional policy is the continuing dual subordination of fiscal arrangements, which was discussed by Philip Hanson. In short, budget revenues from the most important taxes are shared upwards with the federal authorities, while the centre redistributes, often with a considerable time delay and on an ad hoc basis, funds to the provinces afterwards, which leads to open-ended bargaining.

Table 10.9: Main income sources of the consolidated budgets of the Altaiskii and Primorskii kraya, 1992–3 (in million roubles and percentage of the total)

Income Source	1992	AK %	1993	%
Total	33,422	100.0	445,114	100.0
Profit tax	8,078	24.2	89,531	20.1
VAT	4,893	14.6	55,896	12.6
Personal income tax	6,067	18.2	57,399	12.9
Excise duties	2,579	7.7	18,292	4.1
Other	2,594	7.8	28,356	6.4
Total guaranteed income	24,211	72.5	249,474	56.1
Subsidies	5,135	15.4	50,638	11.4
Federal budget	2,926	8.7	96,841	21.8
Federal loans	1,150	3.4	300	–
Credits	–	–	47,861	10.7

Income Source	1992	PK %	1993	%
Total	35,829	100.0	751,905	100.0
Profit tax	9,894	27.6	212,041	28.2
VAT	3,235	9.0	93,701	12.5
Personal income tax	7,819	21.8	97,088	12.9
Excise duties	1,411	3.9	15,516	2.0
Other	4,654	13.0	181,698	24.2
Total guaranteed income	27,013	75.4	600,044	79.8
Subsidies	–	–	72,923	9.7
Federal budget	7.286	20.3	73,792	9.8
Federal loans	1,526	4.3	5,146	0.7
Credits	–	–	–	–

Note: Because of rounded absolute figures for PK, percentage figures are not completely accurate.

Sources: Compiled from Aleinikov and Mikhailyuk (1994, p. 42) and interviews with the deputy heads of the budget office of the PK administration, L. Popova, on 13 and 20 September 1993, and V. Rybakova on 7 September 1994.

Table 10.9 shows a clear decrease in guaranteed income in the AK in 1993, while subsidies and soft credits from the federal budget rose considerably. Moreover, the 10.7 per cent 'credits' were, in fact, loans from local enterprises and organizations,[39] which create additional liabilities and future expenditures. In the PK, in contrast, there was a tendency towards an increasing guaranteed income.

In terms of guaranteed income, the AK was clearly at a disadvantage owing to its high share of agricultural production, for which prices are still not freed, and on which VAT amounts to only 10 per cent. As in the PK, the regional soviet of the AK took the decision, in the summer of 1993, to refuse to allow the payment of R 21.6 bn in overdue federal taxes to be transferred by the Ministry of Finance (AP, 28 August 1993, p. 1). One immediate effect of this challenge was that VAT was left at its full rate in the region in the second quarter of 1994.[40] Table 10.10 shows the main spheres of expenditure in both regions.

Table 10.10: Main spheres of expenditure of the consolidated budgets of the Altaiskii and Primorskii kraya, 1992–3 (in million roubles and as percentage of total)

Sphere of Expenditure	AK 1992	%	1993	%
Total	30,596	100.0	432,379	100.0
Regional economy	10,388	33.9	193,577	44.8
of which:				
Agriculture	1,232	4.0	34,835	8.1
Transport	787	2.6	13,291	3.1
Housing	6,068	19.8	92,471	21.4
Other	2,301	7.5	52,980	12.2
Social and Cultural Sphere	15,631	51.1	180,329	41.7
of which:				
Education	7,235	23.6	98,362	22.7
Culture	955	3.1	10,408	2.4
Health and sports	6,580	21.5	64,748	15.0
Social services	861	2.8	6,811	1.5
Administration	1,205	3.9	16,467	3.8
Other	3,372	11.1	42,006	9.7

Sphere of Expenditure	PK 1992	%	1993	%
Total	31,893	100.0	513,541	100.0
Regional economy	13,242	41.5	245,659	47.8
of which:				
Agriculture	573	1.8	33,076	6.4
Transport	1,446	4.5	19,122	3.7
Housing	1,030	3.2	163,800	31.9
Other	10,193	32.0	29,661	5.8
Social and Cultural Sphere	14,779	46.4	199,489	38.8
of which:				
Education	6,928	21.7	99,482	19.4
Culture	596	1.9	6,984	1.3
Health and sports	6,499	20.4	85,912	16.7
Social services	756	2.4	7,111	1.4
Administration	919	2.9	13,902	2.7
Other	2,953	9.2	54,491	10.6

Note: Because of rounded absolute figures for PK, percentage figures are not completely accurate. It also appears that the figure for 'housing' in the PK in 1992 is not quite accurate, bearing in mind the traditional high subsidies for housing and its high proportional percentage in 1993.

Sources: Compiled from Aleinikov and Mikhailyuk (1994, p. 42) and interviews with the deputy head of the budget office of the PK administration, L. Popova, on 13 and 20 September 1993, and V. Rybakova on 7 September 1994.

While in both provinces the regional economy experienced increasing total expenditure, the social and cultural sphere had a corresponding decline of almost the same percentage share, most conspicuously, in the health service.

However, official budgetary figures do not reflect the whole picture, since various other flows of public money are not included in them. These are federal extra-budgetary resources, or 'off-budget funds', which are channelled through federal institutions at the regional and local level (pension fund, social insurance fund, employment fund, and so on), regional extra-budgetary funds, state programmes, and certain subsidies and soft credits. These resources provide much more scope for autonomous regional development than official statistics would reveal, and help to account for the bargaining power different regions have in reality. At the same time, one has to keep in mind that regional authorities in Russia are currently unable to run significant deficits, since they can neither increase the money supply nor (in practice) issue bonds in order to cover budget deficits (Hanson, 1994, p. 26). Table 10.11 gives a rough estimate of actual regional public-sector income and expenditure in both regions in 1993, incorporating extra-budgetary resources.

Table 10.11 shows that both these provinces had a surplus in 1993. Moreover, we can presume that the amount of state subsidies and soft credits in the PK was much higher than indicated here, since information was, in comparison with the AK, only rarely provided in the local press.[41] The sum of public money embezzled by the PK administration (R 25 bn of the consolidated budget in 1993, as mentioned above) also suggests that much more money was available in the PK's coffers than Table 10.11 reveals. In the case of the AK, the most prominent state programme was that of compensation for the nuclear fall-out from the Semipalatinsk testing facility, for which the authorities received R 40 bn in 1993 alone (Melkov and Gotfrid, 1994, p. 51).

Table 10.11: Comparison of aggregated budgetary and extra-budgetary income and expenditure in the Altaiskii and Primorskii kraya in 1993 (in million roubles)

Source	AK Income	AK Expenditure	PK Income	PK Expenditure
Total regional budget	445,114	432,379	751,905	513,541
Central Bank soft credits	172,300	172,300	45,400	45,400
Memorandum items	70,000	70,000	23,000	23,000
Total	687,414	674,679	820,305	581,941

Note: 'Memorandum items' contain 'off-budget funds', finances from state programmes and subsidies.

Sources: Compiled from tables 10.9 and 10.10, Melkov and Gotfrid (1994, pp. 51–2) and several issues of AP and UR in 1993.

In terms of revenues generated from foreign trade, the PK was naturally in a more advantageous position than the AK due to its close geographical location to Asian–Pacific markets and its disposition of resources that are tradeable on the world market, mainly fish and precious metals.

Table 10.12 shows that the foreign trade turnover of the PK was more than four times higher than that in the AK in 1993. It also indicates what is probably a strong tendency across Russian regions for each region's imports to be dependent on its export earnings, as the centre's control of export earnings declines, and, with that decline, centralized purchasing and regional allocation of imports also falls. As in most of the other Russian regions, the export structure was dominated by natural resources, while consumer goods and equipment were mostly imported into both provinces. Figures for freight transport indicate that capacity was under-utilized. The volume of freight loadings had decreased to 64.3 per cent of the 1992 level in the AK (Sidorov, 1994, p. 4) and to 73.6 per cent in the PK (UR, 3 February 1994, p. 2). This is particularly striking for the PK with its high level of foreign economic activities, associated with relatively high domestic tariffs for transport over long distances from and to European Russia.

Table 10.12: Foreign trade activities of the Altaiskii and Primorskii kraya in comparison with Russia, 1993 (in million US$ and per cent of the total)

Indicator	Russia	AK	% of Russia	PK	% of Russia
Exports	43,000.0	75.4	0.24	42.3	1.0
Imports	27,000.0	95.5	0.32	53.0	0.9
Freight transport (including export and import cargoes, in million tonnes)	3,600.0	27.9	0.8	45.0	1.2

Sources: Compiled from EkiZh, no. 6, February 1994, p. 7, AP, 9 February 1994 p. 2 and UR, 3 February 1994, p. 2.

In this context, an important source for generating income at the regional level is the sale of rights for export quotas on 'strategically important' products (fish, wood, wheat, non-ferrous metals). From this the PK administration earned US$ 3 mn in 1992, which it spent on imports of sugar, frozen and canned meat, and other food products (RFEU, July 1993, p. 7). Export licences are sometimes given only on the condition that food products (butter, meat) are imported by export producers for their hard currency revenues.[42] This system of regional quotas and export licences leaves a strong lever of control over foreign trade for regional authorities. The administrative distribution of regional quotas for fishing in the PK, for example, implies price agreements and financial help for 'Dal'moreprodukt', which leads naturally to new cartels and monopolies (UR, 28 January 1994, p. 2). The total PK quota for fishing within its 200-mile zone is 1.68 million tonnes in 1994, which is 48 per cent of the Russian Far East total and a 70,000 tonne increase over the 1993 quota (RFEU, February 1994, p. 4) However, it was reported that regional quotas were scheduled to be liquidated in summer 1994 and that the PK will sell 30 per cent of the remaining quotas by auction (RFEU, May 1994, p. 5).

A very popular element in the regional authorities' attempt at gaining more scope for autonomous development and the control over territorial resources was the idea, pursued in both regions,[43] of setting up free economic zones (FEZ). The governmental decision to give the AK the status of a FEZ was taken in 1990 on highly political grounds, as part of the struggle of the RSFSR authorities against the Union government and the re-establishment of the German autonomous district in the AK, with the hope of attracting predominantly German capital to that region. The main conceptual inconsistency was, apart from its huge territorial size, the approach of opting to solve internal economic and social problems by introducing a preferential regime of tax holidays and freedom from customs duties, which, in fact, could never be provided in reality, since the regional budget's need for revenue was too pressing.

The concept of setting up a FEZ in Nakhodka originally appeared much more promising. It had relatively well-equipped port, transport and infrastructural facilities.[44] It received, alone amongst the 12 FEZs officially approved by the Russian government, governmental credits of R 2.2 bn in 1992 and R 20.1 bn in 1993 (*Finansovye izvestiya*, no. 58, 10–16 December 1993, II). However, of this money, only R 600 million were invested in port modernization, while 70 per cent of the total reportedly ended up back in Moscow in the accounts of various commercial structures (RFEU, April 1994, p. 7). Other preferential treatment included the right to transfer all revenues from privatization into a special account of the FEZ administration and the reduction of tax payments to the centre by 50 per cent. But the main problems for the setting up of a properly functioning FEZ were, apart from high inflation and the lack of legal regulations, the size of the territory and the multiple power structure in the region, including overlapping and duplication of administrative competencies, which provided openings for the corruption and embezzlement of public money mentioned above (UR, 7 October 1993, p. 2). As a result, the Nakhodka authorities found no common formula to articulate their interests and the preferential treatment originally provided was more and more frozen, including tariff privileges that it had enjoyed (RFEU, April 1994, p. 6). The legal status of a FEZ on the whole territory of Nakhodka was changed by governmental decree in September 1994, reducing preferential treatment to five customs zones in the territory (KD, 14 September 1994, p. 2).

More potential for autonomous regional development towards market reform should also arise from the growth of an autonomous financial sector. So far, this has begun to apply only to the PK. Vladivostok has become, along with Moscow and St. Petersburg, one of the fastest growing financial markets in Russia. This has been due mainly to the high turnover of Siberian natural-resource products on local commodity exchanges and an intensive trade in shares of the fishing fleet and the ship-building industry. The Vladivostok stock exchange had a founding capital of R 390 million and achieved an annual turnover of R 3.6 bn in 1993 (UR, 25 January 1994, p. 2). A few large banks (*Vostokinvestbank, Dal'kombank, Evrobank, Dal'rybbank*) could potentially play an active role in future investment, but this depends largely on macro-economic stabilization and the halting of inflation. In 1992, commercial banks in the PK committed only R 196 mn, equivalent to 4.4 per cent of their individual capital, to funding fixed investment (Savalei, 1993, p. 69). At the present time, options for the issue of municipal loans and tenders for the reconstruction of municipal buildings will be quite difficult to implement under conditions of high inflation and negative real interest rates (in early summer 1994 nominal interest rates exceeded current inflation, but may still have been less than anticipated inflation).

Finally, functioning national party structures in the provinces could provide for a new kind of political integration, but the importance of workplace background was much stronger in the Russian parliamentary elections in December 1993.

The AK is represented in the federal parliament by more members of the executive power and former regional soviet, while PK voters showed a preference for the executive power and the intelligentsia (both deputies from an industrial management background were nominated on a party list). Party affiliation, in general, indicated a divided opinion among the electorate. The important problem to which these elections attested was that the development of party structures in the provinces was only in its infancy. Regional leaders were not subject to party discipline which would make them respond to a national policy agenda. At the moment, the decisive success indicator for them is the amount of soft credits and subsidies they manage to get out of Moscow.

Table 10.13 shows the backgrounds of the new deputies elected to the Russian Parliament from the Altaiskii and Primorskii kraya in December 1993. It will be seen that party affiliation was of less importance in these regional elections than the local interest that was represented. Most of those elected would have been at least nominally independents.

Table 10.13:   New deputies to the Russian Parliament (upper and lower house) of the Altaiskii and Primorskii kraya by workplace background and party affiliation, 12 December 1993

Indicator	AK	PK
Total	8	8
Workplace:		
Executive power	4	3
Regional soviet	2	–
Industrial management	1	2
Intelligentsia	1	2
Party employment	–	1
Party affiliation:		
Russia's Choice	1	–
Agrarian Party	1	–
Democratic Party of Russia	–	1
Liberal Democratic Party	–	1
Women of Russia	–	1

Note: Russian Far Easterners occupied only 3 of the 225 seats of the State Duma, which are all represented by PK deputies. Workplace background and party affiliation overlap in this analysis, unlike the breakdown of candidates in the AK 1994 regional elections in Table 10.5.

Sources: RFEU (February, pp. 6–7) and various issues of AP in 1993.

Conclusions

The aim of this chapter was to examine, with the help of two case studies, the profound conflict between the national policy agenda and specific regional interests, which, in many ways, did not conform to the central leadership's initial approach to radical economic reform. This approach could not be politically enforced owing to the lack of national party structures in the provinces. At the same time, characteristic features of traditional Soviet regional policy, such as excessive metropolitan dominance over peripheral regions and the highly concentrated pattern of urbanization, are still very much in place. It has been shown that there is only a limited potential for autonomous development towards market reform for remote regions in Siberia and the Russian Far East.

Arguments have also been provided to suggest that the existing institutional structure and current incentives, including dual subordination of fiscal arrangements and functional duplication between executive and legislative power, are not conducive to a thorough-going market reform. On the other hand, while the prospects for marketization from below are poor, this is not simply because the regions lack autonomy.

Another main conclusion is that some conflicts between the centre and regions are caused by continuing central price controls of agricultural products and electric power, which are forcing regional authorities, under remaining centralized structures, to seek soft credits, tax relief and other compensations from the centre. Moreover, determined resistance by regional authorities (refusals to transfer taxes, declarations of republic status) could mean, in political terms, that new soft credits and tax exemptions would be 'granted'. 'Off-budget funds' and state programmes widened the limits within which regional authorities could finance activities of their own choice. They also provided additional channels which were open for bargaining and informal networks.

Neither the revival of traditionalists in the AK nor the rise of absolutist executive power in the PK provide new scope for 'reform from below', since both opted out of substantial institutional restructuring (halting privatization and controlling energy prices) and returned to Soviet-style solutions, such as the assertion of administrative and redistributional control by the new regional parliament in the AK or the brutal suppression of political opposition in the PK. Although the PK has a clearly higher potential for rapid market reforms thanks to its favourable geographical location, its richer endowment with natural resources tradeable on the world market and a higher guaranteed budgetary income, it is questionable whether it will, under the current regional leadership, substantially prosper or reform in the near future.

Notes

1.   'Region' refers to the first sub-national administrative unit of the 89 subjects of the Russian Federation (kraya, oblasti, autonomous republics and autonomous oblasti), as was discussed in Philip Hanson's earlier chapter. For more convenience, the following abbreviations will henceforth be used: AK = Altaiskii krai, PK =

Primorskii krai, AP = *Altaiskaya pravda*, UR = *Utro Rossii*, EkiZH = *Ekonomika i zhizn'*, RFEU = *Russian Far East Update* and KD = *Kommersant'-daily*.

2. Kirkow and Hanson (1994, pp. 63–88) and Kirkow (1994, pp. 1163–87). The analysis of this chapter covers the events until early December 1994.

3. Interview with the deputy head of the committee for employment and migration of the AK administration, N. Kargina, on 19 April 1994.

4. Interview with the deputy head of the committee of foreign economic and regional relations of the PK administration, V. Tikhomirov, 15 September 1993.

5. The Far Eastern Basin was the only aqua-territory of the Russian Federation where fishing did not decline substantially (from 2,749,960 tonnes in 1992 to 2,682,000 tonnes in 1993), which meant, in fact, a relative increase in the share of the Far Eastern Basin in Russia's total fishing from 52.7 per cent in 1992 to 63.2 per cent in 1993 (EkiZh, no. 11, March 1994, p. 4).

6. As the author was told during an interview with the head of the free economic zone administration in the AK, V. Kolesova, on 7 April 1994, Yu. Zhil'tsov is today the head of a department of the ministry for fuel and electric power industry in Moscow.

7. Interview on 16 April 1994 with the head of the Altai department of the Siberian branch of the Russian academy of science, A. Loginov, who worked initially as V. Raifikesht's economic adviser.

8. Interview with the representative of the President of the AK, N. Shuba, on 19 April 1994.

9. See AP (23 September 1993, p. 2, 25 September 1993, p. 1, and 27 November 1993 pp. 1–2).

10. Interview with the deputy head of the committee for legislation of the AK soviet of people's deputies, A. Sarichev, on 22 April 1993.

11. Interview with the director of the private company *Akva* and leader of the PRES in the AK, V. Tverdokhlebov, 14 April 1994.

12. In October 1994, Nazarchuk was appointed as the new minister for agriculture (*Segodnya*, 28 October 1994, p. 2), which gives now the agrarian lobby in the Altai direct access to state subsidies and soft credits.

13. Interview with the leader of the regional organization of the KPRF and deputy chairman of the new regional parliament, V. Safronov, 19 April 1994.

14. New entrepreneurs intend to give financial help to organize a proper party structure of 'Altai's Choice' in the whole region for the run-up to the next elections on the federal and regional level in 1996 (interview with the director of the private company *Altakompa*, V. Zlatkin, 6 April 1994) and to prepare for the AK a similar project to that of G. Yavlinskii in Nizhnyi Novgorod (interview with the director of *Altan*, V. Pokornyak, on 15 April 1994).

15. For a comparative analysis of the results of these elections with the PK, see: last section of the chapter.

16. V. Raifikesht had apparently applied for a new job as the cultural attaché in the Russian embassy in Germany, which he did not get in the end (Interview with A. Loginov).

17. Interview with the head of the AK administration, L. Korshunov, on 21 April 1994.

18. This is in line with the outcome in other Russian regions. In Novgorod city, the turnout was never more than 25 per cent in any of the 8 voting districts, while in Novgorod *oblast'* 8 re-elections had to take place altogether (*Moskovskie novosti*, no. 13, 27 March–3 April 1994, p. 7). While the total turnout in Russia was just above 35 per cent, that in the AK was 36.8 per cent (AP, 15 March 1994, p. 1).

19. This he denied later when the author interviewed him on 19 April 1994.
20. Interview with the deputy chairman of the AK parliament, V. Safronov, on 19 April 1994.
21. This information was provided by the head of the economic section of the local newspaper *Utro Rossiii*, D. Gainutdinov, when the author interviewed him on 17 September 1993.
22. This has to be viewed in a nation-wide context. After Yeltsin sacked the governor of Bryansk *oblast'*, the Russian parliament announced new legislation ending Yeltsin's right to appoint or dismiss the heads of administration. Several of these later came into conflict with the President over his showdown with the Russian parliament in September–October 1993.
23. V. Kuznetsov is today the head of the Russian trade mission in San Francisco.
24. It is true that autonomous republics such as Sakha/Yakutiya or Tatarstan keep a higher share of budgetary income at their territories and claim more rights in foreign trade. But this applies also to other regions, which have *krai* or *oblast'* status (Tyumen, Kemerovo). The most obvious advantage of republics is probably the fact that their governors (presidents) are not appointed by President Yeltsin (Hanson, 1994, p. 24). For more on the debate about the constitutional status of federal subjects, see the chapter by Elizabeth Teague.
25. Interview with Butakov on 24 September 1993.
26. The main driving forces in the regional soviet for the adoption of the declaration on a sovereign Primorskii Republic were apparently Nazdratenko's deputies Pavlov, Lebedinets and Shkrabov, who had suggested, only a few weeks earlier, the candidature of Nazdratenko as the new governor (UR, 19 October 1993, p. 2). The mayor of Vladivostok, V. Cherepkov, revealed that they forged his signature on a petition to President Yeltsin to replace Kuznetsov (UR, 8 October 1993, p. 2).
27. This was confirmed by Shkrabov during an interview for the BBC film 'Lord of the East', 28 September 1994: 'Nazdratenko did not conquer power, he was promoted to power'.
28. However, Nazdratenko was increasingly at loggerheads with his closest allies and both Pavlov and Shkrabov departed from PAKT in early summer 1994.
29. *Utro Rossii* reported only on the visit of N. Travkin, the leader of the Democratic Party of Russia (UR, 23 November 1993 p. 3).
30. The third important issue was that of Nazdratenko's attempt at scheduling the election of the governor of the PK for 7 October 1994, a device to get a democratic mandate to concentrate more authoritarian power in his hands, since the success of his manipulated re-election was beyond doubt. This challenge of the centre will be discussed below.
31. *Rezhim khozyaistvovaniya dlya ekonomicheskoi stabilizatsii i razyvitiya Primorskogo kraya*, Kraevaya administratsiya Primorskogo kraya, Vladivostok, 1994, p. 12 (unpublished).
32. Interview with the deputy head of the committee of foreign economic and regional relations of the PK administration, V. Tikhomirov, on 14 September 1994.
33. For some of them, both workplace background and party affiliation were indicated on the candidate list. However, the latter played only a minor role during the pre-election campaign and most of them were proposed by 'voters' groups' (UK, 12 March 1994, p. 2).
34. *Spravka ob itogakh privatizatsii po Altaiskomu krayu na 1 aprelya 1994 goda*, Kommitet po upravleniyu gosudarstvennym imushchestvom administratsii Altaiskogo kraya, Barnaul, 1994 (unpublished).

35.   *Sravnitel'nyi analiz itogov privatizatsii v Rossii, Zapadnoi Sibiri i Altaiskom krae na 1 marta 1994 goda*, Komitet po upravleniyu gosudarstvennym imushchestvom administratsii Altaiskogo kraya, Barnaul, 1994 (unpublished).
36.   Interview with the deputy head of the committee for property adminstration of the AK, T. Bobrovskaya, on 15 April 1994.
37.   For a more extensive discussion on privatization in Vladivostok, see Kirkow (1993b, pp. 768–9).
38.   For cases of harassment of private farmers by collective farmers of *kolkhozy* and *sovkhozy*, including arson attacks and the destruction of crops, but also red tape in village councils in the PK, see UR (30 November 1993, pp. 1–2; 15 and 22 December 1993, p. 2).
39.   Interview with the head of the budget office of the AK administration, V. Aleinikov, on 8 April 1994.
40.   Interview with the head of the budget office of the AK administration, N. Yurdakova, on 8 April 1994.
41.   Budget figures for 1992 show that the PK received R 2.7 bn in the form of grants from Moscow. However, the centre provided the region with an additional R 112 bn for its coal industry and a R 3.9 bn credit for its electric energy industry, which were not identified in the budget. On the expenditure side, the PK allocated R 235 million from its 1992 budget for bread price subsidies and allocated R 179 million for the same purpose from its 1992 extra-budget funds (RFEU, July 1993, p. 6).
42.   Interview with the deputy head of the committee of foreign economic and regional relations of the PK administration, V. Tikhomirov, on 15 September 1993.
43.   For a more detailed discussion of the original concept of FEZs in Russia, see Kirkow (1993a, pp. 229–43).
44.   For more information on various development projects of the Nakhodka FEZ, see Kirkow and Hanson (1994, pp. 76–7).

References

Aleinikov, V. and T. Mikhailyuk (1994), 'Predvaritel'nye itogi ispolneniya byudzheta kraya za 1993 goda', in: A. Sidorov *et al.*, *Ekonomicheskaya reforma: otsenka sostoyaniya ekonomiki Altaiskogo kraya i blizhaishie perspektivy ee razvitiya*, Barnaul, pp. 41–2.

Bradshaw, M.J. and P. Hanson (1994), 'Regions, Local Power and Reform in Russia', in R.W. Campbell (ed.), *Issues in the Transformation of Centrally Planned Economies: Essays in Honour of Gregory Grossman*, Boulder CO, Westview.

Brodyanskii, D. (1994), 'Ne zhdat' chuda of Khlestakovykh', *Utro Rossii*, 13 January, p. 2.

Gainutdinov, D. (1993), 'Pobedili li Primortsy?', *Utro Rossii*, 12 June, p. 2.

Goskomstat RSFSR (1991), *Narodnoe khozyaistvo Primorskogo kraya v 1990 godu*, Vladivostok.

Goskomstat Rossii (1993), *Osnovnye pokazateli raboty predpriyatii razlichnykh form sobstvennosti*, Vladivostok: Primorskoe kraevoe upravlenie statistiki, 30 August.

—— (1994), *Osnovnye pokazateli sotsial'no-ekonomicheskogo razvitiya i khoda ekonomicheskoi reformy v Rossiiskoi Federatsii za 1993 god*, Moscow.

Grigor'ev, S. and Yu. Rastov (1994), *Prichiny passivnosti izbiratelei: urok na segodnya i zavtra*, Barnaul (unpublished).

Hanson, P. (1994), 'The Center Versus the Periphery in Russian Economic Policy', *RFE/RL Research Report*, vol. 3, no. 17 (29 April), pp. 23–8.

Kirkow, P. (1993a), 'Das Konzept 'Freier Wirtschaftszonen' in Rußland. Seine Entwicklung von 1988 bis Herbst 1992', *Osteuropa*, no. 3, pp. 229–43.

— (1993b), 'Regionale Politik und wirtschaftliche Ausdifferenzierung. Eine Fallstudie über Rußlands fernöstlichen Primorskij kraj', *Osteuropa*, no. 8, pp. 754–70.

— (1994), 'Regional Politics and Market Reform in Russia: The Case of the Altai', *Europe-Asia Studies*, vol. 46, no. 7, pp. 1163–87.

— and P. Hanson (1994), 'The Potential for Autonomous Regional Development in Russia: The Case of Primorskiy Kray', *Post-Soviet Geography*, vol. 35, no. 2, pp. 63–88.

Knapp, V. (1993), 'Verkhi uzhe ne mogut, a nizy?', *Utro Rossii*, 12 November, p. 1.

Kurakin, A. (1960), 'Altaiskii ekonomicheskii administrativnyi raion i problemy ego razvitiya', *Izvestiya AN SSSR. Seriya geograficheskaya*, no. 6, pp. 38–46.

Loginov, A. *et al.* (1993), 'Analiz khoda ekonomicheskoi reformy v Altaiskom krae', Barnaul (unpublished).

Melkov, M. and R. Gotfrid (1994), 'Razvitie ekonomiki kraya v federal'nykh i kraevykh programmakh', in A. Sidorov *et al.*, op.cit., pp. 51–2.

Mel'nik, A. and L. Rodionova (1994), 'Zanyatost' i rynok truda', in A. Sidorov, *et al.*, op. cit., pp. 29–30.

Osipov, B. (ed.) (1992), *Ekonomicheskii potentsial i problemy razvitiya Primorskogo kraya*, Vladivostok.

Petrov, N. (1994), 'Regional'nye vybory – 94: itogi i uroki', *Rossiya regionov. Byulleten'*, no. 2, Moscow, Analiticheskii tsentr pri Prezidente RF, Rabochaya gruppa po regional'nym problemam Prezidentskogo Soveta, November.

Rastov, Yu. (1993), 'Sotsial'noe rassloenie i dinamika napryazhennosti v Altaiskom krae v techenie 1992 goda', *Aktual'nye problemy sotsiologii, psikhologii i sotsial'noi raboty*, vypusk 2, Barnaul, pp. 17–28.

Sarichev, A. (1994), 'V zhestkikh usloviyakh. Deputatskii klub kraevogo Soveta: opyt chetyrekh let raboty', *Altaiskaya pravda*, 12 March, p. 2.

Savalei, V. (1991), 'Primor'e: poisk ekonomicheskoi nishi', *Problemy Dal'nego Vostoka*, no. 5, pp. 71–7.

— (ed.) (1993), *Programma mobilizatsii finansovykh resursov dlya razvitiya Vladivostoka*, Vladivostok.

— (1994), 'Realii perevernutogo mira', *Utro Rossii*, 11 February, pp. 1–2.

Savvateeva, I. (1994), 'Evgenii Nazdratenko kak zerkalo Rossiiskikh reform', *Izvestiya*, 1 December, p. 5.

Sidorov, A. *et al.* (1994a), 'Kratkie itogi raboty khozyaistva kraya za 1992–1993 gody', in A. Sidorov, *et al.*, op. cit., pp. 4–5.

Sidorov, A. *et al.* (1994b), *Ekonomicheskaya reforma: otsenka sostoyaniya ekonomiki Altaiskogo kraya i blizhaishie perspektivy ee razvitiya*, Barnaul.

Smirnova, T. (1993), 'Syuzhet dlya dramy', *Utro Rossii*, 23 November, pp. 1–2.

Wishnevsky, J. (1994), 'Problems of Russian Regional Leadership', *RFE/RL Research Report*, vol. 3, no. 19, 13 May, pp. 6–13.

11. Estonia: Radical Economic Reform and the Russian Enclaves

Philip Hanson

Introduction

In 1994 Estonia was being described as one of the success stories of economic transformation. Its policy-makers had decontrolled prices, brought inflation below 50 per cent a year for two years, and made substantial progress in privatization. It was true, as elsewhere, that output and real incomes had fallen, but measured total output (real GDP) had begun to increase in mid-1993 (see Table 11.1).

Table 11.1: Real GDP change (year-on-year %), Russia and Estonia, 1989–94

	1990	1991	1992	1993	1994
Russia	–2.0	– 9.0	–18	–12	–15
Estonia	–3.6	–11.8	–31.6	– 2.1	5

Sources: IMF 1993; Russian press; Statistical Office of Estonia, 1994.

In late 1993 the IMF had predicted that the Estonian economy would exhibit GDP growth of about 6 per cent between 1993 and 1994; this would be the highest growth rate in Europe (IMF, 1993). Output has not grown as vigorously as that, in fact, but it has definitely been moving upwards (*Eesti Pank Bulletin*, 1994, no. 3; EBRD, 1994). Meanwhile a competitively elected-government had established a new constitution. There was a fair degree of order in the country's day-to-day life, notwithstanding the fall of the Laar government in the autumn.

Yet only two years earlier, the prospects of the Estonian economy and polity had appeared to be highly uncertain. In 1990–91 there were several reasons for questioning Estonia's economic and political prospects. This chapter is a consideration, from the vantage-point of late 1994, of one of those grounds for doubt: the risk of political instability associated with the ethnic Russian enclave in Estonia's North-East region, in the towns of Narva, Kohtla-Järve and Sillamae. All three towns have elected local governments, along with 251 other towns and districts of varying (mostly smaller) size. Most residents in them do not, at the time of writing, have Estonian citizenship. The region has a concentration of Soviet-era large-scale industry; it is therefore particularly likely to suffer during macro-economic stabilization and economic restructuring (Raagmaa and Tammaru, 1993, give a detailed account).

This enclave is a feature that is most salient, among the Baltic states, in Estonia. It is true that Latvia had a larger proportion of non-Latvians in its population (48 per cent) at the 1989 census than Estonia had of non-Estonians. On the other hand, there is no Latvian region that is so dominated by ethnic Russian settlement – though the city of Riga itself and the town of Daugavpils are strongly Russian. Lithuania, with an 80 per cent ethnic Lithuanian population, has no comparable problem, apart from the ethnic Polish concentration in Vilnius. Moreover, Estonia's Russian enclave is close to the border with Russia, and Narva is right on that border.[1]

How (so far) has it been possible to proceed so successfully with 'shock therapy' policies in a difficult economic situation, in view of the existence of this fragile corner of the country?

To unfold this story, we begin by reviewing the process of economic change in Estonia, then review briefly the character of territorial administration in the republic, then the issues surrounding citizenship and ethnicity, and finally consider the local politics of the region, as a case-study of adaptation to disruptive change in an ethnic minority enclave.

Economic Transformation in Estonia

In 1990–91 many observers argued that Estonia, the smallest of the 15

Soviet republics, would face the most extreme difficulties if its people tried at the same time to pursue political independence and the establishment of a capitalist economic order. Its small size and relatively large non-Estonian population suggested that it would be politically weak. In addition, there were four considerations that many commentators – not only in Moscow – thought would hamper the successful pursuit of independent economic policies: Estonia's trade dependence on Russia; the terms-of-trade loss and balance-of-payments difficulties that were expected from a shift to trading with Russia at world prices; the specific dependence on Russian energy, and the inflationary consequences of being part of the rouble monetary area – from which escape attempts looked perilous.

It was acknowledged that Estonia started with some advantages: in particular, a well-educated population with living memory of a capitalist system during Estonian independence from 1918 to 1940, and a development level that was above the Soviet average. The difficulties nonetheless seemed rather hefty. Each economic cloud could, however, be found, when closely inspected, to have a silver lining.

The summary of Estonian transformation problems and performance that follows draws heavily on the Baltic states chapter in UN ECE 1992, Hanson (1992) and Hansson (1994a).

Some 90–95 per cent of Estonia's cross-border merchandise transactions were with the rest of the USSR in 1989–90. But these flows were the product of the peculiar and distorting pattern of resource allocation under a system of central administration of the economy. Thus, Estonia delivered livestock products to Russia and fed the livestock in substantial measure with grain imported from Russia. But high dependence on grain as fodder is a peculiarity of Soviet-style farming, and is not cost-effective in market economies. Moreover, much of the grain that was so wastefully used in the Soviet economy was imported, much of it through the Estonian port of Muuga. Again, some part of Estonia's imports from the rest of the USSR was needed to support Soviet military units in Estonia. And when it came to inter-republic flows of food and consumer goods, Estonia was a net exporter – a circumstance that was likely to give it a stronger bargaining position in the new circumstances than total trade figures alone suggested.

As for the trade-balance and terms-of-trade problems that seemed to many to be in store, the re-valuation of inter-republic flows in world market prices, based on estimates carried out in Moscow, was known to be shaky. The rouble-to-dollar-price calculations were based on very broad groups of products. Important elements of the current account balance of payments were left out of the picture: cross-border shopping, the treatment of the Soviet turnover tax in the valuation of flows of goods, and appropriate transit and port fees for Russian imports and exports – all were elements in the relationship that would make Estonia's payments balance with the rest of the USSR less lopsided than the available figures implied (UN ECE, 1992). Even so, the present author calculated in 1991 that the shift to world prices in Estonia's trade with Russia might entail a terms-of-trade loss for Estonia of the order of 13 per cent of GDP, which was perhaps a shade too low (Hanson, 1992, Table 6 for details of the estimate; Hansson, 1994a, estimates a terms-of-trade loss in 1992 equal to 16–20 per cent of GDP).

The nation's energy dependence on Russia was certainly less than that of the other two Baltic states. The reason for this was Estonia's oil-shale deposits, located, as luck would have it, in the north-east of the country. An estimate of net imports of primary energy from the rest of the USSR in 1990, excluding hydro- and nuclear power, puts them at only 20 per cent of Estonian usage of primary energy; and Estonia was a net exporter of electric current, including to Leningrad. However, the location of refinery capacity was such that Estonian dependence on imports of oil products was in fact considerable.

Estonian entanglement in Russian inflation seemed an intractable problem so long as the creation of an independent currency was ruled out. The IMF continued to favour the maintenance of a single rouble currency area until well into 1992. It is natural enough for economists to oppose the splitting of a single-currency area into a territory with several different currencies, under most circumstances. In market economies there is a presumption that, where a single currency operates, the region in which it operates fulfils the conditions of an optimal currency area (on optimal currency areas see Robson, 1987, Chapter 9). In any case, the move from one to several currencies must generally increase transaction costs. But circumstances in the former USSR were not normal.

Several writers, and most clearly and systematically Havrylyshyn and Williamson (1991), argued that a continued currency union among the 15 successor-states entailed, in the absence of a high degree of mutual trust and cooperation, a serious 'free-rider' problem. While one currency, the rouble, could be issued only in Moscow, but rouble-denominated bank credit and budget deficits could be expanded by banks and governments over which Moscow had no authority, each state in isolation had an interest in expanding the rouble money supply, since the inflationary effects were diffused across the whole rouble area.

For a government, in these circumstances, to rein in its spending for the sake of overall macro-economic stabilization would be contrary to its national interests so long as it was believed that other governments would not also exert fiscal discipline. National authorities that allowed the local rouble money supply to expand were giving their firms and households the means to bid resources away from any other successor-state that tried to pursue stabilization policies. Unless there was sufficient mutual trust to set up a single monetary authority and also to exercise joint control over all the 15 state budgets, the creation of separate currencies was the only route to macro-stabilization. With its own currency, a government could not so easily deflect on to others the inflationary effects of its own fiscal improvidence; instead, they would fall on its own national economy.

The establishment of the Estonian kroon in June 1992 was the key to Estonia's progress in economic transformation generally. The lining to this particular cloud was gold, rather than silver. All three Baltic states were due to receive some gold held in Western Europe on behalf of their pre-war independent governments. In the case of Estonia, this amounted to some $130 million at prevailing gold prices.

Estonia was the first of the former Soviet republics to establish its own currency. Along with Latvia, it has also been by far the most successful. Unlike Latvia, Estonia adopted a modified currency-board system for the kroon. Lithuania also adopted the currency-board arrangement in 1994. The essential idea of a currency board is that the nation's issue of notes and coins must by law be 100 per cent backed by another currency. The kroon was pegged to the Deutschmark at 8 kroon (EEK 8) to the DM. This can be changed only by legislation, and at the time of writing has not been altered. The restitution of Estonia's pre-war gold reserves facilitated this, but it has also required resolute and skilful policy-making. The currency board does not provide a wholly automatic determination of the money supply. Kroon emission is not automatically increased when gold and foreign currency reserves rise; but it must be reduced if they fall below an amount equivalent at EEK 8 to the DM to the existing currency issue; and the Bank of Estonia is not allowed by law to lend to the government.

At the same time, the Bank can and does set obligatory reserve ratios for the commercial banks, so that broad money supply is not governed solely by currency-board rules plus prudential reserve ratios determined by the commercial banks themselves. The government managed to keep the overall state budget in surplus in 1991, 1992 and the first half of 1993 (IMF, 1993). Regulation of commercial banks, though no doubt over-stretched, has been better-organized and more forceful than in many other post-communist economies. One commercial bank, the Tartu Commerce Bank, has been closed down, and a number of others suspended and required to reorganize (*Izvestiya*, 29 December 1992, p. 3; *Baltic Independent*, 19 January 1993, p. 4 [references to the *Baltic Independent* here cite the initial date of the week that each issue covers]). Other bank suspensions and closures followed.

In the first quarter of 1994 the rate of consumer-price inflation moved up sharply, and the trade deficit widened. The reasons for the renewal of high inflation were disputed.

The Bank of Estonia tended to play down the role of money-supply growth, even though its own reports show narrow money supply (cash in circulation outside the banks, plus demand deposits) up by 99 per cent in the year through January 1994. The Bank stresses instead the role of cost-push factors: money-wage growth and inflation imported from Russia. The latter has certainly played a part, though probably a smaller part than Bank of Estonia economists have argued. The kroon price of imports from Russia rises when – as has tended to be the case – the rouble falls less against the Deutschmark than its relative inflation rate would justify. However, Estonia's imports from Russia in 1993 were officially only 16 per cent of total imports and therefore only around 10 per cent of Estonian final domestic spending (*Eesti Pank Bulletin*, 1994, nos 1 and 2, and statistics from the Eesti Pank information service). Quantitatively, the direct effects of rouble inflation on the Estonian price level seem likely to be rather less than the Bank has maintained.

Others were more inclined to emphasize the influence of the growth of the kroon money supply. Inflows of aid and foreign direct investment (the latter estimated by the Bank at 9.5 per cent of GDP in 1993) had contributed to a rise in foreign-currency reserves that pushed up the kroon money supply. Under the modified currency-board system, currency emission grew less than reserves, up to end-1993. That left a margin, under the currency-board regime, within which emission could increase when reserves ceased to do so (as they did for most of 1994). In early 1994 critics called for a modification or even abandonment of the currency board.

A strong defence of the currency board was mounted by one of its architects, Ardo Hansson (1994b). He accepted that the linkage from the balance of payments through to the money supply and inflation, via the currency-board arrangements, was a main source of inflation in early 1994. He argued, however, that the currency board contained self-correcting mechanisms, and was still a better means of stabilization than any other available at Estonia's current stage of development. The kroon inflation was already producing a feedback effect, through rising net imports, that was tending to reduce foreign-currency reserves as it began to outweigh the capital inflows; this in turn, through the currency-board link, was beginning to curb the growth of the money supply. And indeed money-supply growth did taper off in early 1994. With a lag, this produced a slowdown in inflation in the second quarter. Towards the end of the year, with inflation having slowed, the margin for additional currency emission left by the reserves was only 10 per cent of the existing cash money supply, so that automatic curbs to monetary growth were close at hand (communication from Alari Purju, December 1994).

Therefore experience in 1994 suggests that the Estonian currency-board approach to macro-economic stabilization may not work perfectly, but does work, and is robust.

In general, all the main policies required in transformation have been followed through. The de-control of prices was mostly carried through in 1991, ahead of Russia, and subsequent macro-economic stabilization brought the inflation rate down sharply in 1992–3. Table 11.2 juxtaposes the Estonian and Russian annual inflation figures, showing both the earlier liberalization and the far more effective stabilization in Estonia.

A private sector has developed relatively rapidly. This has been done by a combination of restitution to pre-communist owners, sales of state property, including sales to foreigners, and the encouragement of new firm creation. It has not been based on mass privatization voucher schemes as in the Czech Republic and (with its own peculiarities) in Russia. The National Capital Bonds (a form of voucher) are primarily intended for housing privatization; they are issued to permanent residents (not only to citizens), in values dependent on number of years' employment in Estonia. Compensation securities are issued for the purpose of restitution to former owners; they will be mainly, though not exclusively, obtained by ethnic Estonians. Purju (1994) suggests, on the basis of restitution claims, that about half of all land, a quarter of housing and 7–8 per cent of non-housing capital assets may be returned eventually to former owners.

Table 11.2: Inflation (end-year/end-year % change in CPI, Russia and Estonia, 1991–4)

	1991*	1992	1993	1994**
Russia	89	2,500	853	220
Estonia	319	953	36	45-50

Sources: UN ECE, 1992; Russian press; IMF, 1993; Ardo Hansson, 1994a; *Estonian Statistics*, 1994, no. 7; Dr Alari Purju.

Note: * 1991 year average over 1990 year average.
       ** Preliminary.

Despite the absence of a mass privatization programme along Czech or Russian lines, the private sector share of the economy has risen fast. The EBRD (1994) puts the private sector share of GDP at mid-1994 at 55 per cent. Problems in the countryside have been considerable, as elsewhere in the ex-communist world, but small-scale privatization has in general moved fast. According to one estimate, in the first half of 1993 86 per cent of retail sales and 67 per cent of wholesale turnover was generated by private firms (*Baltic Independent*, 15 August 1993, p. B1). There have at the time of writing been several rounds of offers for sale of large state enterprises, including 38 in late 1992 and a further 53 in May 1993. By October 1993, 22 of the 91 large enterprises offered had been sold, for a total of $8 million, half of that total coming from foreign investors (Purju, 1994). A further 40 enterprises were put on offer in November 1993.

Several enterprises offered, it may be pointed out here, have been in the 'Russian' towns in the North-East (*Baltic Independent*, 18 December 1992, p. 6; 16 July 1993, p. B1; 5 November 1993). In late 1994 the Kreenholm textile works, a major employer in Narva, was purchased by a Scandinavian company. The deal guarantees jobs for 2,000 workers (admittedly only 40 per cent of the present workforce) and a substantial injection of new money (*Baltic Independent*, 6 January 1995). This should represent a major breakthrough as far as the enclaves are concerned.

Structural change has also been substantial, as Table 11.3 shows.

Table 11.3: **Estonia: structural and relative price change, 1991–1994-I**

(**% shares of GDP by sector of origin, current prices**)

	1991	1992	1993	1994-I
agriculture and fisheries	17.8	9.7	10.9	8.2
mining and water, electricity and gas supply	4.5	8.9	6.6	7.2
manufacturing	46.2	37.0	24.0	19.3
construction	8.2	5.4	5.8	4.4
services	21.2	36.8	52.7	60.9
other	2.6	2.2	–	–

Source: *Estonian Kroon* 2 (November 1993); p. 11; *Statistical Yearbook 1994*, *Estonian Statistics 1994*, no. 7.

Note: The definition of 'services' appears to differ slightly between 1991–2 and 1993–4. In the latter period it includes trade, transport, communications, and other services.

In addition, foreign firms have begun to buy, or buy into, Estonian companies, outside the formal offers for sale, on a scale that is more than trivial. (Table 11.4 shows the official foreign direct investment data for 1992 and the first half of 1993.) Examples include Neste's 55 per cent stake in the new oil products terminal at Muuga, along with a chain of petrol stations; the Swedish company Packline's 50–50 joint venture in ski-box production; Gomab Mobel AB's purchase of a furniture factory, the acquisition of the Kunda cement works, Swedish and Finnish stakes in Estonian telecommunications, and so on, quite apart from the usual hotel and other service-sector foreign investment. According to one assessment, there were in autumn 1993 some 2,000 Finnish firms or Finnish–Estonian joint ventures, employing more than 20,000 people in all, though the cumulative total value of Swedish direct investment was larger than that of Finnish companies (*Baltic Independent*, 18 June 1993, pp. B1, B3; 16 July 1993, p. B1; *Wall Street Journal*, 18 October 1993).

Table 11.4:   Estonia: foreign trade and payments, 1992–3
              (EEK mn: DMI = EEK 8; $1 approx. EEK 13)

Balance of payments, 1992 and 1993

	1992	1993
exports, f.o.b.	5548	10763
imports, f.o.b.	−5412	−12496
transfers, net	1146	1392
services, net	635	1021
current account	1839	493
inward foreign direct investment	705	2129
other capital account	−1047	−1745
capital account	−342	384
change in reserves (- = increase)	−820	−2164
errors and omissions	−677	−877

Source: Statistical Office of Estonia, *Statistical Yearbook 1994*.
Note: F.o.b. stands for free on board, i.e., valued without insurance or freight charges.

The number of private firms is reckoned to have risen from about 1,000 at the end of 1990 to some 20,000 in October 1993, and one in five of those established in 1991 and 1992 was in the industrial sector. By October 1993 private firms were officially estimated to account for about 37 per cent of industrial sector output (IMF, 1993; *Baltic Independent*, 26 November 1993; *RFE/RL Daily Report* [*RFE/RL DR*], 4 January 1994). If it is considered that this share contains none of the semi-formal, insider privatizing that is characteristic of Russia, the conclusion would seem to be that changes in property rights of a kind that should transform enterprise behaviour have gone a long way already in the industrial sector.

The opening up of the economy to the outside world has also been of a radical nature. The kroon is fully convertible for current-account transactions. The pegged rate of EEK 8 to the Deutschmark provided initial protection of domestic producers and encouragement to exporters, because it was a substantial under-valuation. A World Bank study reportedly put the kroon's purchasing power parity with the DM in June 1992 at 2.7, or about a third of the pegged rate (Haav, 1993). Other estimates put the under-valuation of the kroon at as much as a sixth of the pegged rate (private communication from Alari Purju, December 1994). In any case, under-valuation has been the chief form of import protection. Tariff duties are minimal, and restricted to items like cigarettes, alcohol, furs and yachts, while the only export duty is on antiques.

The difficulty of squeezing out inflation overnight has meant that the price level has risen relatively to prices in Western Europe. Between June 1992 and October 1994 Estonian retail prices rose almost 3.6-fold, while inflation has been low in Germany. This appreciation of the real exchange rate of the kroon means that the initial protection of an under-valued currency has been substantially reduced.

Table 11.5:   Estonia: trade-partner composition of exports, 1993 (% of total exports)

Russia	22.6
Finland	20.7
Sweden	9.5
Latvia	8.6
Germany	8.0
Netherlands	4.1

Source: as Table 11.4.

Table 11.5 shows the impressive re-orientation of Estonian trade towards Scandinavian and other Western partners. This is not a mere arithmetical outcome of a drop in trade with the former Soviet Union, though those flows have indeed fallen; it reflects very rapid real growth in trade with Finland, Sweden, Germany and other Western countries. In combination with the fall in output, this means that foreign trade dependence has risen. One estimate is that by September 1993 the Estonian economy's trade dependence (the arithmetic mean of exports and imports as a percentage of GDP) had risen from 45 in 1991 to 63 (Hansson, 1994a). Other estimates are lower, and would still put trade dependence at about 50 per cent.

Exports have been concentrated on traditional strengths: livestock products, textiles, and also timber; the role of metals (largely smuggled from Russia and re-exported, and presumably a less reliable earner in the long term) is significant but not dominant. Services, notably transit and port services, have duly played the part that optimists had predicted in 1990–91 (see Table 11.4). Reportedly, Baltic-states ports in 1993 were handling about a quarter of Russia's exports and imports by weight, despite Russian nationalist huffing and puffing about the need for Russia to develop her own ports (Reuters from St. Petersburg, 26 December 1993; an article on the standstill on oil-terminal development in St. Petersburg in *Izvestiya*, 8 July 1994, p. 2).

This rapid sketch of economic change in Estonia may suggest a free-market utopia. That would be wrong. Unemployment on, say, US definitions, must be well above the 2 per cent rate reported at the time of writing. Many families are worse off than they were in 1988 or 1989. Much of the foreign investment, though by no means all of it, is concentrated in and around Tallinn. It may well be that the more encouraging development is regionally concentrated along the northern, coastal border (information from Ardo Hansson and from Ray Abrams). The point to be made here is simply that, from a precarious starting-point in September 1991, an independent Estonia has pursued liberalization, financial discipline and institutional reform in a determined and consistent fashion; it began in 1993 to experience an economic recovery, and continued to do so in 1994.

Many dangers still attend the further progress of economic transformation in Estonia. The maintenance of existing free trade agreements, especially with Sweden and Finland, is important, and was imperilled by the European Union's protectionism, during the Swedish and Finnish negotiations for entry into the EU. Free trade agreements of some value were signed by the three Baltic states with the EU directly on 18 July 1994 (*RFE/RL DR*, 19 July 1994); here, at least, the Baltic states have the advantage of being small and not threatening. But it is relations with Russia, and therefore also the situation of ethnic Russians in Estonia, that represent what is probably the greatest single threat to further progress.

This threat is reflected in Western markets' assessment of the country, or 'sovereign' risk associated with doing business in Estonia.

The March 1994 *Euromoney* review of sovereign risk worldwide puts Estonia in 105th place out of 167 countries. That is better, for good reason, than Russia (138th). But it is striking that the two countries' scores for 'political risk' are close, and poor, whereas Estonia's score on economic performance, at about 50 per cent, is twice that of Russia (*Euromoney*, March 1994, cited in *Eesti Pank Bulletin*, 1994, no. 2).

In other words, Estonia's economic prospects are affected by what happens in the Russian enclaves for foreign-policy and security reasons, as well as for reasons to do with internal social stability.

Local Government in Estonia and the Ethnic Russian Enclaves

Estonia is divided for administrative purposes into 21 first-tier regional authorities, consisting of 15 counties (*maakond*) and six cities with equivalent status. These are administrative divisions of national government, and have no elected government. Self-government in the Central European sense, that is, elected government, operates at the second-tier level of 254 towns and communes. These have an average population of only about 2,300, but there is a wide dispersion about this mean. Tallinn, for example, is simply one of the 254.

The more or less Russian enclaves in the North-East, Narva, Kohtla Järve and Sillamae are three of the self-governed units. The confining of self-government to the unevenly populated second-tier level has the effect, probably intended, of playing down the significance of the Russian enclaves. They are, after all, large enough to have constituted units of a first-tier sub-national level of government, alongside counties and a small number of other medium-to-large towns. Of the three, Narva, with a 1992 population of nearly 83,000, is close to the average population size of first-tier administrative divisions. So is Kohtla-Järve, with 78,000. Sillamae, as already noted, is considerably smaller, at 21,000 (for details see *Estonia*, 1993, and Sootla *et al.*, 1993).

Political developments in the North-East, and particularly in Narva, are reviewed in the next section of this paper. The recent history of elected local government in Estonia can be briefly summarized.

In March 1990, when Estonia was still part of the USSR, there were elections to the republic's parliament. Local councils had been elected earlier, in December 1989. In those elections, of course, all resident Soviet citizens of voting age could vote and stand for election. The elections were more competitive than the 1989 elections to the USSR Congress of People's Deputies. In Estonia, nationalists of varying degrees did well at the parliamentary level. Of the 105 deputies elected to the Estonian Supreme Soviet, 79 were ethnic Estonians, 20 were Russians, two were of mixed Estonian–Russian background, and there were four others (see Hanson, 1993a, for details). The councils in Narva, Kohtla-Järve and Sillamae were dominated by ethnic Russians, most of whom appeared to be opposed to Estonian independence.

After the failure of the Moscow putsch in August 1991, the councils in these three cities were suspended by the government in Tallinn. Elections were held in October 1991, and reportedly nearly all the former deputies were re-elected. In 1992 the Estonian parliament adopted the 1938 Estonian Citizenship Law and, in June, following a referendum on the constitution, a new constitution. The effect of these pieces of legislation was to leave most, though not all, ethnic Russians in Estonia without citizenship and without the right to vote in national elections until they acquired citizenship. An account of the citizenship, aliens and constitutional positions is given in the next section. The parliament elected in 1992 was entirely composed of ethnic Estonians. The new government, led by Mart Laar, was more nationalist, and also more conservative in economic policy, than its predecessor, even though the previous government had itself pushed for Estonian independence.

In the present context, an important wrinkle in the constitution was that resident non-citizens could vote in local elections. Only later, in 1993, was it established by legislation that non-citizens could not stand for election to local office. It was therefore only in the local elections of October 1993 that the present constitutional order prevailed in local political contests: non-citizen voters joined citizen voters at the polls, at which only Estonian citizens could be elected to office. More will be said about these elections in the next section.

Local budgets appeared in 1993 to be significant and, at the same time, controlled. The most systematic, that is, formula-based, redistribution of funds between levels of government takes place between the national and first-tier levels. In the first half of 1993 county and local budget revenues were 25.8 per cent of total tax revenues, and 23.1 of that 25.8 percentage share came from personal income taxes, which are the dominant source of local budget revenue. In addition, transfers from the national budget added 35 per cent to locally-raised revenue, bringing the sub-national share of total budget revenue to 34.8 per cent. The sum of local budget spending through the first seven months of the year was slightly less than the revenue totals.

The position of the Russian enclave cities in the local budgetary system does not look exceptional. Planned 1993 spending per head of population was about the same in Narva as in the similar-sized, ethnic-Estonian cities of Parnu and Tartu. The figure for the smaller Sillamae is somewhat higher. That for Kohtla-Järve was the highest in Estonia. According to the Bank of Estonia, actual local tax revenue has fallen well short of plan in Narva and Sillamae, because of the particularly weak economic situation in these two cities; but this was offset in the first part of 1993 by larger-than-planned transfers from the central budget (*Eesti Pank Quarterly Review*, 1993, no. 3, pp. 8–24).

It looks as though the public finances of these undoubtedly restive Russian enclaves were being managed in a reasonably fair and orderly way – at least *prima facie*. There is little doubt that the finances of most of their counterpart communities in Russia are a good deal messier.

Estonian Citizenship and Estonia's Russians

'A representative democracy in which nearly forty per cent of the population does not enjoy citizenship rights is far from representative.' This judgement by Helsinki Watch (1993) on Estonia's 1992 constitution cannot reasonably be disputed. The October 1993 Helsinki Watch report from which this sentence is quoted gives a full account of the citizenship and related issues. In this section only a broad outline is provided. Table 11.6 gives a picture of the ethnic population mix.

Table 11.6: Estonia: selected demographic background information

1991 population ('000)	1,582
ethnic Russian share of population (%, 1989)	30.0
'Russian-speaking' share of population (%, 1989)	38.5
Russian emigration, mid-1991 – late 1994 ('000)	90
Russian emigration, 1991–4, as % 1989 Russian population)	c. 19

Sources: *Narkhoz 90*; pp. 67, 73, 81; UN ECE, 1992; p. 160; *RFE/RL DR*, 8 September 1994.

The Estonian legislature had, of course, a rationale for treating post-war immigrants into Estonia and their descendants as non-citizens, and making it possible, though not easy, for them (or most of them) to acquire citizenship by naturalization. This was that Estonia had been forcibly annexed by the USSR in 1940, and that people who subsequently settled there did so illegally. The main legislation affecting Estonia's Soviet-era immigrants has been the following: the citizenship law of February 1992; the law on language requirements for citizenship of February 1993; the aliens law of July 1993, and the re-adoption by referendum of the pre-war constitution in June 1992.

The basis of Estonian citizenship is *jus sanguinis,* the law of blood, rather than *jus solis*, the law of land or territory. In other words, citizenship is based on descent rather than place of birth. In this, Estonia is no different from, for example, Germany. The legislation provides that survivors or descendants of those who were Estonian citizens before the Second World War are automatically Estonian citizens. This category includes a minority of Estonia's ethnic Russian population. In this sense, the automatic right to citizenship entails no discrimination on ethnic grounds.

Those who do not qualify for citizenship in this way may become Estonian citizens by naturalization. The main route to naturalization involves two years' prior residence in Estonia after March 1990, the passing of an Estonian language test, the pledging of an oath of loyalty, and a further one year wait. There are also routes to citizenship in which the residence and language conditions are waived. These routes are open, chiefly, to people judged to have provided special services to the Estonian state and those who registered, before Estonian independence, for citizenship with the Congress of Estonia – a shadow parliament that was created by nationalists alongside the Soviet-era Supreme Soviet. Some categories of residents may be denied citizenship, notably those who served the occupying (Soviet) forces and people without a steady, legal source of income.

A more liberal proposal would have given citizenship to all those legally resident when Estonia regained her independence. This is what Lithuania has done – but then Lithuania has only a 20 per cent non-Lithuanian contingent in its population. Many Estonians feel that they have been both invaded and then had their national and linguistic identity put at risk by an influx of non-Estonians, mostly from the 'imperial' ethnic group and mostly not bothering to learn the local language.

The fact that Estonia's provisions for naturalization are not much different from those of many other countries has damped down objections from Western Europe. Criticism, both within and outside Estonia, centres on the special character of the Russian settlement in Estonia in the Soviet period: often enforced, and occurring within what almost all Russian residents perceived at the time to be a single country. Social survey evidence indicates that many ethnic Russians resident in Estonia consider Estonia their home (many were born there), and that a substantial proportion of them initially supported the drive for Estonian independence (Hanson, 1993a). Another element in the legislation that has attracted particular criticism is the fairly stiff language test, together with the fact that exact requirements for that test remained unclear for a year after the citizenship legislation, and that there has been only limited softening of that requirement for older residents.

The citizenship requirements would have caused less discontent if ethnic Russian residents could easily move to Russia without facing great economic uncertainty and a likely drop in living standards. Moreover, the adjoining Russian territories, such as Pskov, are amongst the poorer parts of Russia. Meanwhile, remaining in Estonia, many face Estonian language tests if they are to keep their jobs, and some apparent legal limitations on their participation in the privatization process and their running of their own businesses (Helsinki Watch, 1993).

The law on aliens, which went into effect on 12 July 1993, was a further source of complaint by Estonia's non-citizens. Instead of automatically acquiring a right of residence, previously registered residents who were not citizens were required to apply for residence permits, and these could be refused to the categories of people from whom naturalization could also be withheld.

The resulting changes in the civil status of the population are hard to track. The rough picture that emerges from the sources studied for this chapter is as follows.

At the January 1989 census, according to subsequent Estonian versions, there was a total population of 1,565,000 (Soviet sources at the time gave slightly higher figures). Of this total (in thousands), ethnic Estonians were 963, others 602, of which Russians were 475. The electorate then has been put at 1140 (*Izvestiya*, 21 September 1992, pp. 1, 2). By the Estonian national election of September 1992, the electorate was about 625 (*ibid.*). The electorate for local elections (see above) would have been approximately the same as the national electorate at the end of the Soviet period, though one had to register to vote, and reportedly only about half of non-citizens did so for the October 1993 local elections (Helsinki Watch, 1993, p. 32).

The way the initial Russian, and other non-ethnic-Estonian, population has subsequently split into citizens, resident aliens and emigrants is also hard to track. Total population fell after independence, reportedly to 1,525,000 at the beginning of 1993 (*Estonia*, 1993). The drop is less than the reported emigration of ethnic Russians alone: 80,000 by mid-1993 (*Baltic Independent*, 5 November 1993, p. 3), and 90,000 by late 1994 (*RFE/RL DR*, 8 December 1994). According to official figures provided to Helsinki Watch, at September 1993 85,000 ethnic Russians had acquired citizenship by descent or survival from the pre-war population, another 15,000 had secured naturalization, and a further 3,000 had qualified for naturalization and were in the waiting period (Helsinki Watch, 1993, p. 9). Reports just over a year later, citing Estonian official sources, put naturalization at 45,000 (*RFE/RL DR*, 8 December 1994).

This picture is compatible with information given this author in the Mayor's office in St. Petersburg for early 1994: 120,000 Russian-speakers had by then obtained Estonian citizenship by one of the 'automatic' routes, and 17,000 had obtained it through naturalization (interview with Vladimir Churov, 28 April 1994).

Finally, it was reported that at the time of the December 1993 Russian elections there were 40,000 people with Russian citizenship resident in Estonia (of whom a quarter took part in the Russian voting, about a third of that quarter supporting the new constitution) (*Baltic Independent*, 17 December 1993, p. 1). Again, this looks consistent with information from the St. Petersburg mayor's office for early 1994: 50,000 Russian citizens resident in Estonia (interview with Vladimir Churov, 28 April 1994).

To sum up (and ignoring natural population change, i.e., births and deaths): it appears that two years after Estonian independence, about one in six of the initial population of non-ethnic-Estonians (loosely, 'Russian-speakers') had Estonian citizenship; slightly less than one in seven had emigrated to Russia (or about one in six of the ethnic Russians); one in 12 of the Russian-speaking population had taken Russian citizenship (few of whom, probably, would have dual Russian–Estonian citizenship[2]). By late 1994 the cumulative total of emigrants was up slightly, and that of naturalized non-Estonian residents up significantly.

On the face of it, and still ignoring births and deaths over the four-year period since the 1989 census, we can guesstimate that some 522,000 non-ethnic-Estonians resided in Estonia in late 1993, of whom just under one in five had Estonian citizenship, leaving some 400,000-plus non-citizens, about a tenth of whom had Russian citizenship and something like 360,000 were stateless, but could – if of voting age – vote in local elections.

By 1993, despite the modest cohort of non-ethnic-Estonians among the citizenry, the national parliament was composed entirely, as was noted above, of ethnic Estonian deputies. Various Russian pressure groups had been set up, but under Estonian law only citizens may form political parties. Probably because of pressure from outside (Council of Europe, CSCE, Helsinki Watch), the President established a Round Table of representatives of both citizens and non-citizen groups in June 1993, but its status and effectiveness were not clear, at least initially (Helsinki Watch, 1993, pp. 34–5).

The local elections of 17 October 1993 gave an opportunity for the non-citizens to express their views and seek representation for them, at any rate at local level. It was an opportunity they took. Overall turnout was reported at 52.6 per cent, with turnout higher amongst non-citizens than citizens (*Baltic Independent*, 23 October 1993, pp. 1, 4; *Nezavisimaya gazeta*, 21 October 1993). (If turnout was measured against those registered to vote in the local elections, however, this report may be misleading, so far as non-citizen activism is concerned; nonetheless, the results were striking.) In Tallinn, where the city council elected in 1990 contained only ten Russians, 31 ethnic Russians were elected out of a total of 64 deputies. All, presumably, were Estonian citizens. The three groupings that specifically sought to represent local Russians were the ethnically-mixed Coalition Party of Tiit Vahi, and the ethnic Russian groupings known as the Russian Democratic Movement and the Revel List. These groupings won 18, 17, and 10 seats, respectively. The turnout in Tallinn was 60 per cent, against only 34 per cent in the second city, Tartu, which has a largely ethnic-Estonian population (*Nezavisimaya gazeta*, 21 October 1993). As will be recounted below, the turnout in Narva and Sillamae was even higher.

For ethnic Russians and other 'Russian-speakers' generally in Estonia, the situation was complicated and, for most people, unsatisfactory. A sizeable contingent, it is true, had become Estonian citizens: 48,491 by nationalization (as distinct from automatically) from 1992 to early 1994 (*OMRI DD*, 7 February 1995). Another 50,000 ethnic Russians had got Estonian citizenship automatically (*Baltic Observer*, 9 March 1995, p. 7). Some 90,000 had simply emigrated. According to the Russian embassy in Tallinn, over 61,000 had opted for Russian citizenship. But a substantial number, of the order of 360,000, were for the time being stateless; they faced language tests for Estonian citizenship, and in many cases, for their jobs, which most of them could not easily pass. On the other hand, Russia was for many of them an unattractive and even impracticable alternative location. At the same time, social survey and anecdotal evidence indicated that a fair proportion had initially supported Estonian independence, though the signs were that this proportion had fallen in the face of legislation that was, to put it mildly, inhospitable to them. Anecdotal evidence suggests that a great many wanted to stay and adapt, were not militant about their status, but were for the time being more apprehensive and bewildered than keen to campaign for a new order. But then bewilderment has been a rather usual state of mind amongst the entire population of the former Soviet Union in the past three years.

A survey of attitudes and opinions, amongst both Russian-speakers and indigenous peoples in all three Baltic states, conducted in September 1993, strongly suggests that the scope for compromise and mutual accommodation in Estonia, between Russian-speakers and Estonians, is greater than the rhetoric of politicians in Tallinn, Narva and Moscow would imply (Rose and Maley, 1994).

Almost two out of three Russian-speakers questioned, and one in two Estonians, considered that everyday social relations between the two groups were good. On Estonian citizenship, only a minority of the Russian-speakers questioned took the view that it should be automatically available either to all former Soviet citizens or to those resident in Estonia when independence was gained. The largest single group, 38 per cent, thought ten years' residence was an appropriate criterion, as did 23 per cent of Estonian respondents. An absolute majority of each group – Russian-speakers and native Estonians – agreed that automatic citizenship should be given either to everyone born in Estonia or to everyone with ten years' residence. Moreover, only 39 per cent of the Russian-speakers took the view that they should not be required to learn Estonian.

The one matter on which the Russian-speakers and Estonians diverged sharply was the Estonian government's treatment of Russian-speakers. Only 29 per cent of the Russian-speaking respondents considered this treatment was fair, and 69 per cent did not. Amongst the Estonian respondents the percentages were 72 and 17, respectively. (In each case, 'don't knows' made up the roughly one-in-ten balance.) Despite this majority view among the Russian-speakers of Estonian policy towards them, most of them saw their future as being in Estonia.

Rose and Maley's main conclusion about Russian-speakers in the Baltic states seems irrefutable: they are 'a category, not a cohesive block opposing the regime'. Their survey evidence supporting this view was assembled two months after the law on aliens came into effect – and had been given a great deal of publicity. And the survey was conducted a month before the local elections referred to above.

The picture they give is consistent with other social survey findings. In particular, a survey conducted in late 1993 and again in late 1994 by the Estonian Open Society (Soros) Foundation enables some assessment of change over time and of differences between non-Estonians in Tallinn and in the North-East to be made ('Mida...', 1994). The survey respondents were put into three categories: Estonians, non-Estonians living in Tallinn, and urban residents of the North-East (who would be overwhelmingly Russian). Asked where they would be happy to live, and given the opportunity to offer more than one answer, the percentage responses were as follows (1993 first, then 1994):

Estonians: in Estonia, in present place of residence: 88.7 and 87.2; in the CIS: 0 and 1.3; in one or other Western country (total of several different possibilities): 63.8 and 74.4;

Non-Estonians in Tallinn: in Estonia, in present place of residence: 87.6 and 87.9; in the CIS (total of several different possibilities): 12.4 and 11.2; in one or other Western country (total of several different possibilities): 97.7 and 61.6;

North-Easterners: in Estonia, in present place of residence: 88.7 and 89.8; in the CIS (total of several different possibilities): 11.9 and 15.9; in one or other Western country (total of several different possibilities): 75.7 and 93.1.

Since respondents were apparently free to indulge their imaginations and give several different desirable locations in one answer, there is a great deal about the interpretation of these numbers that is obscure. What is clear is that Russians in the North-East mostly do not consider a move to Russia or another CIS country desirable, though the small minority that do think this may have increased slightly, and that their feelings on the matter do not appear to differ much from those of Russians and other non-Estonians in Tallinn.

In the 1994 survey, non-Estonians in Tallinn and urban residents of the North-East were also asked to rate as fair or unfair a number of features of the citizenship and residence requirements for those who are not automatically citizens. The responses of the two groups did not differ dramatically. Both groups typically had 20–25 per cent of 'Don't know' answers on each of the seven questions. In Tallinn a majority of these non-Estonian respondents regarded four of the seven requirements as fair, and in the North-East this was true for only three of the seven.

A majority of both groups considered that procedures for getting permanent resident alien status were too complicated, and that having to wait a year for citizenship after passing the language test was unfair. A majority of both groups conceded that it was fair to require a knowledge of Estonian for certain jobs, but there was no majority either way in either group over the 'fairness' of an Estonian language requirement for Estonian citizenship; a plurality of North-Easterners thought it unfair (about two-fifths, against a quarter who thought it fair), while the reverse was true of the Tallinnites.

On the whole, this survey suggests a fair degree of acceptance of the new national order amongst Russians in the North-East, and concerns chiefly about not being unduly hindered in adapting to it. The adaptability looks slightly, but not strikingly, less than that of non-Estonians in the capital city.

None of this resembles the caricature of a persecuted minority that nationalist politicians in Moscow like to draw. Nor do the attitudes of Estonian respondents in the Rose and Maley survey mirror the resentfulness and intransigence towards Russian-speakers that much of the Estonian parliament has displayed.

In the light of this evidence, the approaches of President Yeltsin and Estonian President Lennart Meri to Russian–Estonian relations seem not only more civilized than those of their parliaments, but more realistic. Russian–Estonian negotiations (border disputes apart) narrowed down in 1994 to striking a deal that linked Russia's withdrawal of her last few troops in Estonia to Estonia's treatment of one small (10,000-plus) category of Russian-speakers: military retirees living in Estonia. The agreement between the two presidents on 26 July 1994 – troop withdrawals by end-August in exchange for residence permits for the veterans – is one that, it seems, few people outside the parliaments in Tallinn and Moscow would strongly object to. The troop withdrawal has duly gone ahead. The re-integration of at least some ethnic Russians with Estonian political life was symbolized by the election in March 1995 of six ethnic Russian deputies to the 101-member parliament. They represented an assimilationist party with a rather cloying name: Estonia is our Home. (*Economist*, 11 March 1995, p. 41).

What is noteworthy for the present study is that local government provides a channel of representation for the otherwise disfranchised members of the ethnic minority in Estonia. And the local elections of 1993, in which the parties elected to power nationally in 1992 did poorly, have confronted Estonia's policy-makers with the citizenship issue, which they seem on the whole to prefer to treat as though it were not controversial.

The situation in the ethnic enclaves in the North-East is, nonetheless, a special one. Notwithstanding the evidence adduced above about the mildness of most people's views in the Russian enclaves, the fact remains that, until prevented by Estonian legislation from doing so, the local population repeatedly voted for members of the old local *nomenklatura* who were hostile to the very notion of Estonian independence. It is to this manifestation of local democracy, and particularly to developments in the main enclave, the city of Narva, that we now turn.

Narva

To the foreign visitor in early 1993, the town of Narva presented a split personality. The Estonian flag flew over the *mairie*. The Mayor, Mr Vladimir Mizui, who resigned after the local elections in October and was replaced by an ethnic Estonian (RFE Estonian service from Narva, 25 October 1993; *RFE/RL DR*, 22 December 1993), had business cards printed in Estonian, but was said to be a Belorussian and a native Russian speaker. Across the main square from the Mayor's office, a statue of Lenin stood until it was ordered by Mizui's successor to be taken down (*ibid.*) And the only language to be heard in the streets was (and still is) Russian.

In March 1993, the Swedish Helsinki committee sent a delegation to Narva. The language problem was on their agenda. Curiously, the delegation had brought only a Swedish–Estonian interpreter with them. The Narva town council had to find a Russian interpreter for the

Swedes before the delegation and its hosts could talk to one another (*Molodezh Estonii*, 22 March 1993, p. 1; *Den' za dnem*, 25 March 1993, p. 7).

In spring 1993, according to the Mayor's office, only some 6,000 of Narva's 83,000 population were Estonian citizens (author's interview with Vladimir Mizui, 23 March 1993). That meant that fewer than 10 per cent of the voting-age population could vote in Estonian national elections.[3]

In the March 1990 elections to the Estonian SSR Supreme Soviet, under the old, Soviet rules of the game, Narva returned five deputies, who were all Russian. They were chosen from 23 candidates of whom 16 were ethnic Russians (*Narvskii rabochii*, 1 and 22 March 1990). Up to the October 1993 local elections, the Narva town council, in contrast to the all-ethnic-Estonian national parliament, had three ethnic Estonian deputies out of 42 members (author's interview with Vladimir Chuikin, Chairman of the town council, 25 March 1993).

If the September 1992 Estonian national elections, in which fewer than one in ten Narvans could vote, are put to one side, voting in Narva has reflected two things: the Russian-ness of the town's population, and its apparent support for the old local elite of the communist era. The elections concerned were all contested. There was the March 1990 Estonian SSR Supreme Soviet election. There was the city council election of the same date. Finally, there was a second city council election of 20 October 1991, held after the Estonian government had dissolved the Narva city council following the Moscow coup attempt of August. This second time around, much to the disappointment of politicians in Tallinn, Narva voted back in – admittedly with a turnout of only 38 per cent – the leading members of the old town council. These included the previous chairman of the council, Vladimir Chuikin, who had earlier been the Communist Party secretary of the Narva power station, V. Mal'kovskii, a former party first secretary for Narva, and Yuri Mishin, another former Narva party secretary (Chuikin's biography in *Narvskii rabochii*, 9 January 1990, p. 1; election results in *Narvskaya gazeta* [the same paper, re-named to suit the times], 24 October 1991, p. 1).

There is nothing peculiar to Narva about this voting for representatives of the old order. To be more precise: it follows the normal pattern of voting in ethnic Russian regions and cities in March 1990. In the RSFSR, as it then was, only the two biggest cities, Moscow and Leningrad, elected a clear majority of anti-communist 'democrats'. In the great majority, if not all, of the other 75 regions (oblasti, kraya, republics) it appears, anti-communists were unable to organize and advertise themselves sufficiently well to gain control of the councils (McAuley, 1992; Hanson, 1993a). The explanation for Narva, ruefully given by local critics of the Narva council – 'The local population prefer the devil they know' – applied in 1990 (and might still apply) across Russia as well.[4]

The political importance of Narva in Estonia now stems from its solidly Russian character and its location, not from its containing a large share of the non-ethnic-Estonian population. It contains in fact about one in six of that population. Its salience is enhanced by the fact that it is on the border with Russia. The Narva river forms the present boundary. The bridge between the twin fortresses of Narva and Ivangorod[5] now carries two border posts. The usual sad side-effects of the creation of new boundaries abound. For instance, there are pensioners living in Narva (I was told) with no entitlement to an Estonian pension because they had worked in Ivangorod.

Relations between the authorities in Narva and the national authorities in Tallinn were difficult until the latter changed the rules, and thereby also changed the membership of the Narva Council. My interviews in March 1993 with members of the local leadership of the time and the Estonian government's Commission on the Problems of the Ida-Viru Region, together with a reading of sources in English and Russian, suggest that the main issues explicitly put forward up to that time were the following.

On the side of the Estonian government, there was, until the October 1993 local elections, a belief that the local leadership in Narva (and in Sillamae and Kohtla-Järve) was creating obstacles to the integration of the three Russian-speaking towns into the social and economic life of Estonia. Criticism was directed particularly at the youngish chairman of the town council, Vladimir Chuikin (born 1951; studied in Leningrad, and worked in Moldavian state broadcasting before coming to Narva in 1982). Chuikin, his critics said, really wanted to see a re-established USSR. And indeed, he had said as much in the past (*Estoniya*, 18 June 1992, p. 2). He pushed, in 1990–92, for various objectives that Tallinn governments did not like: adherence to the constitution and laws of the USSR, not those of Estonia, in 1990–91; the creation of a special economic zone in the North-East; a referendum, to be held locally, on the creation of a special autonomous status for the region (*ibid.*). On 17 July 1993 the referendum that

Chuikin and others wanted was held, with agreement or disagreement on the granting of special autonomous status to the towns as the issue. There was a 54 per cent turnout and 97 per cent support for autonomy, reportedly, in Narva, and the corresponding figures for Sillamae were 60 and 95 per cent (*Independent*, 19 July 1993, p. 9; Helsinki Watch, 1993, p. 32). The Estonian Supreme Court chose to regard the referendum as unconstitutional, on the grounds that Estonia was, under the constitution, a unitary state, and nothing much happened.

The view that was expressed to outsiders by the Chuikin group of local leaders in Narva ran as follows (author's interviews of 23–5 March 1993 with Mizui and Chuikin, supported by conversation with some unemployed factory workers at a protest meeting in the council hall). The politicians in Tallinn seem to want to drive us out of Estonia. Unemployment is worse here than in the rest of Estonia but they provide no [special] help (see also *Den' za dnem*, 25 March 1993, p. 9, in an issue devoted to Narva). (The 1993 budgetary evidence discussed below contradicts this judgement.) Government commissions do nothing constructive; they just come and investigate us. The suggestions that we've made, about special economic zones, for example, are ignored. The Estonian language requirements for both citizenship and a great many jobs are excessive: for example, level F for citizenship or for confirmation in the state health service for a psychiatrist, level E for other doctors; people are trying to learn Estonian, but teaching is not readily available in Narva and there is no way of practising Estonian in Narva outside the classes. The doctors in clinics and hospitals in Narva [allegedly] are all about to lose their jobs for this reason.[6] Non-citizens may not form political parties or hold positions in the police or judiciary, and may be subject to limitations in the right to engage in business.[7] In general, the government in Tallinn does not trust us, leaves us with severely constrained municipal finances, and shows no sign of wanting to solve problems here. Clearly, their real hope is that many Russians will leave the region, but the great majority have nowhere to go.

The prevailing assumption in Tallinn about Chuikin and his allies seemed to be that they were representatives of the old *nomenklatura*, as indeed, in background, they were, and that their provenance determined their political stance: in other words, they were presumed to see a future for themselves only in a return to the old Soviet order. They could not, therefore, the argument went, be reconciled to Estonian independence; but in this they were presumed not to be representative of the population of Narva. The awkward fact that this population has twice elected them had to be explained in some other way.

The Estonian government had created three successive commissions on this problematic region. By a decision of 28 August 1991 the councils of Narva, Kohtla-Järve and Sillamae were dissolved and a government commission set up to oversee the region, under Tiit Vahi, pending new local elections. On 31 July 1992 a new commission on Narva was established under Rein Sarap. On 4 November 1992 yet another commission, headed by Andres Tarand, was created (*Den' za dnem*, 25 March 1993, p. 9; at the time of writing, Tarand is Prime Minister). The dissolution of the three councils after the August 1991 coup attempt was not, apparently, on the grounds that they gave any overt support to the coup. It was primarily on the grounds of their earlier (April 1991) declaration of adherence to Soviet, not Estonian, laws.

The *Narvskaya gazeta*, at least, records only one public statement by leading figures in Narva about the rightness or wrongness of the coup while it was still in progress. Oleg Klushin, the Director of the Kreenholm Textile Factory in Narva and a member of the USSR Congress of People's Deputies, reportedly called a meeting at the factory on 21 August – to which few people came – and declared that in his view the coup was illegal. This was reported, it is true, only on 24 August, when the coup had collapsed, but it is quite possible that it could not have been reported earlier. The paper comes out only three days a week. There was an edition of 22 August, but a meeting the previous day might have been too late for inclusion in it (*Narvskaya gazeta*, 22, 24, 31 August, and 5 and 10 September 1991 – all p. 1).

The perception, therefore, of the 1990–93 Narva town council as (from Tallinn's point of view) obstructionist, had some foundation. But it cannot readily be shown that the town council backed the coup, at least in any public fashion, and local leaders had tended, on the whole, to adapt to the shifting locus of power – for example, voting on 26 August 1991 to respect Estonian laws after all. And any suggestion that they lacked legitimacy as elected representatives is hard to defend.

There is a second underlying perception in Tallinn that seems also to be important. It is still important, even after the composition of the Narva town council has changed, however modestly, in a direction that Tallinn wanted. Leading politicians in Tallinn may not consciously entertain the hope that the Russian inhabitants of Narva, Kohtla-Järve and Sillamae will all decamp and go and live in Kingisepp or Pskov, across the border. But the feeling that Estonia has had Russian settlers foisted upon it by Moscow in the past, and that their presence is inherently undesirable, runs deep in Estonian society. It is entirely unrealistic to imagine that anything short of physical aggression will drive large numbers out. They mostly have nowhere in Russia to go, and know they would not be welcome.[8] But the dominant Estonian feeling about the post-war Russian immigrants seems indeed to encourage Estonian politicians to neglect Narva.

A sociological survey of April 1992, covering the attitudes of the non-Estonian population, was interpreted by its authors as showing that Russian-speakers in Narva were not especially anxious about nationality issues, and that anxiety on this score was highest in places where Estonians and Russian-speakers lived alongside each other in roughly equal numbers (such as Tallinn) (Kirch *et al.*, 1992, figures 2.3 and 2.4 and accompanying text). But the same study also shows that non-Estonians in Narva scored below their counterparts in five out of six other areas of Estonia in their integration into Estonian life. The ranking of regions by Russians' anxiety about nationality issues was also extremely close to the ranking by anxiety about economic issues, and anxieties about economic issues are now very high indeed in Narva. The lack of any public demonstration by non-citizens during the September 1992 national elections supports the view that citizenship and nationality issues have not been sharp spurs to action. The deteriorating economy of the Narva region is now the cause of greatest discontent. It does not follow, however, that the economic and nationality issues will necessarily be kept separate. Unemployment and poverty are easily linked with the issue of national identity.

At a meeting in the city council on 25 March 1993, Vladimir Chuikin addressed 300 unemployed people.[9] The exchanges at this meeting displayed the most acute of the current anxieties and tensions in the town. A union of the unemployed had recently been formed; a meeting of union leaders from Narva, Kohtla-Järve and Sillamae on 19 March had called for union action to save jobs, and the three leading state enterprises in Narva, the power station, the Baltiets electronic and electrical engineering works and the Kreenholm textiles factory, were (and still are) all in deep trouble (*Molodezh Estonii*, 22 March 1993, p. 1; *Den' za dnem*, 25 March 1993, p. 3; *Narvskaya gazeta*, 23 March 1993, p. 1; author's interviews in Narva, 23–5 March 1993).

Facing an angry crowd, Chuikin was able to deflect much of the anger and suspicion away from the Narva town council and on to the government in Tallinn. He did this without making any reference to the ethnic division. There were only two references to that divide in what was said from the floor, and even those were oblique. The meeting could have been in any hard-hit Russian town in 1992, with everyone criticizing the Gaidar government. We keep only 18 per cent of the turnover tax collected in Narva, Chuikin said, all the rest goes to Tallinn. We've asked them for help, but they do nothing. He patiently explained the unemployment benefit rules; he told questioners who asked about particular problems (the lack of free medical care for a sick child, for instance) which offices they should apply to; he called for a show of hands from those who were not receiving unemployment benefits, and something like 200 of the 300 people present put up their hands.

Many of the points made from the floor at first were hostile to Chuikin and the council. 'You're not afraid of losing your jobs, are you? And you're not doing a good job, look at the mess we're in.' 'You're all right. You were here [i.e., in office] under communism, and you're still here.' And when Chuikin complained about the costs facing the town budget, somebody called out, 'And the cost of bribes?'

Against what seemed, at first, to be the odds, Chuikin brought the temperature of the meeting down. He pointed out that his job was not secure. They could vote him out if they wanted. He recounted the initiatives that he and the council had taken in pursuit of special treatment from Tallinn. And at one point he turned on a heckler and said, 'You didn't support us when they turned us out in September 1991', referring to the dissolution of the town council by the Estonian government after the August Coup. 'There was no trust then', somebody replied.

The impression the meeting gave was that, if anything, Chuikin and his traditionalist allies were gaining more trust than before. Polling of local opinion over time would be needed to check that this has really been the case, but it seems likely. One unemployed worker, when I asked how he felt about Chuikin, said, 'On borets', ('He's a fighter', – implying, for us). With the town council as the community's only effective elected representatives, and a government in Tallinn that conscientiously eschews subsidies, Estonia's chosen political structure and economic policies could have been designed to strengthen the political base of the ex-*nomenklaturshchiki* in Narva.

The local situation changed with the local elections of October 1993. Their general character in Estonia at large was described in the previous section: they gave ethnic Russians and sympathetically-minded Estonian politicians a far greater voice than they had at the national level, and provided a jolt to the national government and the parliamentary majority. In Narva, the outcome was rather different. Above all, the old guard of local politics was forced out by the requirement that only Estonian citizens could stand for office. Naturally enough, local exemption from this requirement was one of the elements of the special-autonomy status that Chuikin and his allies had been seeking.

In other respects, the outcome in Narva and Sillamae was not so different from that elsewhere, if allowance is made for the very high non-citizen share of these towns' populations. The turnout in Narva was 66 per cent, in Sillamae 67. In the Narva city council election, the successful parties were not local branches of national groupings but movements apparently specific to Narva: the Democratic Labour Party (DLP), the Trade Union Centre (TUC) and the Narva Estonian Society (NES). Of 36 seats, the DLP won 17, the TUC 12 and the NES 7. Of the successful Narva parties, the DLP and TUC have their roots in the local Communist Party and local *nomenklatura*.

Either under pressure from Tallinn or prompted by their own tactical considerations, the new Narva council made Anatoly Paal of the NES the chairman of the council, and deputies from each of the two larger groups his deputy chairmen. To judge by their names, these two were ethnic Russians, unlike Paal, who was reported to be an ethnic Estonian. All had by law, of course, to be Estonian citizens. Following Mizui's prompt resignation from the mayor's office, that post was advertised, with the information that applicants had to be Estonian citizens (which, some informants had told this author earlier in 1993, Mizui was), and that successful applicants did not have to be residents of Narva (*Baltic Independent*, 23 October 1993, pp. 1, 4; RFE service from Narva, 25 October 1993; *RFE/RL DR*, 22 December 1993).

By the time of the national election of March 1995, only 2,000 Narvan Russian-speakers had obtained Estonian citizenship, against 20,000 (a third of the Estonian total) who had opted for Russian citizenship. So at this stage there were still only 7,000 residents of Narva eligible to vote in national elections. According to early reports, few of them supported the ethnic-Russian Estonia Is Our Home party (see above), which was thought to have got most of its support in Tallinn (*Baltic Observer*, 9 March 1995, p. 2).

It would be absurd to say, from the evidence available to outside observers in early 1995, that the Estonian government's difficulties in Narva had been resolved by the new local elections. From Tallinn's point of view, the disappearance from local office of Chuikin and several of his *nomenklatura* allies was a tactical gain. But the success of the DLP and TUC suggests that the old discontents and allegiances of the local population still matter, even when some of the notorious local hard-liners (as Tallinn saw them) have been side-lined. People with Estonian citizenship, it appears, can be found to represent those concerns, as they were in Tallinn and elsewhere. This indicates, though it does not conclusively demonstrate, that the favourite Tallinn conspiracy theory about politics in Narva was not a good account of the facts.

It is also worth pointing out that Narvan politics seems so far to have remained – perhaps unlike local politics in the other two enclave towns – a distinctive, regional politics. Instead of nationally-based political groupings being the main contenders locally, the vote-winners in Narva were localist parties. The proposition that holding national elections first, and local elections later (see Chapter 1), will tend to undermine regional secessionist movements, is not borne out in this case. This is at least partly because the politics of the former Soviet Union are far more complicated, in some respects, than those of Spain's democratization which prompted the Linz and Stepan hypothesis about the importance of the sequence of local and national elections (see Chapter 12).

Estonia, when still part of the USSR, had   elections at what subsequently turned out to be the national and the local level, at a time when everyone in the country was aware of the momentum towards Estonian independence. Therefore a local government in a conspicuous ethnic enclave on the Russian border had time to articulate local interests in secession or regional autonomy. For this reason, it might be argued, the sequence of events in Estonia and Narva does not constitute a test of the Linz and Stepan hypothesis. Another way of putting this, however, is to say that the hypothesis is inadequate to help us understand and predict developments in this former Soviet state.

The Narva Economy

Together with the neighbouring towns of Kohtla-Järve and Sillamae, Narva experienced in 1990–93 an economic deterioration that was more severe than the average for Estonia. This is not because the Estonian government was discriminating against the Russian enclave. Rather, the position is that this enclave has a concentration of the kinds of economic activity that are apt to suffer in the course of transformation; and the Estonian government is not engaging in positive discrimination to offset this.

The Kreenholm textile works is not a Soviet creation, and may have a long-term future. It has already been noted that in December 1994 it was purchased by a Scandinavian firm. But many large enterprises in the region have poorer prospects. The familiar problem of inter-enterprise arrears is particularly severe when the inter-enterprise links concerned are across republic boundaries (as the rouble zone has fragmented). For large enterprises in small successor-states this is especially serious. In 1993, at least, Kreenholm had liquidity problems arising from arrears of payments to it (for example, from Ukrainian enterprises), and its traditional suppliers of cotton in Uzbekistan were withholding supplies. It also had payments arrears to the local power station. It was reported in spring 1993 to be working at 15–20 per cent capacity (*Molodezh Estonii*, 22 March 1993, p. 1; *Den' za dnem*, 25 March 1993, p. 7), and was still operating at this level when purchased by the Swedish firm Borås Wäfveri (*Baltic Independent*, 6 January 1995).

The power station, dependent on high-cost local shale-oil, and under a government that is serious about free-market policies, has put up prices to customers inside and outside Estonia, and is facing payments arrears in part for that reason (*Narvskaya gazeta*, 23 March 1993, p. 1). Baltiets is a former Soviet defence-industry plant, a fact sufficient in itself to ensure that it has problems. According to an unemployed engineer formerly at Baltiets, the labour force employed there in March 1993 was down from 5,000 to 700 (author's interview, 25 March 1993). Uranium-processing at Sillamae (formerly a closed town) was of course also part of the former Soviet military industry sector.

Officially (in Tallinn) registered unemployment in Narva was 3,000 on 1 March 1993, or roughly 6 per cent. Several informants in Narva referred in late March to a 'true' local unemployment rate of about 50 per cent. The gap between these two figures is not as bizarre as it seems at first sight. Under present Estonian rules governing unemployment registration, there are four categories of people who are not registered unemployed but might reasonably be classified as unemployed: workers on 'enforced vacations', receiving no pay but not yet declared redundant (Estonian law provides that they be paid or sacked after six months); people whose severance pay has ended but who are in the 30-day period of official job-searching they must complete before qualifying for unemployment benefit; people who have completed the full six months of receipt of unemployment benefit and no longer qualify (but have not found another job); and 'discouraged' would-be workers whose discouragement is sufficient to deter them from registration, though they would otherwise qualify.

Raul Eamets of Tartu University has calculated that in December 1992, when officially registered unemployment in Estonia was 1.4 per cent, the rate would have been 7.3 per cent if these four categories were added to the members officially registered (Eamets, 1993). Applying the same ratio to the Narva registered unemployed figure for March 1993 would give a local rate of 'real' unemployment of about 31 per cent. People in the unregistered categories could be more numerous in Narva, relative to the registered unemployed, than they were in the country as a whole in December. A 'true' figure of 50 per cent therefore cannot be ruled out, though an estimate of 30–35 per cent could be more readily defended.

In 1993 registered unemployed persons received 180 kroons a month benefit provided they did 80 hours a month community work, and 90 kroons a month if they did not. For comparison, the minimum pension in spring 1993 was 260 kroons a month, the average wage about 800 kroons. In Narva in late March of that year, 180 kroons would have bought 43 Mars bars, 7.3 kilos of ham, 9 kilos of sausage, 18 kilos of apples or about 60 kilogram loaves of bread (author's observation of prices in Narva, March 1993). Most people were paying relatively substantial sums for apartment rent and electric light: *Den' za dnem* of 25 March quoted 135 kroons a month for a one-room apartment and electricity. Clearly, to be unemployed in Estonia at present, as elsewhere in the former Soviet Union, is a harsh fate, even if you are receiving unemployment benefit.

The North-East region, in which Narva is the largest town, has a large share of Estonia's natural resources (notably oil-shale), capital and industrial skills. Unfortunately, many of these apparent assets are liabilities. The Soviet system's propensity to develop high-cost raw material sources and use them wastefully, and to invest heavily in arms production, leaves white elephants all over the former Soviet Union. When such white elephants are located in a small, independent successor-state that has a difficult relationship with Moscow, they are whiter than white.

Rescue by foreign investors looks slightly more plausible now that Kreenholm has been bought up. But other large Narva plants are more problematic. In spring 1993 Narva apparently had no joint ventures or foreign firms (*Spravochnik*, 1992, and early-1993 interviews). Uncertainties about the region, specifically because of its location and its character as a Russian enclave, may continue to inhibit foreign business interest.

The attitude of the Chuikin leadership was not helpful to local economic transformation. Vladimir Chuikin said in March 1993 that he saw the prime requirement as a restoration of former economic links with the rest of the former Soviet Union; and he is sceptical about the inherent virtue of privatization (author's interview, 25 March 1993). The local *nomenklatura* was not, of course, against privatization in practice. The town's executive committee, according to *Den' za dnem* of 25 March 1993, was a major shareholder in the Narva Bank and the Narva Trading House (*Narvskii torgovy dom*). On the boards of these two important semi-private businesses were a former party first secretary for the town (Malkovskii), a former director of Baltiets, replaced by the government for obstructing government policies, and the director of Kreenholm.

Den' za dnem accused these ex-*nomenklaturshchiki* of aiming to control local business. The Narva Trading House, according to the paper, had a general licence from the *mairie* to engage in border trade on behalf of the municipality; former political contacts in Russia allegedly assisted them in doing this. Since his departure from representative local politics, Chuikin has indeed remained in the area, engaged in business.

This general picture resembled that in most regions and cities in Russia. In other words, the political economy of local, *nomenklatura*-guided, selective liberalization is what it is in ethnic-Russian communities, whether they happen to be inside or outside Russia. But in Narva the potential linkage with the nationality and citizenship issues constitute an extra danger, both for local economic change and for Estonia's political stability.

The sheer proximity of Russia adds to the danger. Residents of Narva can enter Ivangorod by walking across the bridge. They do not have to pay the usual Russian visa fees (25 kroons to an Estonian with the new, blue Estonian passport, and 15 kroons to an Estonian resident bearing the old, red Soviet passport, in 1993). In early 1993 they could then buy most everyday items more cheaply in Ivangorod, at the late-March exchange rate of 52 roubles = 1 kroon. Many Narva pensioners do this, and re-sell in Narva to supplement their pensions.[10] Food items were rationed to local residents at the time in Ivangorod, so Narvans bought from individuals outside the shops, presumably at a mark-up above the Ivangorod shop price. They could still make a good profit.

This created a situation where appearance and reality, to many residents of Narva, diverged. The average real wage in Estonia in early 1993 was $65 a month, or 2–3 times the Russian equivalent. Yet most people in Narva, when asked whether people in Ivangorod live better or worse than they do, answered, 'Better, because the prices there are lower'.

So long as the present economic regimes in the two states continue, the prices on the Russian side of the river are likely to stay lower in nominal, kroon terms, even in the face of some real appreciation of the rouble against the Estonian currency. Ivangorod prices will go on rising fast, but remain below market-clearing levels, subject to subsidies and partial controls (including rationing); the unstable rouble will fall relative to the kroon, and the trade will continue. In Narva the shops are well-stocked, there are no queues and prices are relatively stable. The purchasing power of average Narva incomes is almost certainly higher than that of average Ivangorod incomes. But rouble prices on the far side of the Bridge of Friendship will continue to look attractive to people in Narva. All of this tends to impede the implementation in Narva of the generally sound economic policies of the Estonian leadership.

The Narva economy can be considered, not only as just another segment of the Estonian economy, but as a gateway for Russian–Estonian transactions. In this role, it is now handicapped by a poorly-functioning visa regime that impedes the movement of people, including border crossings by the 10,000 St. Petersburg residents who are said by that city's administration to own property in North-East Estonia (interview with Vladimir Churov, St. Petersburg Mayor's office, 28 April 1994).

At the same time, smuggling is universally said to flourish across this border, and the Russian mafia treat Estonia as a route to the rich pickings and efficient financial markets of Scandinavia (Ulrich, 1994). For less exciting currency transactions, between rouble and kroon bank money, correspondent accounts operate more or less effectively in St.

Petersburg banks (Churov interview), as well as in Estonia.

For the time being, it seems that, as a gateway town, Narva is serving the informal economy well enough. However, poor political relations between Estonia and Russia may hinder an upgrading of this role. That there is scope for further development of the gateway is suggested by the new Mayor of Narva, Raivo Murd, calling for cooperation with the city of St. Petersburg in the construction of a second bridge at Narva to accommodate the large flow of goods across the border (*Sankt Peterburgskie vesti*, 23 April 1994, p. 3).

Conclusion

Estonian governments managed in 1991–4 to combine radical reform of the economy with a stance on citizenship for Russian-speakers that was governed by suspicion and vengefulness rather than pragmatism and a search for accommodation. This combination was managed without a destabilizing backlash from the large minority that did not get citizenship. One reason for this fortunate outcome was that Estonia continued to be seen by most of its Russian-speaking residents as a better place to live and work than Russia.

It is even more striking that Russians in the border enclaves of Narva, Kohtla-Järve and Sillamae have not been an especial source of trouble for the national government. Of course, relations between Tallinn and the old leadership in the enclaves were strained until national legislation removed the regional *nomenklatura* from the chance of local office. And economic conditions in the North-East have not been helpful to reconciliation. The scope for local representation of non-citizens in the government of the three enclaves seems to have helped materially in that (provisional) outcome. So, perhaps, has the equitable fiscal treatment of the three towns in a time of great difficulty for them.

There remains a strong case for the Helsinki Watch recommendation that the Estonian citizenship laws be reconsidered and the conditions for naturalization relaxed. If relations with Moscow improve, the intense suspicion that Estonian nationalist politicians claim to feel about Russian-speaking residents may come to seem even sillier than it does now. In those circumstances, the case for cultural autonomy for the enclaves might even begin to be taken seriously. In the meantime it is hard to defend the imposition, for example, of strict Estonian-language requirements for doctors and other professionals in what are, after all, Russian-speaking communities.

Notes

* The author is grateful to Ülari Alamets and Alari Purju for reading and commenting on an earlier draft. They corrected several errors and provided additional information. They are not responsible for those shortcomings that remain in the paper.

1. Estonia has territorial claims on land on the other side of the Narva River, including what is at present the Russian town of Ivangorod. This is a further complication in the life of the region.

2. It appears to be legally possible for those Russians who 'inherited' automatic Estonian citizenship to hold Russian citizenship simultaneously, since dual citizenship is allowed to such Estonian citizens. Anyone acquiring Estonian citizenship by naturalization may not hold another passport. The purpose of this distinction, in the eyes of the policy-makers, is to allow émigré Estonians resident in, say, Sweden, to acquire Estonian citizenship without having to forgo their Swedish citizenship. But it would seem to have the effect of allowing for the possibility of *some* overlap between Estonian and Russian citizens resident in Estonia.

3. On the citizenship legislation, see *Kak stat' grazhdaninom Estonii. (How to become a citizen of Estonia)*, Kohtla-Järve, 1992. At the time of the USSR-wide local and republic elections of March 1990, the number of registered voters in Narva (under USSR rules of the game) was 51,900 *Narvskii rabochii*, 4 January 1990, p. 1). If the share of voting-age population in total population was about the same for Estonian citizens in Narva as for the town's population overall, less than 4,000 of the population would be Estonian citizens of voting age.

4. Author's interview with El'dar Efendiev, 25 March 1993. Efendiev is the director of the Narva museum; he is not an ethnic Estonian, but he is an Estonian citizen and a member of the government's Commission on the Problems of the Ida-Viru Region (i.e., the North-East), and has stood unsuccessfully for election in Narva. For the record, it should be said that Efendiev is also a critic of some of the Estonian government's policies on Narva and the North-East.

5. Jaanilinn, in Estonian. The Estonian Republic has a claim on a strip of land on the eastern side of the river, including Ivangorod/Jaanilinn, which was recognized as Estonian in the 1920 treaty with Russia. But the Estonian government can hardly want to incorporate any more Russians.

6. *Molodezh Estonii*, 22 March 1993, p. 1, under the headlines 'Doktor, pokazhite yazyk' ('Doctor, show me your tongue'; the Russian for 'tongue' and 'language' is the same). In the Kohtla-Järve paper *Severnoe poberezh'e* of 23 March 1993 (p. 1) it was reported that even ethnic Estonians living in the region had called, at a meeting in Sillamae on 19 March, for a relaxation of the language requirements.

7. *Den' za dnem*, 25 March, 1993, p. 6, describes the border guards' efforts to learn Estonian. The constitution guarantees Estonian citizens the right to engage in business. It also guarantees that right to non-citizens, but 'subject to Estonian legislation.' There is therefore said to be a fear that laws might be introduced prohibiting non-citizens

from certain types of business.
8. The general housing shortage in Russia and the influence of refugees from the Transcaucasus and Central Asia that has already occurred are two powerful reasons. Another, according to some Narvans I spoke to, is a special resentment against people returning from the Baltic states: You went and lived the good life in the Baltic states when we had it much tougher here, and now that times have changed you want *us* to help *you?*
9. I attended the meeting, and the following remarks are based on my own observations. I interviewed Mr Chuikin afterwards, and he appears to have been unaware that any outside observers had been present at the meeting.
10. The trade is described in *Den' za dnem*, 25 March 1993, p. 4, and can be seen in the streets of Narva. The paper gave Narva and Ivangorod prices for 14 food items on 18 March. Only three (pork, chicken and butter) were cheaper in Narva. The unregistered average price ratio was 0.73 (Ivangorod price over Narva price at 50 roubles to the kroon.)

References

Eamets, Raul (1993), 'Labour Markets and Employment Issues of Transition Economies in the Case of Estonia', Tartu University, mimeo.
EBRD (1994), European Bank for Reconstruction and Development, *Transition Report*, London, October.
Estonia: A Reference Book (1993), Tallinn: Estonian Encyclopaedia Publishers.
Girnius, Saulius (1994), 'The Economies of the Baltic States in 1993', *RFE/RL Research Report*, vol. 3, no. 20, 20 May, pp. 1–15.
Haav, Karel (1993), 'Big problems of Small Business in Estonia', paper presented at the Second Freiberg Symposium on Economics, Bergakademie Freiberg, 9–11 September.
Hanson, Philip (1992), 'Centre and Periphery: The Baltic States in Search of Economic Independence', *Journal of Interdisciplinary Economics*, vol. 4, pp. 249–67.
— (1993a), *Local Power and Market Reform in the Former Soviet Union*, Munich: RFE/RL Research Institute, RFE/RL Studies.
— (1993b), 'Local Power and Market Reform in Russia', *Communist Economies and Economic Transformation*, vol. 5, no. 1, pp. 45–61.
Hansson, Ardo (1994a), 'International Trade and Transformation in Estonia', paper presented at the European Forum Group conference on 'The role of international trade in the transition process', Prague, 29–30 January.
— (1994b), 'Why Estonia's German Mark Peg will be maintained', *Baltic Independent*, 3 June, p. B4.
Havrylyshyn, Oleh, and John Williamson (1991), *From Soviet DisUnion to Eastern European Community?*, Washington, DC: Institute for International Economics.
Helsinki Watch (1993), 'Integrating Estonia's Non-Citizen Minority', New York: Helsinki Watch, October.
IMF (1993), *Economic Review 1993*, no. 4, Estonia, Washington, DC: IMF.
Kak stat' grazhdaninom Estonii (1992), Kohtla-Järve: no publisher identified.
Kirch, Aksel, Marika Kirch and Tarmo Tuisk (1992), 'The Non-Estonian Population Today and Tomorrow. A Sociological Perspective', Tallinn: Estonian Science Foundation, preprint.
McAuley, Mary (1992), 'Politics, Economics and Elite Realignment: A Regional Perspective', *Soviet Economy*, January–March, pp. 46–89.

'Mida...' (1994), 'Mida arvavad Eestist mitte-eestlased?', *Hommikuleht*, 17 November, p. 17.

Purju, Alari, (1994), 'Privatization with Vouchers in Estonia', Stockholm Institute of East European Economics, March, mimeo.

Raagmaa, Garri, and Tiit Tammaru (1993), 'The Unemployment in the Large-Scale Factories of North-East Estonia as the Biggest Problem of Estonia. Historical Background, Present Situation and Future Strategies', paper prepared for the European Regional Science Conference, Moscow, August 1993.

Robson, Peter (1987), *The Economics of International Integration*, London: Allen & Unwin.

Rose, Richard, and William Maley (1994), 'Conflict or Compromise in the Baltic States?' *RFE/RL Research Report*, vol. 3, no. 28, 15 July, pp. 26–36.

Sootla, Georg, Madis Kaldmae and Ardo Almann (1993), 'The Reform of Local Self-Government in the Course of Transition to Democracy in Estonia', paper prepared for the seminar on The Process of Institutionalization at the Local Level, Oslo, June.

Spravochnik predpriyatii razlichnykh form predprinimatel'stva v g. Narve (1992), Narva: Gorispolkom.

Statistical Office of Estonia (1994), *Statistical Yearbook 1994*, Tallinn.

Ulrich, Christopher J. (1994), 'The Growth of Crime in Russia and the Baltic Region', *RFE/RL Research Report*, vol. 3, no. 23, June, pp. 26–33.

United Nations Economic Commission for Europe (1992), *Economic Survey of Europe in 1991–1992*, New York: United Nations.

Van Arkadie, Brian, and Mats Karlsson (1992), *Economic Survey of the Baltic States*, London: Pinter.

Part IV. Conclusions

12. Decentralization and Change in Post-Communist Countries

John Gibson and Philip Hanson

The studies presented in this book reveal an array of different developments in different ex-communist states. The observation that these countries are not to be lightly generalized about has become a cliché but it is certainly true so far as devolution is concerned. We shall generalize nonetheless – though not, of course, lightly.

Devolution and Liberalization in General

The first question we raised in the Introduction concerned the circumstances in which progress was made towards political and economic liberalization, and the circumstances in which it was not.

A provisional answer, for devolution in the countries covered in this book, would be that nothing succeeds like success. Compare Estonia, Poland, Hungary and the Czech Republic, on the one hand, with Russia, Moldova and Romania, on the other.

Relatively orderly and liberal devolution in the first group has been accompanied by the curbing of inflation to less than 50 per cent a year by 1993 and an upturn in output by 1994 at the latest (EBRD, 1994). In the second group, Russia and Moldova have, to put it mildly, disorderly relations between the centre and the regions, and Romania, though less disorderly in this respect, still seems – from Adrian Campbell's account – to lack what he calls a 'pluralist conception of centre–local relations'. In these countries inflation remains dangerously high and real GDP continues to fall (Russia and Moldova) or at any rate (Romania) has not yet clearly turned upwards.

The other country whose local government is considered in this book – Lithuania – seems an intermediate case: perhaps a somewhat delayed economic stabilizer and at the same time a country in which, as Artashes Gazaryan and Max Jeleniewski suggest, local self-government is beginning to work more effectively in representing minorities and linking local and national politics.

No doubt the links between relative economic success and progress in devolution, if they exist, are of many kinds. Those societies that have so far proved better at managing economic transformation may have done so for reasons that also make constitutional and political reform proceed more smoothly. But for the time being we can simply note that progress in economic adaptation will tend to ease resource constraints that can bedevil centre–region relations.

Estonia provides a good example. It began its post-communist independent existence with a larger proportion of non-Estonians in its population than Moldova had non-Moldovans or Romania non-Romanians. Moreover, the history and geography of Estonia's ethnic minorities – chiefly Russian, chiefly a product of recent Russian annexation, and with enclaves on the Russian border – gave Estonia a larger initial ethnic-minority handicap than even the numbers alone would suggest. On top of that, the evidence of official trade statistics in 1988–90 suggested, as was argued in Chapter 9, that Estonia's economic dependence on Russia was almost total.

In the event, the success of Estonia's macro-economic stabilization, together with the (related) progress in attracting foreign investment, has helped to contain the problems of the Russian enclaves. Narva and the other ethnic-Russian enclaves of the Estonian North-East have suffered more during the painful economic adjustment than most of the rest of Estonia, but the region has begun to attract foreign investment, and an embryonic system of formula funding has produced net transfers of public money to the area.

The Estonian example suggests that relatively successful economic adjustment can produce a virtuous circle of developments that mitigate potentially serious ethnic tensions. Conversely, the lack of progress in stabilization in Moldova and Ukraine, for example, can hardly have helped resolve the ethnic and separatist conflicts that they face.

The institutional inheritance

Institutions themselves play a role in adaptation. To say this is to raise the question how particular institutions came to be what they are, and why they themselves cannot be adapted to facilitate political and economic liberalization. But if we are trying to understand short-to-medium-term problems of liberalization, it is reasonable simply to accept that each of the countries studied by our authors has inherited certain institutions, and that changing institutions is costly and difficult. With that premise, we can consider institutions as an influence in their own right.

Hungary stands out, amongst the countries studied here, for its adaptive design of government institutions. Kenneth Davey points out that Hungarians started early on the design of their post-communist state structure, and their policy-makers consulted widely before the first round of legislation on that structure. The second round of legislative reform, in 1994, was, in Davey's words, a matter only of 'fine tuning'. In contrast, legislative change after the initial reforms has been frequent in Russia, delayed in Poland, and more than a matter of fine tuning in the other countries studied.

The approach to reform of the state structure in Hungary, as Kenneth Davey describes it, is reminiscent of the process of consultation and debate that preceded the introduction of the Hungarian New Economic Mechanism (NEM) in 1968. True, the NEM was not entirely successful, and was subject to frequent amendment later on. But it is perhaps the best example we have of the conscious design of a national economic system. Is it too fanciful to suggest that Hungary, alone amongst ex-communist countries, inherited from the communist period not just institutions but a tradition of conscious re-design of institutions as a matter of public policy?

This suggestion should not be interpreted to mean that Hungarian policy-makers have a special capacity for the design of public institutions in general. If they had, their country would be as near a Utopia as such institutions can contrive. That is hardly the case. As the economist Janos Kornai has argued, Hungary may well suffer from some severe institutional problems, including what he has called a 'premature welfare state' (Kornai, 1994), but it may be that the peculiar communist-era pre-history of reform in Hungary confers benefits now on public administration as well as on banking, commercial law and other market institutions.

Finally, as far as our review of circumstances favouring or hindering liberalization is concerned, there is the matter of another sort of inheritance: the communist-era elites. In Russia, as Elizabeth Teague, Adrian Campbell, Philip Hanson and Peter Kirkow all emphasize, regional and local elected assemblies and administrations have been dominated by members of the old *nomenklatura*. In Romania and Moldova (and Ukraine) the old elites have continued to dominate politics at both national and sub-national levels. In Poland, Hungary, the Czech Republic, Estonia and Lithuania, in contrast, new people ('democrats', nationalists, anti-communists) have come into positions of political leadership at all levels – albeit not at first in Estonia.

One particular development in this third group of countries deserves attention: the return of reformist, ex-communist social democrats to national power (often as coalition partners) in all these countries except the Czech Republic. (In the case of Estonia, this is a development that has just occurred at the time of writing, and it is too early to say anything more about it.)

It is clear from the chapters on these countries, as well as from Adrian Campbell's chapter on Romania and Moldova, that ex-communists in the national leadership have tended to be wary about, if not plain hostile to, the devolution of state powers. However reconstructed these politicians may be on issues such as macro-stabilization and privatization, they still like a good, clear hierarchy. The ex-communists in Poland and Lithuania – not to mention those in Romania and Moldova – have been true to type. As Anna Cielecka and John Gibson observe, the Social Democrat–Peasant Party coalition in Poland has stalled further reform of local government; as Artashes Gazaryan and Max Jeleniewski point out, in the case of Lithuania, the Brazauskas leadership has been more wary of devolution than the Landsbergis team had been.

Once more, however, Hungary is different; its most recent legislative reforms, as has already been mentioned, did not alter the devolved, two-tier structure of directly and indirectly elected sub-national government. But then the Hungarian ex-communists are themselves not very true to type. Kornai (1994) judges them (and not merely their Free Democrat coalition partners) to be more disposed to follow orthodox monetary and fiscal discipline than their Hungarian Democratic Forum predecessors in office.

Authoritarian Modernization?

We have been concerned in this study with only one aspect of authoritarian modernization: the maintenance of a strong central state machine with very limited territorial devolution, as a means to pushing through radical economic change: price de-control, macro-stabilization, privatization, the introduction of new commercial legislation, and the re-shaping of economic activity.

In fact, territorial devolution is rather limited in all our countries, except Hungary (by design) and Russia (by inadvertence). Only in Russia, Hungary, Romania and Moldova are upper-tier regional governments directly or indirectly elected. Only in Russia and Hungary do sub-national governments spend a substantial share of GNP. Only in Hungary, it seems, is there much sub-national discretion in the setting of tax rates and tax bases. In Romania and Moldova monitoring and control from the centre are extensive, even though there is an elected first-tier regional authority. In Russia central monitoring and control by prefects and presidential representatives are meant to be extensive, but in practice are not.

What can be said – and it is not exactly news – is that top–down control is not enough to secure economic transformation. As Adrian Campbell has shown for Moldova and Romania, the avoidance of substantive devolution may be rationalized as a means of pushing through economic reform, in countries where reform is not, in fact, being successfully pushed through.

At the same time, the studies assembled here do not provide a case for the opposite view: that highly devolved government helps or at any rate does not hinder economic transformation. Hungary's track record in post-communist economic adaptation is less impressive, on balance, than those of the Czech Republic, Poland or Estonia, where devolution is more limited.

What can perhaps be said, if only tentatively, is that progress in developing a market economy can be seen in those of our countries where centre–local relations are relatively orderly. The case of Estonia, discussed above, is in this connection an impressive one, given Estonia's starting conditions. The case study of Českij Krumlow by Daniel Hanšpach and Zdenka Vajdová shows the mayor of a small town exercising a considerable degree of initiative and cooperating with members of the new business class in a strategic development plan for the community. In contrast, Peter Kirkow's research on Primorskii krai shows a regional political leader, appointed by Moscow, busily distorting the privatization programme of his region to suit a bunch of cronies, and suppressing critics and opponents. Clarity and order in centre–local relations are probably more important for economic development than any particular formal structure.

Developing Democratic Institutions

It is still rather early to draw conclusions about the functioning of local government as a school of democracy in the ex-communist countries. Putnam's question is nonetheless a starting-point: does local politics attract serious politicians?

None of the papers in this book was intended to give an account of the development of regional and local elites, though the case studies of the Polish town of Raciborz by Andrzej Bukowski and of two Russian regions by Peter Kirkow provide some insights.   Only a few observations, derived from these studies and from the various national structures of local government, will be offered.

The search for elected local office in several of these countries leads in many cases only to rather small empires. Where only the lower tier of sub-national government is directly elected, the average population size of the territory is of the following order: 16,000 in Poland, 2,300 in Estonia, 7,100 in Romania, 3,100 in Hungary, and 67,000 in Lithuania. In Romania and Hungary, there is then indirect election from the lower to the higher tier, but Adrian Campbell's account of the Romanian case suggests that top–down control of both tiers in that country is quite strong.

Lithuania and Hungary apart, this suggests rather parish-pump politics. The exceptions would be in a handful of big cities. In Russia and Moldova there is direct election at the upper level of sub-national government. In Moldova the average population size of the upper tier is quite modest (110,000), and prefectural influence there is in any case strong. In Russia prefectural (gubernatorial) influence is meant to be strong, but governors have in fact been relatively independent of the centre; the population size of the average province (including the republics, where the leaders are not, even nominally, appointed from Moscow) is of the order of 1,662,000: larger than the whole of Estonia.

A priori, then, one might guess that, outside the capital and a few other major cities, people seeking a national career in politics would not pursue elected local office, except perhaps in Russia and Hungary and possibly in Lithuania. But this is merely a simple deduction from the barest bones of the institutional structure. Other considerations might make a difference.

The development of a functioning party system – probably necessary in the long run for effective democratic government – entails a linking of national and sub-national politics. Independents can and do play a large part in local politics even in quite developed modern states, but if the parties that compete in national elections have little or no presence on the ground outside the capital city, and play little or no part in provincial politics, conflicts of interest between centre and regions will be harder to manage. Effective government in general may be correspondingly harder to achieve.

The extension of national-party organization into local politics might be expected to take time. Andrzej Bukowski's study of the collapse of an electorally successful anti-communist coalition in the Polish town of Raciborz shows just how shallow the social roots of such early political groupings can be, and therefore how detached from the everyday concerns of members of the local community. Similar conclusions can be drawn from Adrian Campbell's sad tale of the deepening disarray of initially 'democratic' elected city governments in St. Petersburg and Ekaterinburg.

In the light of this evidence of the difficulties faced by new political groupings, the fact that about 50 per cent of seats in the Czech November 1994 local elections were won by independents looks, on the face of it, quite encouraging. It may well be entirely compatible with the development of a coherent political structure linking local and national politics.

In Russia, on the other hand, the development of parties has been chiefly the prerogative of Moscow and St. Petersburg. Party organization outside those cities is minimal, except in the case of the Communist Party. Moreover, the parties or political movements that do exist are highly fissile and unstable. A certain appearance of party representation in the regions has been produced by the legislation on national elections. Half the members of the Duma (lower house) are elected on party lists. A new electoral law passed in early 1995 maintains this arrangement. As all the chapters in this book that deal with Russia make plain, however, national-party affiliations are of minor importance, in reality, at the regional and local levels. As these chapters make equally clear, the unresolved centre–regional conflicts are an enormous hindrance to liberalization generally in Russia.

An interesting institutional device in the Lithuanian legislation of 1994, pointed out by Artashes Gazaryan and Max Jeleniewski, is the requirement that local elections can only be contested by parties. In other words, independents are simply not allowed. This seems a rather artificial contrivance. Its consequences cannot be judged here. The March 1995 local elections in Lithuania came just as this book was being completed, and have not yet been analysed in detail. To what extent real national-party organization on the ground was brought along by this legal requirement, we cannot say. It appears, however, that – just as in the Estonian local elections of 1993 – a shift in national mood and popular demands was signalled by the upsets to governing parties in the Lithuanian local elections.

Coping with Ethnic Minority Regions

Of the countries considered here, the Czech Republic, Poland and Hungary might reasonably be said to have no significant ethnic minority problems. The others have, though in varying degrees. From the point of view of regional devolution, it is compactly settled minorities that matter. Romania has its Hungarian minority (7 per cent), mainly in Timisoara and neighbouring towns. Lithuania has more ethnic Poles than Lithuanians in the capital city, Vilnius. Estonia has its ethnic-Russian enclaves close to its North-East border. Moldova has, most notably, the Gagauz and the ethnically-mixed separatist Transdniester region. Russia has its patchwork of ethnic, or nominally ethnic, republics. Details are given in the chapters on these countries.

As we noted in the Introduction, Linz and Stepan (1992) have advanced a hypothesis about territorial devolution in newly-democratizing countries with compactly settled minorities or potentially separatist regions or both: if national elections are held ahead of local elections, the tendency will be for parties to be formed along the lines of cleavages in nation wide policy issues, cutting across regional concerns; at subsequent regional or local elections, the prior existence of such parties will make it less likely that the sub-national elections will be fought on regionalist agendas. Conversely, holding regional elections first will make it more likely that regionalist groupings will be formed, making the maintenance of a unified state more problematic than it would be with the national-election-first sequence. Their main example of the integrating effects of the first sequence is Spain; their examples of the disintegrative effects of the second sequence are the USSR and Yugoslavia. (They treat the 1989 elections to a Soviet assembly as not sufficiently free to count, and the 1990 elections to the parliaments of Soviet republics as being the first truly competitive elections.)

The countries with potentially separatist regions studied in this volume do not fit the Linz and Stepan hypothesis well. In the former Soviet Union elections at what are now national level (Russia, Estonia, Lithuania, Moldova, etc.) in March 1990 took place at the same time as local elections within these countries. Subsequent developments in the contentious regions have little to do with electoral sequences. In Estonia non-citizens (who so far constitute the majority of adult residents in the Russian enclaves) can vote only in local elections. The combination of relatively successful economic adjustment and the institution of a large number of mostly very small territories for elected local government seems to have helped keep the peace and hold the country together, as Chapter 11 recounts.

In Moldova, according to Adrian Campbell's account, momentum towards a break-up followed the national election of a government with a programme of merger with Romania. Any subsequent success in containing the problem seems more to do with a shift away from the goal of unification with Romania than with electoral sequences.

In Lithuania, local elections that allowed, for example, an explicitly ethnic Polish party to gain a majority on Vilnius city council are thought to have helped integration by giving the Polish minority a stronger voice – though it is too early to judge the effects of an election that has, at the time of writing, only recently taken place.

In Romania, the relatively quiet state of affairs in Timisoara does not seem to have anything particularly to do with a sequence of elections. The strong element of top–down government in Romania, and the small average size of both tiers of sub-national government, may be more relevant.

As for Russia, the first post-communist (though not the first fairly free) elections were at the national level in December 1993, with local elections following, in the sequence approved by Linz and Stepan. The invasion of Chechnya came after both. The decline of more general centrifugal tendencies that occurred in late 1993 came before either of these elections and seems mainly to do with the President's show of force against the Russian parliament. This decline in centrifugalism may prove to be temporary, since the basic weakness of the Russian state has since been made abundantly clear.

How Different is Russia?

Of the countries studied in this book, the ones in which centre–regional relations now appear most incoherent and problematic are Moldova and Russia. In quite different ways, the other former Soviet states considered here – Estonia and Lithuania – have coped with regional devolution, so far, reasonably well. No doubt it helps that they are both very small countries. But Estonia has had to cope, despite its own tiny size, with a serious risk of secession by its mainly Russian North-East.

For the rest of the world, it is the centre–periphery mess in Russia that matters most. We therefore conclude with some observations on Russia's regional muddle.

What impediments that muddle brings to the process of economic change have been set out in Chapter 9. They need not be repeated here. More fundamental, in a way, are the social and political circumstances that have created this disorderly state of affairs.

The two chapters that deal directly with this subject are the first two in the book, by Elizabeth Teague and Adrian Campbell. They take rather different views of the problem. Campbell stresses the historical background. In Chapter 4, when he is putting developments in Romania and Moldova in context, he remarks that the Russian Federation has inherited a system of territorial management that is capable both of extreme centralism and of great regional autonomy – what he refers to in Chapter 2 as (sub-national) 'rebel autocracies'. This system, he suggests, 'has a well-established logic of its own'.

Elizabeth Teague is more concerned with the present need to construct a political system that works than with establishing a family tree for today's Chechnya, Tatarstan and Primorskii krai. She sees the treaties between Russia and Tatarstan, Russia and Kabardino-Balkaria and Russia and Bashkortostan (we must now add the most recent one, with North Ossetia) as devices for gaining a breathing space, or a lull in hostilities, during which all concerned can think out some more solid basis for the government of what is at present Russian territory.

Both authors find a logic of sorts in the present Russian regional disorder. Both also see the present situation as unsatisfactory. Campbell draws attention to, among other things, the weakness of local administration, with its 'skeletal' staffing. National government is weak in the same way. Oddly, Russia's development may well be handicapped by a shortage of bureaucrats.

More bureaucrats, however, will not help much when rules, procedures and institutions are so unstable. This is the point that Elizabeth Teague stresses. Ambiguity in the design of the Russian constitution and Russian centre–periphery relations, she argues, may serve as a useful device for keeping the peace while putting off the making of coherent arrangements for the longer term. But the notion embodied in the makeshift treaties with Tatarstan and other republics, of a sovereign state within a sovereign state is a nonsense. A rule of law and a coherent constitutional order are still needed. The difficulty Russia has in arriving at these is one of the most debilitating of the legacies of the Soviet and Russian past.

References

EBRD (1994), European Bank for Reconstruction and Development, *Transition Report*, London: EBRD, October.

Kornai, J. (1994), 'Lasting Growth as the Top Priority: Macroeconomic Tensions and Government Economic Policy in Hungary', EBRD working paper no. 15, December.

Linz, J.J. and A. Stepan (1992), 'Political Identities and Electoral Sequences: Spain, the Soviet Union and Yugoslavia', *Daedalus* 121: 2 (spring), pp. 123–41.

Index

in Romania 82, 83, 86
in Russia 17, 196-198, 233, 251
Greece 6, 78
Greeks 79
Grigor'ev, S., 231, 259
guberniyas 19
Gypsies 79, 167
Haav, Karel 271, 298
Hahn, Jeffrey W., 5, 9, 184, 215
Hannum, Hurst 35
Hanson, Philip 1, 36, 179, 189,
 192, 204, 210, 214, 215, 217,
 218, 229, 234, 245, 247, 250,
 253, 259-261, 263, 264, 274,
 277, 285, 298, 303, 305
Hanšpach, Daniel 163, 307
Hansson, Ardo 263, 264, 267,
 268, 272, 298
hard currency 192, 193, 195, 210,
 212, 238, 252
Havrylyshyn, Olen 264, 298
Helf, G., 5, 9, 184, 215
Helsinki Watch 275, 277-279,
 286, 296, 298
Henze, Paul 14, 36
Hill, Ronald J., 41, 43, 55, 92,
 111
Hirschman, Albert 4
Homeland Union 63
Horvath Consulting 172
hospitals 90, 150
Hough, Jerry F., 5, 9
household income tax 195
housing 34, 47, 69, 122, 163-166,
 168, 174, 176, 188, 196, 200,
 216, 239, 249, 250, 267, 268,
 288
housing construction 69, 164
housing policy 163, 165, 166, 176
housing privatization 188, 267
housing stock 165, 166, 168, 174,
 188, 239
Houston 210
Hungarian Democratic Forum 119,
 123, 306

Hungarian Institute of Public
 Administration (HIPA) 116
Hungary 2, 7, 8, 73, 74, 79,
 115-117, 122, 125-127, 163, 179,
 303, 305-308, 310, 313
Hungary, local government Chapter
 5 *passim*
Ikar 234
Iliescu, Ion 74, 77, 88, 97, 111
Illarionov, A., 187, 188, 215
Illner, Michael 6, 8, 9
IMF 261, 264, 266, 268, 270, 299
Imperial Tradition 38
imports 76, 208-211, 235, 237,
 252, 271
income tax 68, 69, 121, 140-142,
 161, 195, 247, 248
individual family-owned houses
 164
individual housing 164
industrial, and state enterprise,
 subsidies (including demands for)
 in Lithuania 62
 in Racibórz 155
 in Russia Chapter 9 *passim*, 185,
 186, 194, 196
inflation 106, 157, 165, 169, 180,
 201, 222, 225, 227, 253, 254,
 261, 264, 266-268, 271, 303
Ingushetia 15, 16, 20, 28, 182,
 190
Inkatha Freedom Party 3
inter-enterprise arrears 292
international capital 170
Internationalization 193, 207
Ipatov, V., 238
Ishutin, Anatoly 49, 50
Italy 3, 181
Ivangorod 297, 285, 295
Ivanovo 190
Jaanilinn 285, 297
Jałowiecki, B., 160, 161
Japan 219, 236
Jeleniewski, Max 57, 304, 306,
 310